CW00651872

The Knights Templar

The Knights

The Knights Templar

History & Mystery

Tony McMahon

PEN & SWORD
HISTORY

First published in Great Britain in 2024 by
Pen & Sword History
An imprint of Pen & Sword Books Limited
Yorkshire – Philadelphia

ISBN 978 1 03611 348 3

A CIP catalogue record for this book is
available from the British Library

Typeset by Mac Style
Printed in the UK by CPI Group (UK) Ltd, Croydon, CR0 4YY.

Pen & Sword Books Limited incorporates the imprints of After
the Battle, Atlas, Archaeology, Aviation, Discovery, Family History,
Fiction, History, Maritime, Military, Military Classics, Politics,
Select, Transport, True Crime, Air World, Frontline Publishing, Leo
Cooper, Remember When, Seaforth Publishing, The Praetorian Press,
Wharncliffe Local History, Wharncliffe Transport, Wharncliffe True
Crime and White Owl.

For a complete list of Pen & Sword titles please contact

PEN & SWORD BOOKS LIMITED
47 Church Street, Barnsley, South Yorkshire, S70 2AS, England
E-mail: enquiries@pen-and-sword.co.uk
Website: www.pen-and-sword.co.uk
or
PEN AND SWORD BOOKS
1950 Lawrence Road, Havertown, PA 19083, USA
E-mail: uspen-and-sword@casematepublishers.com
Website: www.penandswordbooks.com

For Peter and Alice

Contents

List of Illustrations

1. The author at the Templar fortress in Mogadouro, a town in north-east Portugal
2. The Palatine Chapel in the Norman palace at Palermo in Sicily shows the fusion of Islamic art in the ceiling and Byzantine mosaics on the walls
3. Medieval re-enactors process in the annual Viagem Medieval at Santa Maria da Feira, Portugal
4. The author in the ruins of Fountains Abbey in Yorkshire, one of the richest Cistercian abbeys in England before the Protestant Reformation
5. Hugh de Payens, first grand master of the Knights Templar
6. Seal of the Knights Templar
7. The claimed site of the crucifixion of Jesus in the Holy Sepulchre, Jerusalem – venerated by the Templars
8. Praying at the Western or "Wailing" Wall in Jerusalem – part of King Herod's second temple
9. Temple church in London with the distinctive circular shape mimicking the Holy Sepulchre rotunda in Jerusalem
10. Church of San Jacopo in San Gimignano, Italy that began life as a Templar-run hostel for pilgrims on the Via Francigena leading from Canterbury in England to Rome
11. The Hagia Sophia in Istanbul – vandalised by crusaders during the Fourth Crusade
12. Byzantine emperor makes donation to the church – mosaic in the Hagia Sophia in Istanbul
13. William of Tyre discovers that the future King Baldwin IV has leprosy
14. The author at the gateway into the Templar fortress at Tomar, Portugal where a bloody battle was fought against the Almohads
15. The Siege of Ascalon 1153 from a fifteenth-century depiction of this Templar victory
16. Third Reich stamp depicting the Wagner opera Parsifal and the Holy Grail
17. The crypt at Saint Seurin church in Bordeaux dates to the fifth century with medieval claims it was consecrated by Jesus Christ himself. Bordeaux was the seat of the Dukes of Aquitaine

Templar Timeline

1095	Pope Urban II calls for a crusade at the Council of Clermont
1069–1099	First Crusade
1099	Jerusalem captured by a crusader army
1113	The Knights Hospitaller recognised by Pope Paschal
c.1118	The Knights Templar are formed
1118–1136	Hugh de Payens, first Templar grand master
1139	Papal bull, Omne Datum Optimum, issued by Pope Innocent II
1139–1149	Robert of Craon, second Templar grand master
1144	Edessa falls to the Seljuks
1147–1151	Everard des Barres, third Templar grand master
1147–1149	Second Crusade
1147	Lisbon in Portugal captured by Afonso Henriques
1148	King Louis VII of France defeated at Mount Cadmus
1149	Seljuk leader Nur ad-Din takes Antioch
1153	Bernard of Clairvaux dies
1153	Bernard de Tremelay killed at the Siege of Ascalon
1153–1156	André de Montbard, fifth Templar grand master
1171–1179	Odo of St Amand, eighth Templar grand master
1174–1193	Reign of Saladin, founder of the Ayyubid dynasty
1177	Battle of Montgisard
1184–1189	Gérard de Ridefort, tenth Templar grand master
1187	Battle of Hattin
1191–1193	Robert de Sablé, eleventh Templar grand master
1186–1192	Reign of Guy de Lusignan as King of Jerusalem
1189–1192	Third Crusade
1190	Frederick Barbarossa drowns while on crusade
1190	Siege of Tomar in Portugal
1191	Richard the Lionheart takes Cyprus
1198	Teutonic Knights recognised by Pope Innocent III
1202–1204	Fourth Crusade
1204	Constantinople sacked by crusader armies
1212	Battle of Las Navas de Tolosa

1209–1229	Albigensian crusade against the Cathars
1217–1221	Fifth Crusade
1228–1229	Sixth Crusade
1229	Jerusalem handed over to Frederick II
1247–1250	Guillaume de Sonnac, eighteenth Templar grand master
1248–1254	Seventh Crusade
1249	Damietta taken by the crusaders
1250	Defeat at Mansourah and capture of King Louis IX of France
1285–1314	Reign of Philip IV 'the Fair' of France
1291	Fall of Acre to the Mamluks
1292–1312	Jacques de Molay, twenty-third Templar grand master
1311–1313	Guillaume de Nogaret, Chancellor of France
1314	Jacques de Molay burned at the stake in Paris

The Templar Series

This book, *The Knights Templar: History & Mystery*, is part of a three-book series on the history and mystery surrounding the Knights Templar by author and TV historian Tony McMahon.

The second instalment will be *Downfall of the Templars*, followed by the third instalment, *The Knights Templar and Freemasonry*.

Maps

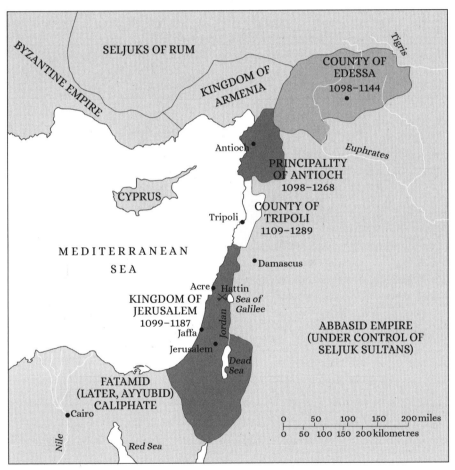

The crusaders states of Outremer at their maximum extent in the early twelfth century CE.

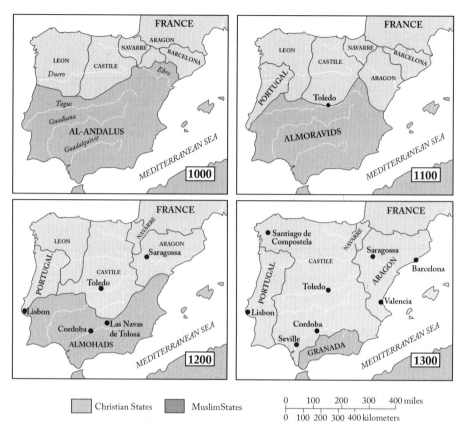

Christian States   Muslim States

The "Reconquista" of Spain and Portugal showing shifting boundaries between Muslim and Christian kingdoms on the Iberian Peninsula.

Introduction

On 18 March 1314, four dishevelled knights were led through the streets of Paris, shackled at the hands and feet, to be given one last chance to save their lives. They appeared before a panel of the church's greatest leaders in France who were prepared to show mercy as they had confessed to their terrible sins. But to the amazement of everybody present, the oldest of the knights retracted his confession. The last grand master of the Knights Templar, Jacques de Molay, refused to grovel to these puffed-up prelates for a second longer. He had languished in a dungeon cell for seven years and had no intention of spending a day longer behind bars.

His stubborn defiance was a death sentence. Alongside him, the Templar master of Aquitaine, Godefroi de Gonneville, also took back his confession. Confounded, the church worthies ordered the men back to prison. Hours later, De Molay was brought back to the centre of Paris, only this time a pile of wood and a stake had been prepared. The French king had intervened, demanding the death penalty. The grim scene that ensued ended 200 years of crusading and fighting for Christ by the Knights Templar.

From the flames, De Molay cursed the king and the pope. He summoned them to appear before the throne of God in just a few months. It was a curse that would be realised with the deaths of both men within the year. But already, by that fateful day, the Templar order was being broken up – its assets divided. All evidence that these holy warriors had ever existed was being eradicated. They had been found guilty of the most monstrous crimes and subjected to seven years of investigation. Now it was time to erase them from history.

Yet the Knights Templar have refused to fade away. They have endured while the names of other military orders from the Middle Ages are forgotten. Their rapid rise, and fall, has puzzled and enthralled generations of history enthusiasts. Countless legends and myths have grown up about the knights. Did they possess the Holy Grail? Had they discovered knowledge that threatened the Roman Catholic church? Were they suppressed because they had grown too rich and powerful?

The usual stance of academics is to roll their eyes at the conspiracy theories and esoteric histories about the Templars. Stick to the facts and strip out the fanciful nonsense. Tell a strictly linear narrative from their founding around the year 1118 to the execution of the last grand master in 1314 and ignore centuries of embellishment that followed. But it's not that easy. Because the conspiracy theories and fake news about the Templars began at the very start. Throughout their existence, medieval chroniclers, jealous of their success or suspicious of their motives, trashed the knights. As will be seen, unfounded allegations were made by scribbling bishops and monks to traduce the knights. Their own version of events has tragically been lost to history.

The calumnies against the Templars were relentless. A constant stream of reputationally damaging comments behind their backs. Their bravery in battle was derided as opportunism. When they stormed into an enemy fortress ahead of everybody else, it was because they were after the spoils. Their financial acumen was really a combination of greed and fraud. The monastic lifestyle led by the knights was a cover for diabolic initiation rituals and heretical beliefs. As for their loyalty to the Christian cause, they were treacherously doing deals with the Saracens or Mongols whose company they clearly preferred. All these things were said while the knights still lived and breathed.

Some have mocked the Knights Templar as semi-literate mediocrities, out of their depth in the stormy political situation of the time. Evidence cited is that when they stood trial, on what were undoubtedly trumped-up charges, they had little to say in their defence. De Molay even admitted that he was not a great legal mind. The knights, with some notable exceptions, seemed dazed and confused by the whole experience that led to so many being burned at the stake.

Yet at the height of their powers, the Knights Templar were a unique and compelling proposition. They conceived of something that had never been seen before. A professionalised military order of knights that operated to a rule book, punctuated the day with prayer, dressed the same, and led a highly regimented existence. On the battlefield, they terrified the enemy as they charged in strict formation, a thunder cloud of flowing white mantles emblazoned with the distinctive red cross of martyrdom. First into battle and last out was their motto. All individuality suppressed to achieve their mission.

Across Europe they established a network of agri-businesses and, ahead of their time, developed sophisticated financial instruments. So impressed were the monarchs of the Middle Ages that on occasions they handed over the state finances to the Templars to run. These were medieval bankers and investment managers, who amassed incredible wealth in a relatively short space of time. Their houses came to be seen as the safest place to deposit one's money while on crusade.

They captured the imagination then as they still do today. The quintessential crusader fighting for the cross and only accountable to the pope. Yet they have also been depicted as an order operating to their own agenda. This was at the core of the accusations made against them when the arrest warrants were issued in 1307. But what was that agenda? This has intrigued people down the centuries. Were they set up by a secret, shadowy organisation operating in the shadows? While based in Jerusalem on the Temple Mount, did they unearth holy relics, such as the Holy Grail, that they kept for themselves? Did the knights imbibe forbidden belief systems, including ancient forms of Christianity long condemned by the Catholic church?

The linear history of the Templars including the many battles and plots are detailed here but alongside that runs the whispered allegations levelled against the order as well as the outlandish conspiracy theories from the medieval period to the present day. By absorbing both the history and the mystery, we get the full picture of this incredible order of knights. Armed with all the information, the reader can decide who and what were the Knights Templar. Let the journey commence.

Chapter One

The Crusades: 'Deus Le Vult!'

In the year 1095, Pope Urban II made an impassioned speech at Clermont in France urging a new kind of religious war – a crusade. Several versions of what Urban said that day have come down to us but it's the blood-curdling account by the medieval chronicler Robert the Monk that really grabs one's attention. Here was the supreme pontiff, Christ's vicar on Earth, bellowing over the rim of the pulpit, terrifying his audience with fearful tidings from fellow Christians in the east. It must have mesmerised and horrified those gathered to hear the terrible news His Holiness had to impart – and Urban spared no details.

Christianity was under attack. Urban told those present that 'a horrible tale has gone forth and very frequently has been brought to our ears'. Violent armies from 'the kingdom of the Persians, an accursed race, a race utterly alienated from God' had descended on what had been up to now Christian lands. These monstrous invaders pillaged, burned, and put innocent people to the sword. Captives had been led away and others broken by torture.[1]

And there was worse. Churches had been levelled and their altars defiled in various unpleasant ways. Christians had been forcibly circumcised. Then, the pope raged, these merciless thugs shot men to death with arrows and raped their wives and daughters. Urban went on to describe one bizarre form of torture that still makes difficult reading in our own time. The gist of this gruesome address from the leader of the Roman Catholic church was that territory in the east, populated and governed by Christians for centuries, was falling to the forces of Islam. It was a race against time to save the cross from being overwhelmed by the crescent.

The pope's incendiary words roused everybody and his call to arms was greeted with a thunderous cry: 'It is the Will of God!' Deus Le Vult in church Latin. The Holy Father was visibly moved by this universal acclamation. He proclaimed that in the wars to come, those who charged at the enemies of Christ should repeat that very same cry. God had clearly placed those stirring words into the mouths of all those present that day at Clermont. This was a glorious moment of divine intervention, and the course of action was now obvious. Thousands must take the cross, go into battle, and die for Christ. And in doing so, their sins would be wiped away, clearing the path to eternal, heavenly glory.

This was not a war to be fought somewhere far away. It was on Rome's doorstep. From Pope Urban's perspective, the battle lines between Christianity and Islam stretched from the Atlantic shores of Portugal, through Italy, and on to the Middle East. The military fortunes of the two faiths varied along that perilous divide. In some places, the cross was defeating the crescent while in others the situation was reversed. It was this shifting frontier that the Knights Templar would undertake to defend as the shock troops of Christendom. But their arrival on the scene was still two decades away.

Only a hundred years before Urban's speech, Muslim forces were finally dislodged from the French mainland around Marseilles, after a century-long presence. Their pillaging expeditions extending up the Alpine passes into modern Switzerland. Grenoble had been despoiled in the year 954, and the Benedictine monastery of St Gall, a major centre of learning, sacked. Cities as far apart as Vienne, Nice, Geneva, and Lausanne came under sustained onslaught. While in Italy, Pisa was stormed by Muslim armies in 1004 and 1011, while an attempt to conquer Sardinia required a previous pope, Benedict VIII, to get actively involved in organising the fightback.[2]

Across the Iberian Peninsula (modern Spain and Portugal), Christian-led armies were pushing back the long-established Islamic caliphate that had once exercised near total dominance from its glorious capital of Córdoba. Cities like Toledo and Coimbra were wrested from the control of Islamic rulers by the rapidly expanding Christian kingdoms of Léon and Castille. What would come to be termed the 'Reconquista' (reconquest) of the Iberian Peninsula was well underway by the time Urban rose to speak.

Rome itself had not been immune to Islamic military might at the height of its power. Arab raiders had ransacked St Peter's Basilica, in Rome, in the year 846 CE, leading to the building of the Leonine Wall by the popes. The loss of rich liturgical vessels and jewelled reliquaries was still an open wound in Rome. This had been followed by repeated unsuccessful attempts by Muslim forces to invade southern Italy. They had come alarmingly close to success. At the Battle of Stilo in July 982 CE, a huge Christian army led by the Holy Roman Emperor Otto II was defeated in Calabria by Emir Abu'l-Qasim. Fleeing for his life, the emperor was forced to swim out to sea, rescued by a passing ship.

That victorious emir was the ruler of Sicily. Today an integral part of Italy but for two centuries, this large island was a Muslim emirate. Only four years before Urban addressed the council at Clermont, Norman knights had finally managed to overrun Sicily with the blessing of His Holiness.[3] They built a fortress-like palace in the capital, Palermo. Its chapel, the Cappella Palatina, still stands, blending the architectural and decorative styles of the Christian invaders and the defeated Muslims, evidencing the blurring of cultures that occurred along this long frontier between the two Abrahamic faiths: Christianity and Islam.

In Iberia and Sicily then, Christianity was on the march. The cross was pushing back against the crescent. However, in the east, events were moving in the opposite direction. A new kind of Muslim invader had arrived on the scene. First, striking terror into fellow Muslims. But then turning their attention to a rich, fertile Christian empire that unexpectedly found itself on the verge of being snuffed out. In desperation, it turned to the west begging for help.

At Clermont, Pope Urban referred to atrocities allegedly being committed in Christian lands to the east, now falling to a new, determined wave of Muslim invaders. He was talking about a realm centred on Asia Minor, ruled for a thousand years by what is usually termed the Byzantine Empire. This was a vast and ancient Christian kingdom in the Middle East with its sumptuous capital of Constantinople, circled by impregnable walls. Largely Greek speaking and Christian, but not Roman Catholic. This empire spanned the vast Anatolian peninsula, Greece, the Balkans, and large parts of Bulgaria.

It was the great survivor. Although we call it the Byzantine Empire, that name would not have been recognised by its rulers or subjects. They regarded themselves as the unbroken continuation of the eastern half of the Roman Empire. An empire that stretched right back to Augustus Caesar and Mark Antony through to Hadrian, Marcus Aurelius, Constantine, and Justinian, with the people still proudly calling themselves Romans. Given the key role the Byzantines played in sparking the Crusades, it's worth taking a brief detour into their history.

In the late Roman imperial period, the centre of power moved from Rome in Italy to the 'new Rome' of Constantinople, named after the Roman Empire's first Christian emperor – Constantine (reigned 306 to 337 CE). He needed a capital strategically positioned to stare down at the Persians on one side of the Bosphorus, the sea strait cutting through the city dividing its European and Asian halves, while being in closer proximity to the encroaching tribes north of the river Danube. Rome was useless for this objective. Constantinople, though, was ideally placed. Constantine also desired a capital that reflected his newly chosen religion: Christianity. This city would brim with glittering churches and basilicas – not pagan temples.

Christianity had been born in the Middle East. Its first centuries saw state persecution and hostility. Yet now, Constantine sanctioned, promoted, and funded Christianity from the state coffers. But the new state religion was an unfinished work. Its doctrines needed to be more rigorously defined. Unlike the original Christians of Galilee, fired up by faith alone, the Greco-Roman world demanded philosophical and theological clarity. A series of church councils were set to work by successive emperors to shape the new faith. Nearly all these councils were held in the eastern Roman empire.

In 380 CE, emperor Theodosius I declared that the version of Christianity agreed at the Council of Nicaea (325 CE) would be the only permissible version of the religion. All other doctrinal positions to be banned on pain of death or banishment. The Nicene Creed is still recited in Roman Catholic and eastern orthodox churches today, with its belief in one God and three persons (Father, Son, and Holy Spirit), who have co-existed for all time. This dogma would be enforced by the five Christian patriarchs, most of whom were in Asia or North Africa. These were the patriarchs of Constantinople, Antioch, Jerusalem, and Alexandria while the fifth was the Bishop of Rome – who was just another patriarch, despite emerging claims to overall supremacy.

While the western half of the Roman empire fell in 476 CE to 'barbarian' rulers, splintering into several fiefdoms, the eastern half carried on with its borders intact. A concerted attempt under the emperor Justinian in the sixth century CE to retake the west resulted in Italy, part of Spain, and north Africa being reconquered. But this put an enormous strain on imperial resources. It also led to a devastating war with the Persian Sasanian Empire, which for two decades occupied Jerusalem, even taking the holiest of relics, the True Cross, deep into modern Iran, though it was later recovered.

By the seventh century CE, a weakened eastern Roman Empire was confronted by an unforeseen armed host inspired by the new faith of Islam that burst out of the Arabian desert. What is now Egypt, Israel, Syria, Jordan, and Lebanon were seized by the seemingly unstoppable Islamic caliphate. Muslim warriors even massed at the gates of Constantinople, but the walls held firm. However, the loss of so much territory transformed the mindset of the empire, turning it from Roman to something we would recognise as Byzantine. No more dreams of recreating the Rome of the Caesars, as the empire fought endless defensive wars against Bulgars in the west, and Muslims in the east. It would never again be the empire that believed its destiny was to rule the world.

It was a huge blow to both the Byzantines and the Catholic church in the west to see Jerusalem taken by Caliph Umar ibn al-Khattab (c.582–644), the second ruler of the Rashidun caliphate, after a siege. The loss of Bethlehem, birthplace of Jesus, and Jerusalem, the site of his death and burial, was an enormous blow to the Roman Catholic church. Especially those thousands of European pilgrims who trekked to the holy sites at considerable personal risk. It would be their security that the Knights Templar would claim to be defending when they were set up in the year 1118.

The Muslim caliphs were overjoyed to control the holy city from where, according to Islamic scripture, the Prophet Muhammad ascended to heaven. They gave architectural expression to this joy, building the Dome of the Rock on the Temple Mount, the very place where Jews had long hoped their temple would rise once more following its destruction by the Babylonians, and then by the Romans. The golden dome on the new building intentionally outshone the nearby Christian church of the Holy Sepulchre, moving the whole focus of the city to this Muslim shrine. Its grandeur perfectly expressed the triumph of the crescent over the crucifix.

How did Christians in the region react to their new Muslim rulers? The life and writings of John of Damascus (675–749 CE) throws some light. Born to a prominent Syrian, Arab Christian family, John carried on the family line of work, becoming a senior civil servant to the Umayyad caliphs. In the early years of Muslim rule, Greek was still used in government and the new rulers seemed like a light touch compared to the Byzantine emperors with their incessant bullying over how to pray properly, plus their constant need for higher taxes. Maybe Muslim rule would work out better than being governed from Constantinople.

In 726 CE, the Byzantine emperor Leo III forbade the worshipping of icons by all Christians, whether under his direct rule or in the Islamic realms, arguing that venerating images of Christ and the saints amounted to idolatry. This was a total reversal from his predecessors who had even put the face of Christ on the coinage. John was opposed to the smashing up of icons and roused his fellow Christians to oppose it, believing Syria's Muslim rulers would support him. A rather curious tale recounts a forged letter then being sent by the emperor Leo to the caliph implicating John in a plot to surrender Damascus to the Byzantines. The caliph was convinced and ordered John's right hand to be cut off. However, a little later, the severed hand was returned and miraculously reattached itself to John – after some prayer.

Already by the time of this disagreeable incident, John had moved on from the civil service to become a full-time monk. In his new role, he penned increasingly vitriolic tracts on Islam. His works would exert a tremendous influence among Christians. He argued that Islam was just one of many heresies giving a false account of the nature of God. John popularised the term 'Saracen' to refer to Muslims, who he believed were descended from the tempestuous first son of the Hebrew prophet Abraham and an Egyptian slave woman, Hagar. It was widely thought that the Bedouins were descended from Ishmael, who God passed over to make a covenant with Isaac, Abraham's second son from his wife Sara. So, the Muslims were dismissed as Ishmaelites and Hagarites, part of an inferior family branch unfavoured by the Almighty and seduced by the antichrist.[4]

In John's life we see a process whereby the region's Christians were initially relieved to see the back of the Byzantines, or at least have an Islamic buffer between themselves and the imperial authorities in Constantinople. But over time, as it became clearer that the new religion was not a mere distraction but a new state-backed orthodoxy, Christians bristled. Being anti-Byzantine did not mean cheerleading for Islam.

Christians in the Levant were fed up of being told how to pray and what to believe by the authorities. They wanted to be left alone. As Muslim rulers took over Jerusalem, they found a population that was majority Christian. The upper class were Greek-speaking Byzantines. The lower class were a diverse Syriac-speaking people adhering to many different Christian sects, some of which were deeply hostile to the Nicaean brand of Christianity forced on them by Constantinople. The Byzantine emperors had tried in vain to find a compromise theological solution that would please everybody. When that failed, they resorted to oppression, torture, and execution.[5]

The emperors hated disunity. Religion was the ideological glue that held the empire together. It was the means of controlling millions of minds from Carthage to Damascus and Athens. So, strict orthodoxy was enforced. Troublesome priests were exiled or silenced. Patriarchs were ordered to fall into line. Heretics were punished, sometimes by death. Therefore, when the Muslim armies swept in, some Christians dared to hope for a lighter-touch regime.

Islam's holy book, the Qur'an, touches on some of the bitter disputes within Christianity in the seventh century CE. It's even argued that the Qur'an is influenced by some of the dissident Christian sects that were proselytizing in the Middle East at that time. For example, Muslims and Gnostic Christians shared the view that Christ was not really crucified. His death on the cross was an illusion, where a doppelganger was executed while the real Jesus ascended to heaven. Some Gnostics argued that the man who offered to carry the cross of Jesus, Simon Cyrene, ended up nailed to it. Jesus 'transfigured' Simon to look like him and endure the worst form of Roman execution while the Son of God 'assumed the form of Simon and stood by, laughing at them'.[6]

In 1945, a series of Christian Gnostic writings were discovered at the Egyptian town of Nag Hammadi. Thirteen leather-bound papyrus codices written in Coptic and comprising fifty-two Gnostic texts had been buried in the fourth century CE. They included gospels that never made it into the bible such as The Gospel of Thomas, The Apocalypse of Paul, and The Holy Book of the Great Invisible Spirit. These ancient writings evidenced the diversity (and confusion) of thought that existed in early Christianity.

Gnosticism argued that the material and spiritual worlds were entirely separate – a dualist view. The material world is utterly evil and corrupt while the spiritual world is pure and good. Humans should reject all things material, even their own bodies, as sinful. Instead, they should strive for a higher truth – the 'gnosis' (Greek for knowledge) – that can be found on a higher plane of existence. Everything down here on planet Earth is a foul distraction.

The body of Jesus seemed physical, but the divine spirit entered at his baptism and left just before the crucifixion. The idea that God could have been polluted by an earthly form, experiencing the act of birth and the pain of death, was ridiculous. However, in the official version of Christianity, sanctioned by the emperor in Constantinople, that is exactly what the mainstream church insisted had happened. God assumed human form and suffered as a man on the cross, sacrificed for our sins. And anybody who disputed would end up paying with their life.

Yet there were a dizzying number of Christian heresies that endured for centuries despite being outlawed by the imperial authorities and the official church. For example, those who preached that Jesus had not co-existed for all time with God the Father but was created by him (Arianism). Jesus only had a divine nature and not a human one (Monophysitism). The Antidicomarianites (Opponents of Mary) believed that Mary was not a virgin until her death while the Nestorians argued that Mary only gave birth to the human part of Jesus, and not the divine. Over such hair splitting, Christians killed each other.

Today, the last remaining Gnostic sect survives in Iran and Iraq, though their numbers are tiny because of continuous persecution. The Mandaeans retain a 2,000-year-old conviction that while John the Baptist was a great prophet, Jesus of Nazareth was a fraud. Their sacred texts, boldly asserting this, are claimed to predate the scripture of both Christianity and Islam. And the language they speak today is said to be the only surviving dialect of Aramaic that dates to the Roman period. The language spoken by Jesus Christ and John the Baptist.[7]

Mandaeans had long been prominent as goldsmiths and silversmiths. One theory is that their metalworking skills brought them into contact with the Knights Templar during the Crusades. This contact began with mere commercial transactions but as the knights socialised with them, they imbibed their ideas. Maybe they were surprised by these variants of Christianity long suppressed by the popes in the west. Did it cause them to question their own faith, everything they had been taught?

When the Templars were outlawed and put on trial, they were accused of many heretical crimes including the worship of a strange head, spitting on the crucifix, and inappropriate kissing during their initiation rites. Some have speculated that the Templars were indeed guilty of these charges and that these bizarre practices had been learned from sects such as the Mandaeans in the Middle East.

It's been suggested that the venerated head could have been that of the decapitated John the Baptist, beheaded at the request of Salome, stepdaughter of the king Herod Antipas. Could the Templars have come to believe that he, and not Jesus, was the true Messiah? Eight days after arrest warrants went out for the Knights Templar in the year 1307, bringing the order crashing to an ignominious end, a senior Templar under interrogation confessed that the grand master of France, Amaury de la Roche, had told him that Christ was a false prophet and not God.[8] How could such ideas have infiltrated the Knights Templar?

Gnosticism was repeatedly denounced for centuries but it refused to go away. Indeed, it may have travelled from the east to the west like a tropical disease carried home by crusaders and Templars. During the Templar period from the twelfth to the fourteenth centuries, a Gnostic-influenced movement swept through southern France. Aristocrats and serfs converted to the Cathar heresy with huge enthusiasm. They rejected the obscene wealth of the medieval church, all its sacraments, everything in the material world, and allowed women to play a priestly role.

While crusades were being fought against Islam in the Iberian Peninsula and the Holy Land, Pope Innocent III launched the Albigensian Crusade to crush the Cathars in France. An enemy believing it represented true Christianity against a devilish church. It took twenty years, from 1209 to 1229, to eradicate the Cathars, involving mass burnings and indiscriminate slaughter. At one siege in July 1209 at the town of Béziers, the papal legate notoriously advised the crusaders to annihilate the entire population with the words: *'Kill them all, let God sort them out.'*[9]

Many of the methods used to crush the Cathars were later deployed against the Knights Templar. The knights, once heralded as champions of the pope and the Roman Catholic church, found themselves in the year 1307 condemned as the most damnable of heretics, deserving nothing more than to have their bodies broken in dark dungeons. The merciless torturers and inquisitors got to work on the knights with the tools tried and tested on the Cathars. There was a particular viciousness when it came to Rome stamping out false belief within the Christian fold that outshone the brutality against other faiths during the Crusades in the Holy Land.

This has fed speculation, especially in recent decades, that the Knights Templar were sympathetic to the Cathars and were conspicuous by their absence in the Albigensian Crusade, though they did have their hands full on the Iberian Peninsula and in the Holy Land.[10] Some have claimed that Templar properties in southern France harboured Cathars seeking a hiding place from the church and even buried them when they died. All of which paints a picture of an order of knights that started life as faithful sons of the Roman Catholic church but ended up riddled with heresies.

The impression we get from both contemporary sources and later writers is that the Knights Templar, for whatever reason, seemed to soak up forms of Christianity that the popes in Rome and emperors in Constantinople had done their level best to wipe out without success. Whether this is true is what will be investigated. It is indisputable, however, that the Templars were repeatedly depicted as practisers of diabolic rites based on banned scriptures. All these ideas had been picked up during their crusading in the Middle East.

The destruction of the Knights Templar was over two centuries in the future as Urban addressed his council at Clermont. He spoke as the Middle East was plunged into bloody turmoil. Rival Shi'a and Sunni Muslim caliphates fighting for control of the region and in turn attacking the Christian Byzantines. Very soon, the pope would be adding to the chaos with thousands of crusading knights loyal to Rome. Their stunning early successes would be in no small part due to divisions among their enemies.

Islam had arisen 450 years before, transforming Arabia, north Africa, and the Levant. Up until the seventh century CE, the region had been divided between the eastern Roman (or Byzantine) empire on one side and the Sasanian Empire, centred on modern Iran and Iraq, on the other. This duopoly, with Romans facing off Persians, seemed eternal. Since Cleopatra, Egypt had been ruled by Romans, along with the Levant and Asia Minor. Facing them were the Sasanians, who for four centuries dominated Persia, which adhered to the Zoroastrian faith that shared the Gnostic belief in a universal battle of good and evil. But that duopoly was about to end.

The two superpowers were rocked to their foundations by the explosion on to the scene of Muslim armies storming out of the Arabian Peninsula. The Rashidun caliphate wiped out the Sasanians and tore away a big chunk of the Byzantine Empire. But it failed to take Constantinople. As a result, the Byzantines endured. After a period of internal strife and licking their wounds, the empire struck back, regaining lost territories and its self-confidence. A new divide emerged between the Christian, Greek-speaking Byzantine Empire and an increasingly wealthy Islamic caliphate ruled initially from Damascus and then

Baghdad, after the Abbasid dynasty took over. The Abbasids claiming descent from the Prophet Muhammad's uncle, Abbas ibn Abd al-Muttalib (566–653 CE).

Constantinople and Baghdad were exceedingly rich cities. Both sat on major trade routes taxing everything that passed through. Silk, honey, slaves, soap, spices, metals, and glass were some of the myriad goods that enriched the elites. Skimming the merchants funded palaces and magnificent places of worship. In the process, the two cities became very competitive. On one occasion, two Byzantine ambassadors were given a guided tour of the caliph's palace that featured a park with a silver tree, golden leaves, and some kind of mechanical singing birds.[11] Not to be outdone, a Muslim chronicler, Ibn al-Faqih al-Hamadani, reported that the Byzantine emperor Constantine V (718–775 CE) impressed his Abbasid guests by turning copper into gold and silver using a mysterious powder.

Throughout the ninth and tenth centuries CE, the Islamic Abbasid caliphate presided over a cultural golden age we associate with the Tales from the Thousand and One Nights. A magical world of sultans, sorcerers, and scheming viziers.[12] It was a time of remarkable tolerance and openness to ideas with Muslim intellectuals absorbing and adding to the combined wisdom of Rome, Greece, and Persia, making great advances in science and the arts.

But just as the Golden Age of Islam was reaching its peak, a group of nomadic raiders, far away near the Aral Sea in central Asia, decided to up sticks and migrate. They had long eked out a precarious existence on the Eurasian Steppe, a vast stretch of grassland and shrubs, extending for thousands of miles from eastern Europe to China. It was a harsh environment, plunging to freezing in winter and baking hot in the summer. The land was fit for little more than grazing cattle. And according to one theory, extreme weather events in the tenth and eleventh centuries caused by climate change, resulting in famine, forced tribes on the steppe to emigrate or die.[13]

These steppe people lived on horseback, herding their flocks and raiding more settled communities or other tribes. As warriors, they moved quickly, wearing light armour, fighting other tribes, and sometimes striking terror into nearby empires. The steppe had produced fearsome foes before, such as the Huns, Ostrogoths, Avars, and Pechenegs. Fighters whose disinterest in urban sophistication might explain why they torched so many great cities to the ground without a second's thought.

Among the steppe tribes was a tribal federation known as the Oghuz Turks. Back in the tenth century, the leader of an Oghuz clan – a man called Seljuk Bey – moved south into what is now Kazakhstan. Encountering Muslim merchants, he converted from shamanism to Islam around 985 CE. After that he announced his refusal to pay any more taxes to the unbelievers in the Oghuz federation.[14] In the next century, his grandsons struck out in the direction of the Abbasid caliphate. An audacious move but also well-timed. The Islamic world had begun to fracture, with rulers in Muslim-ruled Spain and Egypt no longer recognising the supremacy of the Abbasid caliphate. The Seljuks sensed weakness.

As they advanced across modern Iran, the caliph was powerless. He made a series of concessions to the Seljuks, granting them control of territory in the hope they might be appeased and cease their forward march. That tactic failed miserably. In the year 1055, the Seljuks entered triumphantly into his capital of Baghdad. Without even bothering to meet the caliph, they proceeded on towards the city of Mosul. Henceforth, the Abbasids ruled in name only while real power lay with the determined newcomers.

Ironically, the Byzantines had come to rely on the Abbasid caliphate as a buffer between them and any marauding steppe people. Nomadic warriors had headed in their direction before, normally taking a northern route to bypass the caliph's forces. That at least delayed their arrival in Byzantine territory. But now, the Abbasids were under the Seljuk thumb. The caliph was their compliant puppet. This created a menacing situation for the Byzantines with a vast throng of land-hungry steppe warriors right on their doorstep.

The ghosts of the long-gone but not forgotten Huns must have loomed large in the Byzantine imagination. Another steppe people who had ravaged the western and eastern halves of the Roman Empire during the fifth century CE. Only this time, the new arrivals were inspired by the Islamic faith. It was like the Huns and the Rashidun caliphate rolled into one new super-threat. Combined with economic instability that led to cuts in imperial military spending; civil war between the Byzantine nobility; and a neglect of the eastern frontier – the Seljuks rightly sensed the Byzantine Empire was vulnerable.

On Friday, 26 August 1071, the world was turned upside down. The unthinkable happened. Not only was a Byzantine army defeated by the Seljuks in the Battle of Manzikert, but the emperor, Romanus IV Diogenes (c.1030-c.1072), was captured. Covered in dust and dishevelled, he was paraded before the Seljuk leader, Alp Arslan (c.1029–1072), who then used the imperial personage as a human footstool to mount his horse.[15]

Nothing like this had been seen since the capture of the Roman emperor Valerian in 260 CE. At the Battle of Edessa, the Sasanian king, Shapur I, had taken that emperor prisoner. He too was used as a footstool. In some accounts Valerian grew old as a slave. In other versions, he was killed by having molten gold poured down his throat or flayed alive and then stuffed with straw as a gruesome exhibit. In contrast, Romanus was set free by Alp Arslan but then deposed and blinded by his own nobles on his return to Constantinople, dying in agony from infected wounds.

In just a few hours of fighting at Manzikert, the empire had lost the Anatolian plain. Its breadbasket, source of recruits for the army, and land link to Persia and beyond. The Seljuks essentially hollowed out the Byzantine realm, leaving the emperor with a coastal strip and his capital city. To add insult to injury, the invaders chose Nicaea as their capital. A city just fifty miles away from Constantinople.

This was a battle defeat that sent shockwaves through both the Islamic and Christian worlds. The Byzantines were viewed as an increasingly spent force. They would linger for another four centuries, but the overall trajectory of these descendants of the Caesars was downwards. For their part, the jubilant Seljuks named their newly acquired territory the Sultanate of Rûm – a translation of the word Rome. This tribe from the steppe had done its ancestors proud. They had conquered the Roman Empire.

By the 1090s, the Byzantine emperor Alexios I Komnenos (1057–1118) was forced to swallow his pride and pen a begging letter to the princes and prelates of the west. Grovelling for help from the pope in Rome. Hard to imagine that just four centuries before, the Byzantines had so dominated the whole of Italy that they were able to arrest Pope Martin I, transport him to Constantinople, humiliate him in public, and then exile the beaten-up pontiff to the southern Crimea. All because he objected to the emperor's preferred definition of Christ's true nature. But by the eleventh century, those days were long gone. The papacy had powerful western backers.[16]

Relations between Constantinople and Rome had soured in the years before the Battle of Manzikert. On 16 July 1054, the legate of Pope Leo IX (1002–1054), Cardinal Humbert of Silva Candida (1015–1061), strode into the Hagia Sophia, the seat of the city's patriarch, Michael Cerularius (1000–1059), just as afternoon prayers were about to begin. He slammed a bull of excommunication from the pope onto the high altar, delivering a few cursory words in bad Greek to everybody present. Then wheeled round and exited before a shocked congregation. This was the serving of divorce papers by the Roman Catholic church on the eastern Byzantine church.[17]

Like most divorces, the danger signs had been present for a while. On the surface, it was all about differences over priests marrying, the kind of bread used in communion, fasting days, and so on. Really, it was a power struggle between the Latin and Greek churches. The papacy was flexing its muscles in the eleventh century, demanding that all secular powers bow to its authority, based on the assertion that the popes were the successors of Saint Peter, and therefore their jurisdiction should cover both the western and the eastern churches. The Byzantines, who had controlled the popes like puppets 400 years before, were having none of this.

A religious turf war raged as new peoples were converted to Christianity. Roman Catholic and Byzantine orthodox priests rushed to persuade pagan converts that their version of the faith was superior. This unseemly jostling for position also extended to existing Christian areas. For example, when Norman knights pushed the Byzantine military out of southern Italy, Constantinople-appointed bishops were kicked out and replaced by Catholics loyal to the pope. The emperor and his patriarch reacted by closing Catholic churches within his realm. This petty ecclesiastical tit-for-tat undermined any trust that once existed between the eastern and western churches.

The bull of excommunication itself was entirely over the top. It accused the patriarch of Constantinople of endorsing the worst heresies that had ever arisen in Christendom. For example, he was alleged to be a promoter of the Valesians, a bizarre group of Christians who forcibly castrated passing travellers and any guests who were unwise enough to visit them. The patriarch was also said to sanction Nicolaism, a heresy mentioned in the New Testament that incorporated orgies and wife swapping into their church services.[18]

The pope excommunicated the patriarch in 1054, and Michael Cerularius reciprocated by excommunicating the pope. This acrimonious split came to be known as the Great Schism. Rome engaged in a public relations exercise to portray Cerularius as an overbearing patriarch daring to imagine he was superior to the pope and so arrogant that he even wore purple shoes, the very height of presumption. The two churches would never reunite, although in 1965, Pope Paul VI and Patriarch Athenagoras finally decided to lift the 900-year-old mutual excommunication.

Thirty-five years after the schism, and the emperor Alexios had no time for this theological squabble. The Seljuks had overrun much of his empire and were in control of nearby Nicaea. He was also fighting the Normans in southern Italy and what is now Albania and northern Greece. However, not all Normans were enemies. One Norman knight – Robert, Count of Flanders (c.1035–1093) – was returning from a pilgrimage to Jerusalem in 1086 and resolved to help Alexios fight the Seljuks, which he did with considerable bravery. The two men struck up a friendship.

So much so that Alexios wrote him a letter to be circulated to western rulers and the pope when he got back home. The first part detailed the atrocities against Christians that Urban would later read out at Clermont. The second part described the miserable state of his empire. And the final part listed all the holy relics and riches that he would gladly give away to knights from Europe if they came to his aid. Better his entire treasury fell into their hands than the 'pagans'.

Alexios certainly knew how to make his western target audience lick their lips. The priceless relics on offer included the head of John the Baptist with hair and beard still present; fragments from the five loaves and two fishes left over from the miraculous feeding of the multitude by Jesus; and the pillar to which the Messiah was tied when he was scourged before the crucifixion. The emperor pledged to throw in the whip as well. But if relics were not enough for the knights, Alexios offered 'the treasure vaults of the churches of Constantinople'. All the gold, silver, gems, and silken vestments in his own capital could be taken in return for military aid against the Seljuks.

Not surprisingly, some have suspected that this letter, which played a key role in sparking the crusades, was a forgery by greedy, western knights.[19] Would the emperor really have invited foreign soldiers to come and ransack his city taking as much treasure as they could carry away? This was his worst nightmare, surely. The letter has been a source of contention, with some believing there was an original version that was then heavily doctored, or that the whole document was a fake.

What we can say for certain is that Alexios wanted some well-trained mercenaries from the west to come and help him push back the Seljuks. Nothing could have prepared the emperor for what Pope Urban was about to unleash. A new form of Christian warfare undertaken by countless thousands of crusaders.

So, what was Pope Urban's thought process as he developed the idea of a war for God and Christ in the Middle East? Expansion of his powerbase is the most credible answer. The papacy had been mired in corruption in the previous century. A period referred to as the Rule of the Harlots and even the Pornocracy. One pope (John XII) was elected in his teens while another (Benedict IX) put the papacy up for sale to the highest bidder.[20] Urban and his predecessor but one, Gregory VII (c.1015–1085), set about cleaning up the church and firming up its authority.

Pope Gregory resolved to put the church above all secular kings and princes. Key to this was the power to make all ecclesiastical appointments across Europe. However, many European monarchs baulked at this power grab from Rome, preferring the Byzantine model where the emperor controlled his patriarch. They felt the church should be subject to them. This would underscore future conflicts over the independent operation of the Knights Templar. The Holy Roman Emperor, whose realm centred on modern Germany, even backed a rival pope, Clement III, who was duly crowned in opposition to Pope Gregory and took control of the city of Rome. Not for the first or last time, there were two rival popes staring each other down. All because the Holy Roman Emperor believed the church in his kingdom should answer to him, and not the pope.

When Urban was elected pope in 1088, he was unable to enter Rome. The 'antipope' Clement was still in control and Urban only got entry to the papal palace, the Lateran, two years before his speech at Clermont. Norman and French knights helped Urban seize Rome from the clutches of Clement. So basically, brute force got him to the papal throne. This lesson in the importance of the sword in matters spiritual would not be lost on Urban.

Neither was the fact that great armies were making significant gains in the name of Christ in southern Europe. It was the clash of steel that was driving back Islam, not prayers and incense. Christian kingdoms in Spain and Portugal were inching forward using force, believing they were waging a just war, as defined in the fifth century after Christ by that great church father, Saint Augustine, who taught that war was admissible in the cause of peace and the snuffing out of evil.[21]

Norman knights who had originally served as mercenaries for the Byzantines had now turned on their paymasters and taken southern Italy from them, as well as capturing Sicily from the Muslim caliphate. Islam had once seemed invincible, conquering everything in its path. But during Urban's papacy, the Catholic church dared to dream of extending its power and influence eastwards. Why should the Byzantines rule once more in Jerusalem when the pope could command armies to do his bidding, bringing the holy sites under Rome's total control?

The only question was how to achieve this goal. Jerusalem had been in Muslim hands for over 400 years. To replace the crescent with the cross would be a huge undertaking. However, Urban hailed from the French knightly nobility. By virtue of his upbringing, he instinctively realised the desire of many knights to feel that their acts of slaughter and maiming had a higher purpose. Even the most bloodthirsty of them lived in constant fear of purgatory or eternal hellfire after death. Urban realised he had the unique authority to sanctify their acts of extreme violence. He could offer them a road to heavenly glory contingent on maximising their brutality.

And Urban's instincts were proven right. After his incendiary Clermont speech, crusading fever swept Europe. Letters sent by Urban to bishops and princes express his delight on hearing that knights and nobles were rushing to board ships for the Holy Land. Though the pope also sent some stern missives to monasteries demanding that monks and priests stay put unless their bishop gave them permission to leave. He also instructed young married men not to depart 'without the consent of their spouses'. Urban was already having to restrain some of the fervour he had unleashed.

Their destination was an unhappy city. From the start of the eleventh century, Jerusalem had been plunged repeatedly into violence and destruction. After falling to Muslim control in the seventh century, it had been ruled by the Rashidun caliphate, the immediate successors of the Prophet Muhammad (634–661); then the Umayyads, who built the Dome of the Rock (661–750); after them, the Abbasids, who had little interest in the city (751–969); followed by the Shi'a Muslim Fatimid caliphate that ruled out of Egypt (970–1071); who were then forced out of the city by a Seljuk force led by a terrifying warlord, Atsiz ibn Uvaq al-Khwarizmi (died 1079).

While Atsiz was off on campaign trying to take the Fatimid capital, Cairo, the people of Jerusalem rose in revolt and drove out the Seljuks. A furious Atsiz sped back and massacred thousands of the city's rebels including those who had holed up in the Al-Aqsa Mosque believing its sanctity to Muslims would protect them. This slaughter foreshadowed another bloodbath to come in just under three decades, only on that occasion inflicted by invading crusaders.

The most sacred site for Christians in Jerusalem was the Church of the Holy Sepulchre. It's a curious, sprawling church containing both the site of the crucifixion of Jesus and the empty tomb where he was buried then resurrected. It would be a place of huge spiritual importance for the Knights Templar. Many of their churches were built in imitation of the Holy Sepulchre's circular construction. But by the time the Templars arrived, the original Roman building and many Christian churches in the city had been wrecked in the year 1009 by the 'mad caliph', Al-Hakim (985–1021).

Abu Ali Manur, more commonly known as Al-Hakim, was a Shi'a Muslim Fatimid caliph who rejected the traditional policy of tolerance towards Christians, Jews, and even Sunni Muslims, viewing their beliefs as an offence to God. Things had started out more promisingly when the well-educated young man took power. His lands included Egypt, Sicily, Syria, north Africa, and the holy cities of Islam on the Arabian Peninsula. Many expected yet another cultured and refined caliph who would encourage learning and inter-faith dialogue. They were soon disabused.

The 'Nero of Islam', as some dubbed him, ordered the destruction of all churches, synagogues, and other religious artefacts throughout his domains.[22] On 18 October 1009, the Church of the Holy Sepulchre was levelled in an act of crazed vandalism. The official reason given by Muslim chroniclers was Al-Hakim's objection to an annual Easter miracle involving priests entering the tomb of Jesus from where an eerie light emanated. A column of fire was said to miraculously appear from which the congregation lit their Paschal candles. Al-Hakim bristled at this superstitious idolatry.

The demolition of Christendom's most revered place of pilgrimage sent shockwaves across Europe. Up until then, Christian pilgrims made the long journey to Jerusalem in the belief that the only danger lurked on the roads in the form of cut-throats and thieves. But now, the city's Jews were forced to carry a bell while Christians had to wear a cross that was at least two feet in length and width. This was a disturbing departure from the relative tolerance practised by the Sunni Muslim Abbasid caliphate. In its realm, Jews and Christians were reduced to an inferior 'dhimmi' status, forced to pay the 'jizya' tax, but not subjected to this kind of persecution.

Now, this Shi'a Muslim Fatimid caliph was displaying aggressive intolerance towards two large religious groups within his kingdom – even though Al-Hakim relied on people from other faiths and ethnic backgrounds to run his administration up to the highest levels.[23] Harshest of all his discriminatory measures was a clampdown on the freedom of women, with a bizarre ban on shoemakers making and selling footwear for female customers. He also forbade a certain culinary dish because the Umayyad caliphs had enjoyed eating it. Finally, he ordered the extermination of all dogs in Egypt. Which might explain why on one of his regular nocturnal horse rides in the hills, where he went to meditate, Al-Hakim failed to return. His horse and some bloodstained garments were later retrieved. The Nero of Islam was dead. Possibly at the hands of dog lovers.

Jerusalem recovered slowly after the demise of this mercurial monarch, but the memory of his wanton destruction lingered and was referenced decades later by Pope Urban at Clermont. The message was clear. To make the Holy Land safe for pilgrims, Christians needed to be back in control of Jerusalem. And so, the Crusades were underway.

Some years before Urban's speech, a priest from Amiens, a city in northern France, had gone on pilgrimage to Jerusalem. His name was Peter, and he was deeply distressed by what he witnessed in the holy city. Infidels and godless men defiled the sacred Christian sites. The offerings of the faithful were plundered. Pilgrims subjected to extortion and physically attacked. Angered, Peter forced a meeting with the patriarch and fumed about the situation. The ageing Christian leader shrugged, responding:

> 'Most faithful of Christians, how can you thus upbraid and trouble a patriarch whose power and authority are like a tiny ant's before the overweening might of such enemies? My life is ransomed only by constant payments, without which I face torture and death. I fear the threats will grow daily unless Christendom sends help. You must be my envoy to summon it.'[24]

Whether this encounter really happened is a matter of some conjecture. Especially given that one account has Jesus appearing to Peter in the church of the Holy Sepulchre urging him to organise a crusade. Scepticism aside, what the story established was that a military response was required, and that Peter was its natural leader. This French priest's name has endured to the present day as Peter the Hermit, prime mover of the People's Crusade, an early response to Urban's speech. A hugely controversial mass movement of 'the celibate, the unchaste, adulterers, murderers, thieves, perjurers, bandits' who joyfully assembled to reclaim the Holy Land with a promise of total remission of their past sins.

The first action of this vast horde of the faithful was a frenzied pogrom directed against the Jewish populations of the Rhineland in modern Germany. The monastic chronicler Albert of Aachen, writing a few years later, described a 'large and innumerable host' of Christians from France, England, and Flanders turning up at several cities and falling upon the Jewish populations. They wounded and killed men, women, and children then torched their homes and synagogues. It is alleged that some Jewish families committed suicide rather than face this crazed throng.

> 'The women girded their loins with strength and slew their own sons and daughters, and then themselves. Many men also mustered their strength and slaughtered their wives and children and infants. The most gentle and tender of women slaughtered the child of her delight. They all arose, man and woman alike, and slew one another.'[25]

There is a rather snobbish notion that these attacks were perpetrated by the common people, bent on looting Jewish property, whereas the crusader knights of nobler birth had loftier motives, eschewing sectarian violence. This is nonsense. In the months after Urban's speech, French Jews warned their Rhineland brethren of the rapidly growing movement of both high- and low-born Christians. Some well-heeled crusaders engaged in extortion from Jewish merchants as they made their crusading journey through Europe.[26] This included noble knights like Godfrey of Bouillon (1060–1100), who would become the first ruler of Christian-controlled Jerusalem from 1099, and the notorious Emicho of Flonheim.[27]

While Godfrey was successfully palmed off with silver, Emicho's antisemitism was not so easily assuaged. His band of knights slaughtered 500 Jews at Worms before storming the walled city of Mainz. Within the walls, Archbishop Ruthard attempted to protect the city's Jewish population but allies of Emicho opened the gates and over a thousand Jews are estimated to have been hacked to death. One medieval Jewish account described how families hid in their innermost rooms to escape the swirling sword. But there was no escape. Emicho continued this grim activity, moving on to Metz, Neuss, Wevelinghofen, Eller, and Xanten.

Antisemitism was not a new phenomenon in medieval Europe. But Urban's call mobilised anti-Jewish mobs into crusader armies. Whether the pope intended this outcome is open to question. But Jews were widely perceived as a cursed race, forever forced to bear the responsibility for Christ's death. They were the subjects of lurid myths involving the sacrifice of Christian children in strange blood rituals. Despite the complete lack of evidence, these tales gripped the medieval mind. It was exactly this kind of mass credulity that would sink the Knights Templar in a welter of accusations involving pornographic rituals and devil worship.[28]

To many of the first crusaders, killing Jewish people was viewed as a necessary first step on their divinely inspired mission. Godfrey of Bouillon declared that he would be unable to fulfil his crusading obligations until he had avenged 'the blood of the crucified with the blood of Israel'.[29] It is a moot point whether the Knights Templar subscribed to such virulent antisemitism. Some believe the knights displayed greater tolerance to the Jews and as will be examined, this may have been related to the involvement of both the knights and prominent Jews in the world of medieval finance.

Antisemitic crusaders were influenced not just by the New Testament account of Christ's life but a slew of material originating from outside the authorised bible. Emicho may have been inspired by a myth circulating in the Middle Ages that a 'Last Roman Emperor' would emerge who would either convert or destroy the Jewish people, enabling the Second Coming of Jesus Christ and the end of the world. This myth was popularised by a seventh-century CE document, written in Syriac, known as the *Apocalypse of the Pseudo-Methodius*, that was a bestseller in its day.[30] Very much a reaction to the rise of Islam, it predicted the rise of this Last Roman Emperor who would defeat the antichrist, march on Jerusalem, and place his crown on the True Cross.

Like Peter the Hermit, Emicho also claimed to have met Jesus in a vision. And the Messiah had promised the knight that he was destined to become the Last Roman Emperor.[31] His first task was to reach Constantinople and be crowned, after which the End Times would begin. While Emicho's religious delusions may seem absurd, there were far stranger beliefs among those on the People's Crusade. One group, for example, venerated a goose that they believed had divine instructions to liberate the Holy Land. While Albert of Aachen mentions a she-goat believed to possess similar sacred powers.

This first wave of Christian zealots, the People's Crusade, snaked through eastern Europe on to Constantinople and from there, to Jerusalem. The Jewish writer Solomon bar Simson was not sorry to see them go: *'They decorated themselves prominently with their signs, placing a profane symbol – a horizontal line over a vertical one – on the vestments of every man and woman whose heart yearned to go on the stray path to the grave of their Messiah.'*[32] At their head was Peter the Hermit, who was now so revered that the faithful even tore clumps of hair off his mule as holy keepsakes.

This ragtag army made its way through Hungary and Bulgaria, earning an appalling reputation along the way. They arrived in Constantinople by August 1096 with the city registering a noticeable surge in criminal activity and general rowdiness in just a few days. The emperor Alexios ferried these 'Franks', as they became known in the east, across the Bosphorus. These were not the well-disciplined faithful soldiers of Christ he had been hoping for. Bidding them a not very fond farewell, Alexios warned the westerners not to engage the Seljuk enemy until more experienced knights turned up from their homelands.

However, religious zeal trumped common sense. The boisterous Christians went in search of the Seljuks, no doubt hoping to inflict on them what had befallen the Jews of the Rhineland. But fate had something else in store. In October 1096, thousands of Franks were wiped out by the Seljuks at the Battle of Civetot. Peter the Hermit was within the walls of Constantinople at the time and survived, but his popular crusade was essentially over. From now on, kings and princes would take the lead alongside the Knights Templar, and other military orders that would be formed.

The remnants of the People's Crusade folded into armies led by nobles like Bohemond of Taranto (c.1054–1111), the son of Robert Guiscard (c.1015–1085), a Norman warrior and count of Apulia and Calabria who conquered Sicily from the Muslims. Bohemond cut his teeth fighting the Byzantines in southern Italy and although he was now rushing to the aid of Constantinople in its fight for survival against the Seljuks, Emperor Alexios Komnenos treated him with kid gloves, insisting on an oath of loyalty. This scorpion dance between the Byzantines and Franks would become a constant feature of the crusades.

Some in Constantinople – a minority one imagines – were fascinated by the new western arrivals. The daughter of the emperor, Anna Komnene, was a remarkable woman who wrote a history of the period. She left us a very revealing pen portrait of Bohemond as a towering physical figure with a dangerous personality:

> *'There was a certain charm about him, but it was dimmed by the alarm his person inspired. There was a hard, savage quality to his whole aspect. Even his laugh sounded like a threat.'*[33]

While aristocrats like Bohemond would lead the Crusades from now on, the ranks still contained many desperate characters. Penniless before they arrived, these wretched people marched barefoot, bore no arms, were entirely filthy and naked, and lived on the roots of plants. The chroniclers referred to them contemptuously as 'Tafurs'. At the Siege of Ma'arra in the second half of 1098, a city between Antioch and Damascus, Christian chroniclers accused the Tafurs of cannibalism.

Ralph of Caen spared no details describing how the flesh of killed Saracen soldiers was tossed into the cooking pot while dead children were roasted on spits.[34] Fulcher of Chartres specifies which bits of the Saracens were cut off and how hungrily they were devoured, while Albert of Aachen mentions that the Tafurs tucked into both human and dog flesh. On the Arab side, these atrocities lived on in infamy for many years. But some have questioned whether the Tafurs have received an unfairly bad press over the centuries. Were they scapegoats for barbaric practices that were indulged in more widely, at dire moments in the crusades? Was their poverty unavoidable or did they choose to crusade with no money, shoes, or steel armour? A picture emerges of a body of people who voluntarily gave up everything and threw themselves into the thick of battle with suicidal passion for the cause.

Seen in this light, there is a foreshadowing of the Knights Templar with their vow of poverty and hatred for ornament and personal wealth. Also, like the Templars, the Tafurs seem to have had their own version of a grand master, referred to as King Tafur. Allegedly a high-born French knight who had given up all worldly goods to command this ragged but devoted throng. For the crusading nobility, there must have been some propaganda advantage in making it known to the enemy that such fearsome creatures existed in their ranks. Human flesh-eating fanatics would surely instil fear among the Muslim forces.

In July 1099, the crusaders arrived outside the walls of Jerusalem. The holiest city in Christendom where Jesus had been crucified, buried, resurrected, and from where he ascended into heaven. The thrilling anticipation of taking Jerusalem inspired some, maybe including Tafurs, to throw themselves recklessly at the walls. Arrows, giant boulders, and boiling oil from on high soon convinced everybody that a more strategic approach was required.

The crusader nobility – Godfrey of Bouillon, Raymond of Toulouse, Robert of Flanders, and Robert of Normandy – marshalled their forces, building siege towers and scaling ladders. Also playing a leading role in the siege of Jerusalem was Bohemond's nephew, Tancred (c.1075–1112). They faced the city's Fatimid occupiers who had taken Jerusalem back from the Seljuks.

The Fatimid governor, Iftikhar al-Dawla, anxiously awaited a relief force reported to be marching north from Egypt. So, the crusaders realised that time was not on their side. Swift action was needed. On 14 July 1099, they mounted a determined assault, initially meeting stiff resistance. But the following day, the Franks stormed the city walls, swarming into Jerusalem's narrow streets. There was no mood for clemency among the crusaders.

The Christian chroniclers outdid each other in detailing the scale of the massacre that ensued. Even by medieval standards, the savagery was unprecedented. One account, the *Gesta Francorum*, boasted that the crusaders were cutting down so many Fatimid defenders the blood coated their ankles. Even allowing for a degree of hyperbole, the besiegers must have been electrified by their success. Setting foot in a place they had only ever heard about from priests in the pulpit.

The terrified inhabitants sped towards places of worship, seeking sanctuary. Jews headed for the synagogues while Muslims, or 'Saracens' as they were termed by the chroniclers, made for the Temple Mount. Known to them as the Haram al-Sharif – the very spot where the Prophet Muhammad had ascended into heaven. As for the city's eastern Christians, it was claimed they had been cleared out in advance of the siege in case they collaborated with the crusaders. However, that was never a given as their religious loyalty was to the patriarchs of the east and not the pope.

Interestingly, Fulcher of Chartres points to the multi-ethnic profile of the population, calling them 'Arabs and Ethiopians'. The citizenry was clearly composed of a diverse mix of people from the Levant as well as north Africa. About 20,000 people lived within its walls and despite the Muslim conquest having occurred four centuries before, Christians may still have been a majority.

As the crusaders surged through Jerusalem, Muslims climbed on top of the Al-Aqsa Mosque and shut themselves inside the Dome of the Rock – two buildings sacred to Islam that would be renamed by the crusaders as the Temple of Solomon and Temple of the Lord respectively. They huddled, frightened and powerless, expecting the worst. Robert the Monk later mocked their hopeless predicament. Did those on the mosque roof imagine 'they could have grown wings and flown away'? Instead, he sneered, nature denied them wings while the crusaders inflicted 'a miserable exit from their wretched lives'.[35]

In death, there was no dignity. The crusaders split open their bellies in response to rumours that the Saracens were swallowing their money, 'bezants', as the local coins were called, literally consumed to prevent that wealth falling into greedy western hands. The bodies were then burned, and the charred carcasses picked over for any traces of treasure. By this stage of the barbarity, according to Raymond of Aguilers, the blood of the enemy had risen to knee level and splashed on the bridles of the horses. All of which gave him cause for celebration:

> *Some of the pagans were mercifully beheaded, others pierced by arrows plunged from towers, and yet others, tortured for a long time, were burned to death in searing flames. Piles of heads, hands and feet lay in the houses and streets, and indeed there was a running to and fro of men and knights over the corpses.*[36]

The Christian world rejoiced at the news that Jerusalem was now back in Christian hands after over four centuries of Muslim rule. Days later, Godfrey of Bouillon was proclaimed Defender of the Holy Sepulchre, turning down the title of King of Jerusalem as the only legitimate king of the city had been Christ himself. Nevertheless, Godfrey was in complete control. He had realised the crusading vision so forcefully articulated in Clermont years before, by Pope Urban. Sadly for Urban, he died just two weeks after the crusaders broke into the city and never received the news.

Chapter Two

Mysterious Origins of the Knights Templar

In either 1118 or 1119, a group of nine knights, down on their luck, gathered in Jerusalem and moaned about their predicament. The glory they hoped for had failed to materialise. Their sacred mission sullied by everyday politics. Disenchanted, they even considered turning their back on the secular world and entering monastic life. The vow of poverty would have been easy given their reduced circumstances. Their leader was a minor noble from the Champagne region of France who had been crusading in the Holy Land for two decades. Many of his associates were second or third sons of noble families who, faced with the prospect of never inheriting a title, sought a role through crusading. They were desperate to find a sense of purpose.

How or why this bedraggled group of soldiers ended up forming the Knights Templar is something of a mystery. Was it their own idea? Was it suggested to them by King Baldwin II of Jerusalem? The usual line is that they themselves conjured up the idea of a new type of military order to protect Christian pilgrims on the roads into Jerusalem. Their leader, Hugh de Payens (1070–1136), was reportedly shocked by the massacre of hundreds of pilgrims by brigands at the river Jordan in Easter, 1119. These defenceless people, weakened by religious fasting, had trekked to the spot where Jesus was baptised by John the Baptist only to be set upon and either murdered or sold into slavery. The banks of this sacred river had been left strewn with the eviscerated corpses of the Christian faithful.

News of this atrocity had spread like wildfire back home. Hardly good PR for the crusader endeavour in the Holy Land. So much for Jerusalem and the other holy places being safer to visit now they were back in Christian hands. As they disembarked from ships in the port city of Jaffa, pilgrims nervously took the road for Jerusalem not knowing whether they would make it alive. Beyond the walls of crusader-controlled cities was the unpoliced countryside. As for the future network of mighty crusader castles, these were still at the planning stage.

As with so many wars in history, the crusaders discovered that it was one thing to take territory but quite another to govern it. Godfrey of Bouillon had died a year after taking the title Defender of the Holy Sepulchre but never being declared king. This may have reflected tensions within the Frankish forces over whether the ruler of Jerusalem, the holiest of cities, should be a churchman or a prince. Godfrey's brother Baldwin (c.1060s-1118) swept aside such arcane considerations. He was far less shy about assuming full regal powers and had himself crowned as the first crusader King of Jerusalem in 1100, reigning until 1118 when he died attempting to invade Egypt. He was then succeeded by his cousin Baldwin of Bourcq, crowned Baldwin II (c.1075–1131).

The kingdom of Jerusalem was one of four crusader realms established after the First Crusade that also included the County of Edessa, the County of Tripoli, and the Principality of Antioch. Together, these kingdoms were referred to as 'outremer', a French term for overseas. All ruled by Roman Catholic princes brought up in the Latin rite of Rome and firmly rejecting the Byzantine Greek Christian rite long established in the region. These invaders were referred to as Franks – 'Frangoi' by the Byzantines and al-Ifranji by the Muslims, even though they were not exclusively from France. The Franks (crusaders) found themselves in charge of a restive population of Muslims, Jews, and Christians who worshipped very differently to them and resented their presence.

Into this unstable situation came nine knights viewed as a solution to the problem of how to solidify Christian rule over the Holy Land. Their names: Hugh de Payens, Godfrey de Saint-Omer, Payen de Montdidier, Archambaud de Saint Amand, André de Montbard, Gondemar (or Gundemar), Rossal (or Roral), Geoffroy Bisol, and Godefroid. Two of them, Hugh de Payens and André de Montbard, would go on to become grand masters of the new order of holy warriors: The Poor Fellow-Soldiers of Christ and of the Temple of Solomon. Better known by the truncated title – the Knights Templar.

What differentiated these knights from their secular counterparts? The whole notion of such a brotherhood of holy knights is often assumed to have been obvious to everybody at the time. But what is often overlooked is that the crusades unleashed by Pope Urban had created a whole new political paradigm. Not since the Roman conquest of the Middle East had European soldiers carved out chunks of the region creating new realms. However, holding on to these gains so far from their homelands was a huge challenge for the crusaders, most of whom were used to seasonal periods of warfare, between which they returned to run their estates. In effect, the Knights Templar offered themselves as a permanent private army to the rulers of outremer and their proposition was irresistible.

To make such a commitment required an ethos where duty came before personal interest. In the medieval context, that could only entail being bound to a sacred cause. It meant creating a new kind of soldier who was more than a brute swinging a sword or an axe, but part of a united corps imbued with one aim: to serve God and the church. How Hugh de Payens and his band of knights arrived at this conclusion is lost in the mists of time. Some have argued that they were influenced by the Peace of God movement in the eleventh century when the church sought to use its power to combat generalised violence between warlords across Europe. Another influence might have been the long-established military interpretation of the term 'jihad' among Muslim warriors compelling them to take up the sword against the infidels. The Templars were therefore the Christian expression of this Islamic model.

Whatever inspired them, this group of knights created a new military order that combined the role of knight with that of a church canon. That meant conducting drills and training for battlefield conditions while also observing the monastic routine of prayers at intervals from dawn to dusk. And like monks, these knights would observe the vows of poverty, chastity, and obedience. Not for them the carousing, hawking, hunting, gambling, and womanising much beloved of secular knights. This was a tremendous personal sacrifice of pleasure and leisure for these individuals, but they clearly believed that theirs was a higher calling that would clear the path to eternal glory.

The chroniclers agree that their primary aim was to protect pilgrims journeying to Jerusalem from the depredations of robbers and brigands. It was unacceptable that the roads to the holiest city of Christendom were littered with the bleached bones and emptied purses of the faithful. It's usually assumed that these were a mix of opportunistic robbery and murder combined with a violent political statement against the occupying crusaders.[1] However, it's worth noting that Muslim pilgrims journeying to Mecca also faced the risk of being fleeced and killed in similar attacks conducted well within the Fatimid caliphate.[2] Banditry, then, was a Frankish and a Saracen problem.

For the rulers of outremer, there was the additional dimension of being an alien occupying force tackling an enemy within that was constantly trying to loosen their grip, through a relentless campaign of violence that we would call terrorism or guerrilla warfare today. This enemy was referred to variously as 'Turcomans', 'Saracens', and 'Bedouins'. Disaffected people that may have included Muslims, Jews, and Christians as well as a mixed ethnic profile of Arabs and those of Turkic origin. They are usually characterised as nomadic but might have adopted this lifestyle relatively recently because of constant warfare in the region or factors relating to climate change that made a peaceful, pastoral existence no longer tenable.[3]

Whoever these brigands were, they were not only terrorising the countryside but also extending their campaign of murder, kidnapping, and robbery into Frankish-controlled cities. And the authorities felt powerless to contain the problem. The chronicler William of Tyre (c.1130–1186) summed up the paranoia that was gripping Frankish populations. Christians, he wrote, could not pass from one place to another within the Kingdom of Jerusalem without risk to their lives. The crusader kingdoms were 'inhabited by infidel Saracens, who were most cruel enemies of our people'.[4] They were a 'pest' and any Christians who had come to live in outremer and imagined they were safe behind their front door were deluded:

> 'Nor was it on the highways alone that danger was feared. Even within the city walls, in the very houses, there was scarcely a place where one could rest in security. For the inhabitants were few and scattered, and the ruinous state of the walls left every place exposed to the enemy. Thieves made stealthy inroads by night. They broke into the deserted cities, whose few inhabitants were scattered apart, and overpowered many in their own houses.'[5]

The Knights Templar, then, were not just about providing an armed escort for pilgrims visiting the Holy Land they were in the business of internal security. In this regard, they had to go above and beyond the secular knights, being committed ideologically to the crusades and present full-time. They positioned themselves as an elite force with a permanent presence in outremer. While others serving in the Holy Land felt obliged to return home, to defend their estates from predators or other considerations, the Templars were in place all year round. Maintaining order, engaging the enemy, and providing protection to outremer's Frankish rulers.

The main threat was not just from Fatimid and Seljuk caliphs, and their military forces, but men and women of violence who to modern eyes might be characterised as petty criminals, terrorists, or freedom fighters according to your point of view. These nomadic thieves and murderers took advantage of the absence of any form of state authority in large swathes of the region. They acted with seeming impunity, striking at their targets then either retreating into the mountains or escaping across what passed for a frontier between the Christian and Muslim kingdoms.

This threat was to be tackled by the Knights Templar over the next 200 years with the construction of a string of impressive fortresses from which knights could ride out to enforce the law at the tip of a sword. But it was a constant battle of cat-and-mouse, as the bandits conducted a raid then melted into the ether.

If we take the account of chroniclers like William of Tyre at face value, then the soon-to-be Templar knights began talking about their new idea to King Baldwin II of Jerusalem and the Latin patriarch, Warmund of Picquigny (c.1060s-1128) in 1118 or 1119. The Latin patriarchate had been established after the conquest of Jerusalem in 1099, and set about enforcing the primacy of Roman Catholicism, to the fury of Greek and Syriac Christians. But there was little sympathy among the crusaders for those strange variants of Christianity long suppressed and forgotten in the west that still thrived in the east. Warmund was no mild-mannered cleric. He led crusader armies besieging Tyre in 1124 and Belhacem in 1128. So, both Baldwin and Warmund were military men, open to what the knights had to propose.

There is no reliable fly-on-the-wall account of what was said in these talks. The gist is that the nine knights undertook to live as a religious community, rather like the Augustinians. They committed to a semi-monastic life, renouncing all private wealth, and embracing the vows of chastity and obedience. This did not mean retreating behind the walls of a monastery. Far from it. While they would live together, as monks do, they would very much operate in the outside world, combining the role of knight and holy person. Crucially, they undertook to protect the roads leading into Jerusalem.

What they lacked was a base of operations. Where were these knights, pledging to live as a semi-monastic community, going to be? Baldwin offered them space in the south wing of the royal palace, in what had been (and is today) the Al-Aqsa Mosque. After the crusader takeover of Jerusalem in 1099, this building was renamed the Temple of Solomon in the firm belief, among the crusaders, that it was the site of the original Jewish temple, built by King Solomon, that once housed the Ark of the Covenant – a sacred vessel containing the Ten Commandments. The Ark had gone missing during the Babylonian destruction of Jerusalem in 587 BCE and was never seen again.

Their headquarters gave rise to the order's name: The Poor Fellow-Soldiers of Christ and of the Temple of Solomon, shortened to the Knights Templar, or just Templars. The decision to be based on the Temple Mount has generated a slew of conspiracy theories centred on the idea that the knights had an ulterior motive. Primarily the notion that while outwardly proclaiming their mission as the protection of pilgrims, they were busy tunnelling under the Temple of Solomon in search of sacred treasures including the Ark of the Covenant, Holy Grail, and even the head of John the Baptist.

This is not entirely far-fetched. Many Christians down the centuries had come to Jerusalem seeking physical items mentioned in the Bible. The mother of the first Christian Roman emperor Constantine, Helena, visited the Holy Land for two years on pilgrimage in 326 CE. In an impressive haul of relics on just one trip, she managed to retrieve the True Cross upon which Jesus was crucified; the wooden panel affixed to it with the mocking words 'Jesus the Nazarene, King of the Jews'; nails used in the crucifixion; the stairs Jesus ascended at the Palace of Pontius Pilate; and the holy crib including some of the original hay. These items can still be viewed in Rome today.[6]

When the crusaders were struggling to hold on to Antioch in June 1098, a rather scruffy Provençal peasant named Peter Bartholomew claimed Saint Andrew had appeared to him in a dream and told him where to find the Holy Lance that had pierced the side of Christ. It was under the cathedral of Saint Peter where, a little later, Peter dived into a hole and found a rusty old spear tip. However, many remained sceptical, believing he had planted the object in the ground. On Good Friday in April 1099, an exasperated Peter agreed to undergo an ordeal by fire carrying the Holy Lance through a narrow gap with massive piles of blazing wood on either side. He suffered horrific burns, dying shortly afterwards. But the lance made its way to Constantinople and then Rome where it was venerated.[7]

So, the idea of the Templars going on their own relic hunt is within the bounds of possibility. Especially as the Temple Mount is honeycombed with tunnels, cisterns, and chambers. An underground vault believed to have been the stables of King Solomon was used by the Templars for their horses. But did they lay down their swords for picks and shovels while they were below ground? If so, this would have been viewed as an act of sacrilege by Jews, Muslims, and many Christians.

Tunnelling underneath the Temple Mount has remained contentious from the Middle Ages to the present day. Nineteenth-century excavations by British explorers led to a bitter clash with the Ottoman authorities.[8] In recent decades, attempts by Israeli archaeologists to explore these underground spaces have led to fights inside the tunnels with Palestinians who view it as the desecration of a holy place.[9] However, if the Templars had been digging, they would have faced no effective opposition.

Adjacent to the Temple of Solomon was the Dome of the Rock, the seventh-century octagonal structure with its distinctive golden dome built under the Umayyad caliphate – one of the oldest surviving Muslim buildings in the world. Believed to be the place where God began the act of creation; brought Adam into existence; ordered Abraham to sacrifice his son; and to Muslims, it is from where the Prophet Muhammad embarked on a spectacular journey upon a winged horse meeting Musa (Moses), Ibrahim (Abraham), and conversing with God.[10] It had been renamed the Temple of the Lord (Templum Domini) by the crusaders and was occupied by Augustinian canons, who converted this Muslim place of worship into a church, replacing the crescent on its dome with a cross.

The Augustinians gave the Templars permission to use a square near the palace for military drills. In addition, Baldwin and Warmund – as well as other church and secular leaders – lent or donated gifts to the knights to pay for food and clothing. In the first decade of their existence, the Templars wore secular clothing, not the white mantle with a red cross that we associate with them. If we are to believe the chronicler William of Tyre, who was very suspicious of the Templars, the order seems to have been stagnant in its first phase of existence. After nine years, he claimed, there were still only nine knights. But that was all about to change.

Who were these nine knights bent on creating a new kind of knightly order? The two knights initially petitioning the King of Jerusalem and the Latin patriarch were Hugh de Payens and Godfrey de Saint-Omer. De Payens is an enigmatic figure about whom our knowledge is patchy. He became the first grand master of the Knights Templar and undoubtedly played a critical role in getting the order recognised and funded.

Hugh was the vassal of another Hugh, the count of Champagne (c.1074-c.1125). To be a vassal in the medieval system of feudalism meant that De Payens enjoyed the protection of the count in return for pledging homage and fealty. Count Hugh went on crusade twice in the years 1104 to 1107 and again in 1114 to 1116. De Payens, as his vassal back in France, joined his liege lord but seems to have remained in Jerusalem when the count returned home. Though in 1125, when the Templars were well established, the count came back to outremer and resolved to stay, never to see his homeland again. At this point, close to death, he became a Templar himself.

The County of Champagne was a French principality to the east of Paris renowned for its agricultural and trading prosperity in the Middle Ages. The city of Troyes played host to two fairs each year, the summer 'hot fair' of Saint Jean and the winter 'cold fair' of Saint-Remy, where traders, hawkers, and buyers swarmed to do business. The term 'troy ounce' originates from these markets as a measurement of weight. But what is noteworthy, with regard to the mindset of those future Templars who grew up in this region, was that the Troyes fairs were known throughout both the Christian and Muslim worlds.

During these commercial gatherings, the young De Payens would have witnessed the intermingling of thousands of people from Venice, Cologne, Bruges, Paris, and much further afield. Silks, spices, and perfumes arrived after a long journey from the east. Wool and linen were transported from Flanders and England. So lucrative were the fairs that the counts of Champagne went to great lengths to protect traders as they came and went, also ensuring that Jewish merchants were not subject to abuse or violence. One must wonder whether the Templar mission of policing roads (and protecting Jews, as the Templars did) originated in the running of the Troyes fairs.

The fairs involved not just an interchange of goods, but an interchange of ideas. Trade routes were transmission belts for dangerous religious heresies as well new forms of architecture, fashion, and ways of doing business. At Troyes, merchants experimented with state-of-the-art bookkeeping and new concepts of transferring money. The Knights Templar are often credited with inventing the idea of the cheque. They held money for wealthy people travelling on crusade who could then withdraw amounts at any Templar commandery like a twentieth-century bank branch. This idea may have come from the Troyes fairs, and it may even be conceivable that the alleged exposure of the Templars to heretical ideas could have started at those great commercial gatherings.

On Christmas Day in 1119, the nine knights of the new order took their vows before the Latin patriarch at the Holy Sepulchre. Official recognition for the Templars and their mission came at the Council of Nablus about three weeks later, on 16 January 1120. This meeting convened the secular and spiritual rulers of outremer and was intended to draw up a more robust legal system for the crusader-controlled territories.[11] It also agonised over the growing sinfulness of crusader-held Jerusalem.

Church leaders at the council upbraided the secular representatives, claiming that various woes that had befallen the city were entirely due to wicked behaviour. How else to explain plagues of locusts and mice that had afflicted Jerusalem? There was also considerable concern expressed about adultery and same-sex relations among the Franks. Those accused of the former sin were to be subjected to the ordeal of hot iron – carrying a heated piece of metal to prove their innocence. While those engaging in homosexual relations were to be burned at the stake.[12]

This concern about homosexuality may have been based on the belief that Baldwin I had engaged in same-sex relations. Modern historians and experts on the crusades are very open to the idea. Jay Rubenstein suggests Baldwin 'lived in a chainmail closet' while veteran Templar experts Malcolm Barber and

Christopher Tyerman have also pondered whether Baldwin could have been homosexual.[13] At the time, William of Tyre intimated as much, though of course the terminology and awareness of matters relating to sexuality were very different in the twelfth century. The church's attitude to homosexuality would become more hostile in the next two centuries and the Templars themselves would be subject to lurid allegations of inappropriate kissing at their initiation rites.

There was clear friction between church and state at Nablus. In what was essentially a frontier society, the church believed that ungodly conduct could bring the wrath of the Almighty down on the crusades. With that in mind, Baldwin II was asked to hurry up and pay the church tithes due on his estates in outremer. Incredibly the monarch apologised, and the patriarch absolved him of his sin. This kind of drama between spiritual and secular, where the church made a public display of its power over earthly rulers, was part of the new movement directed from Rome to make kings everywhere bend the knee to bishops. Then the council was asked to recognise this new religious band of knights, answerable only to the pope. Overwhelmingly, the council gave the Templars its blessing.

The first few years of the Templars are a bit of a blank. Though there are indications that they proved themselves a cut above other knights and of considerable use to King Baldwin. In 1127, the king was involved in a flurry of diplomatic activity with the west. More crusaders were needed to mount a daring assault on Damascus, and there was the question of the succession in his kingdom. Baldwin wanted to get his eldest daughter Melisende (1105–1161) married to Fulk V, count of Anjou (c.1089–1143), who would then inherit the Kingdom of Jerusalem on Baldwin's death. Among those sent back to Europe to achieve these aims was Hugh de Payens, the first Templar grand master.

Hugh already knew Fulk as this French noble had been on crusade in 1120 and according to the English monastic chronicler Orderic Vitalis (1075-c.1142) became attached to the newly established Templar order. Fulk left behind a hundred knights to help defend Jerusalem and after returning in 1121, started to subsidise the Templars. So, he was an early enthusiast for this small band of holy warriors, which would stand them in good stead when he not only married Melisende but also became King of Jerusalem in 1131.

De Payens spent about two years touring western Europe to not only drum up support for the crusades but also to explain and promote the Knights Templar. At the same time, he was fundraising – encouraging nobles to gift land and other resources to the knights. Hugh must have realised that the order needed to move on from a hand-to-mouth existence and build a network of wealth-generating nodes in the west that could channel much needed resources eastwards to his knights in the Holy Land.

Fortunately for him, Christian kings and nobles across Europe had caught Templar fever. On arriving in France in the autumn of 1127, Hugh was showered with grants of land, silver, horses, and armour. A few months later, he was in England where King Henry I lavished the Templar master with further donations of gold and silver. While in London, Hugh established what would become in effect the Templar headquarters in England at a location now occupied by a nondescript office block.

He then journeyed on to Scotland. There he met King David I, who had spent his formative years growing up in Normandy as well as at the Anglo-Norman court of England's King Henry I. Consequently, he was imbued with Norman values, which influenced his policies after inheriting the Scottish throne. That included installing French and Flemish nobles as landlords in southern Scotland and adhering to Rome's Gregorian reforms, where the state would show deference and respect to the church. He also encouraged the foundation of new monasteries encouraging both intellectual life and economic activity.[14]

Far from being at the remotest fringe of Europe, David's court was plugged into a Norman network stretching from England down through Normandy and on to southern Italy. When De Payens showed up to sell his new order of monastic knights, David was very receptive. This fitted in well with his expansion of monastic centres across his realm. The king had no difficulty with a Frenchman setting up a religious community in Scotland as he had already invited monks from Tiron, near Chartres in France, to set up a monastery at Selkirk in 1113. So, Hugh was given the green light to establish a Templar headquarters at Balantrodoch, by the river Esk in Midlothian.

Decades later, the order would build a preceptory, or commandery, as their estates came to be known, at Maryculter in Aberdeenshire. This being Scotland, it became the subject of a Templar ghost story. A knight, Godfrey Wedderburn, was badly wounded in battle in the Holy Land but nursed back to health by a Saracen woman, a Muslim, who was then rejected by her own people for helping a Templar. Grateful, the knight returned to his assigned preceptory at Maryculter with his female Saracen companion. His attempts to explain to the local Templar master that their relationship was purely platonic fell on deaf ears. Remember that all Templars, like monks, had to take a vow of chastity.

Dejected, Godfrey just happened to run into Jesus Christ who miraculously appeared before him. The son of God shone his love on the disgruntled knight and assured him all would be well. The Templar master begged to differ. He doubted the encounter with Christ and was not about to let a Saracen woman live at the preceptory. Now driven to an uncontrollable rage, Godfrey struck the master and for that sinful assault was sentenced to die by his own hand. As he plunged the dagger into his own heart, the unnamed Saracen woman took a ring off Godfrey's finger and forced it onto the master's hand. In a flash of light and a blue bolt of fire, the master disappeared into the earth. To this day, on the anniversary of this event, a deep depression in the ground at Maryculter, known as the Thunder Hole, glows eerily and Godfrey with his Saracen lady friend are seen walking together.[15]

While in Scotland, De Payens met a family that plays a minor role in the mainstream history of the Knights Templar but a significant part in various fringe and esoteric theories about what happened to the Templars after they were crushed from the year 1307. Including the notion that this Norman-Viking line of nobles helped the knights escape from persecution in Europe following ancient Viking routes to reach the New World. The family in question were the St Clair, also spelt Saint Clair and Sinclair, who were the barons of Rosslyn (or Roslin), building the chapel there made famous by the author Dan Brown in his novel *The Da Vinci Code*.[16] The myths and legends surrounding their association with the Templars will be examined.

Hugh's mission to Europe culminated in diplomatic efforts to get the papacy to back the Templars. Success came with the convening of the Council of Troyes under the auspices of Theobald II (1090–1152), who had succeeded Hugh as count of Champagne after the death of his father in 1125. His mother, Adela of Normandy (c.1067–1137), was the daughter of William the Conqueror and his brother Stephen would become king of England between 1135 and 1154. All around the Templars was an interconnected Norman and French aristocracy who stepped forward as their secular champions.

Pope Honorius II (1060–1130) was represented by his legate, Matthew of Albano. This pope, like his predecessor Urban, was still very much in the business of extending papal power in medieval society. Even if that meant clipping the wings of the long-established, wealthy, and overpowerful Benedictine order of monks. Honorius favoured new monastic orders like the Cistercians who displayed a refreshing obedience as well as a healthy contempt for the ornamentation and easy living that had become the hallmark of the Benedictines.

The Knights Templar developed a close relationship with the Cistercians through that order's leading voice, Bernard of Clairvaux, who happened to be the nephew of one of the Templar founding knights, André de Montbard. This would prove to be a very fortuitous connection. In effect, the Templars evolved to become the military wing of the relatively new Cistercian order. Both organisations working in synch, for example in Portugal where Cistercian houses popped up behind Templar battle lines as the Muslim enemy was pushed back.

What happened at Troyes was incredibly important for Hugh de Payens and his Templar knights. It conferred legitimacy, triggering an avalanche of recruits and donations. Judging by how the Knights Templar grew as an organisation after Troyes, it clearly bolstered their confidence enormously. All they lacked was a recognisable image. So, the question of what we would now call branding was addressed. The knights were given permission to wear a white mantle signifying purity. The distinctive red cross would be added later. Their logo in modern parlance.

The council also agreed the first 'primitive' rule of the Templars adapted from existing monastic rule books. It was uncompromising in its severity. This was the mission statement, and it transformed the Templars from a group of secular knights who were especially pious to an officially sanctioned holy order within the Roman Catholic church. The rule began with an appeal to secular knights who fought for 'humans only, and in which Christ was not the cause', to 'associate yourself in perpetuity with the Order of those whom God has chosen from the mass of perdition and has assembled for the defence of the Holy Church'.[17] Then it got down to detailing a spartan life for these knights.

Every aspect of their daily routine was covered. The saying of prayers during the day; the reading of scripture at meals; the amount of meat and vegetables that could be eaten and on what days. Hair should be cut short, and heads tonsured like monks. Pointed shoes and laces were a Saracen affectation and to be banned. Bridles, breastplates, stirrups, and spurs were to be devoid of gold and silver and if a donated item had such decoration, it should be painted over. As for trunks and bags, there must be no lockable clasps as the master might want to look inside and inspect a knight's belongings for anything forbidden.

The Templars were to have no private life. Going for a random walk was out of the question, and letters home to parents could only be sent with the master's permission, who could insist on the contents being read out loud in his presence. Behaviour was to be strictly regulated. Knights were not allowed to gossip or even 'boast' about their own faults to effect humility. Provoking a fellow Templar to anger was also a punishable offence. Consorting with women was prohibited even down to exchanging a kiss of friendship with a sister or aunt.

Punishments ranged from the sort of thing one might have experienced in a nineteenth-century English boarding school, such as being flogged or denied privileges, to being expelled from the order. Expulsion might be occasioned by the discovery that a knight was married; had undisclosed debts; or had not admitted to some or other disease. But punishment could be even more extreme. The former commander of Ireland, Walter le Bachelor, was brought to the

London Temple in 1301 and accused of financial malpractice. Found guilty, he was then locked in a penitential cell and starved to death.[18]

By any measure, Hugh de Payens' mission to Europe was a resounding success. The Knights Templar now enjoyed the papal stamp of approval and a rule book. King Baldwin's daughter, Melisende, married Fulk V, count of Anjou, in Jerusalem on 2 June 1129, thereby ensuring the kingdom's succession. While the *Anglo-Saxon Chronicle* reported that Hugh had taken with him more crusading recruits to Jerusalem than had swarmed there in the First Crusade. But they were in for an ugly shock. Or as one twentieth-century Templar historian put it, a baptism of blood.[19]

Hugh arrived back with many Europeans eager to cut their teeth in battle and become fully fledged crusaders. They were not all bound for the ranks of the Knights Templar. Most would fight as ordinary grunts. But their first taste of action, for many, would be their last. The crusaders were about to make a grave miscalculation that would alter the character of the crusades in outremer by degrees from offensive to defensive. The first in a series of setbacks that would end the initial surge of optimism and bravado that had seen the Franks carve four kingdoms out of the Muslim-controlled Levant.

Baldwin and Hugh de Payens began the Damascus campaign of 1129 in high spirits. Baldwin had a son-in-law and future heir, Fulk of Anjou. Hugh had papal recognition for his order and the money was flowing into Templar coffers. The king had long decided that taking the city of Damascus would strengthen the Frankish hold on outremer and had already launched raids into Damascene territory in 1125 and 1126. For the next two years he did nothing – most likely building up his forces. By late 1129, he felt ready to act. And there was a bonus reason to attack in that Damascus had sunk into murderous political turmoil.

The city had been overrun by a death cult known to history as the Assassins. These mysterious, dagger-wielding figures operated in the shadows directed by a supreme leader dubbed, in Frankish accounts, the Old Man of the Mountain (Shaykh al-Jabal). The roots of the Assassins dated back to the very dawn of Islam. The religion founded by the Prophet Muhammad that had expanded rapidly across the Middle East and north Africa in the seventh and eighth centuries. When the prophet died, the question arose: who should succeed him? The best-qualified person to lead the growing caliphate or somebody who stood in the bloodline of the prophet.

This created a division within Islam between the majority Sunnis and the minority Shi'as that continues to the present. The name of the latter derives from the Arabic: partisans of Ali. This refers to Ali ibn Abi Talib ibn Abd al-Muttalib (c.600–661), who was the fourth and last caliph of the Rashidun caliphate – the first Islamic dynasty after the death of the Prophet Muhammad. His credentials to be caliph were impressive. His father was the custodian of the Ka'aba in Mecca and an uncle of Muhammad. Ali had been a faithful servant of the prophet in his lifetime, helping him during his flight from Mecca to Medina and then fighting to regain control of Mecca.

But his reign as the fourth caliph was cut short when he was murdered with a poisoned sword while at prayer in 661 CE. This led to a succession dispute that Ali's followers lost, leading to the foundation of the Umayyad caliphate. Those loyal to Ali never accepted this outcome, becoming the Shi'a sect within Islam, making up about 15% of all Muslims today and concentrated in modern Iran and Iraq. In 1129, they ran the Fatimid empire in Egypt (even though that country's Muslim population was majority Sunni) while the Sunni-adhering Seljuk-dominated caliphate paid nominal homage to the caliph in Baghdad (which today is in Iraq where most Muslims are Shi'a).

Within the Shi'as, there were further divisions. The Fatimids belonged to the Isma'ili branch with an empire stretching from Morocco to Jerusalem including the holy sites of Mecca and Medina. Within the Isma'ilis was yet another sub-group, the Naziris. It was from among these Shi'as that the Assassins would emerge. The Naziris tended towards a mystical view that Islam's holy book, the Qur'an, had both a surface meaning and a secret, coded meaning. Those who espoused this were referred to as Batiniyya and their activists were referred to as the 'dai'. One of these mystics, Hasan i-Sabbah (1050–1124), founded the Assassins. A shadowy group that would terrify the medieval Levant. In 1090, he and his band of devotees captured Alamut castle in Iran, which sat atop a mountain, making it their base of operations.[20]

It was also a training camp for his Fedai, or fanatical followers. They were, in effect, a terrorist organisation bent on using murder as a political weapon.[21] According to the Venetian explorer Marco Polo (1254–1324), when recruits were deemed good enough to be sent on a mission, they were given a sleeping potion. When they woke up, they found themselves in a paradisical garden surrounded by beautiful women. The young men were then sent back to sleep again only to wake up in front of the Old Man of the Mountain. He then explained that the pleasures they had seen would be experienced after their death and the only route there was glorious martyrdom.

The hold that the Old Man had over these impressionable minds was such that it was said he could command them to leap from a great height to certain death and they would do his bidding. Even allowing for some exaggeration by Marco Polo, we know that these adepts were dispatched across the Middle East to assassinate both Muslim and Christian leaders who had been designated as enemies of the Assassins. Initially, it was the Seljuks who experienced these medieval terrorist outrages, but the crusader kingdoms would encounter their daggers soon enough. And they would cross swords with the Knights Templar in the years ahead.

So powerful did the Assassins become that they were able to take control of entire towns or even cities. By 1128, they were running Damascus. The Seljuk emir, Zahir al-Din Tughtegin, was dying while his vizier (prime minister), Abu Ali Tahir ibn Sa'd al-Mazdaghani, was a puppet of the Assassins and secretly negotiating with Baldwin to hand over Damascus in exchange for crusader-controlled Tyre, to where the Assassins and their pet vizier could then relocate.[22] As far as Al-Mazdaghani and most of the city's population was concerned, they would soon be living under the Franks whose military superiority was beyond question. Baldwin and Hugh de Payens held the same view, and the Knights Templar were relishing the prospect of a great victory. When the emir died, the crusaders and Templars swung into action.

But so did factions within the emir's court in Damascus eager to save the city from Baldwin. A plot was hatched to remove the treacherous vizier and wipe out the Assassins. An Arab chronicler based in the city, Ibn al-Qalanisi (c.1071–1160), detailed the bloody events that ensued. On 4 September 1129, the vizier held court with political and military leaders at the Rose Pavilion in the citadel. The affairs of state were duly gone through but as the vizier rose to leave, he was struck over the head several times and then decapitated. Both head and body were dragged to the 'ashheap' at the Iron Gate and burned.

A population sickened by the overbearing Assassin presence in their midst rose up and gave the homicidal zealots a taste of their own medicine. Using swords and 'poniards' (daggers), they slew the cult members wherever they could find them and chucked their corpses onto dung heaps like abandoned carrion. By the next morning, not one Assassin was left 'and the dogs were yelping and quarrelling over their limbs and corpses'.[23] Those identified as Assassin leaders suffered the agonising indignity of being crucified, nailed to the battlements of Damascus.

One can hardly imagine the glee that Baldwin and Hugh must have experienced on getting intelligence reports about what was happening inside the city. More good news came when the Assassin governor of the city of Banyas reacted to the massacre of his comrades in Damascus by handing over Banyas to Baldwin without a fight. All of this looked like a sign from God that the crusaders and Templars were favoured by the Almighty. The king and Templar master duly led their army towards certain victory at Damascus. A mix of the new European recruits and levies from across outremer.

They stopped a few miles short confronted by the forces of the new emir, Taj al-Muluk Buri (died 1132). He had fought Baldwin twice before, the second time with his father at the Battle of Marj al-Saffar in 1126. That had been an earlier crusader attempt to take Damascus that was only just foiled. This time though, the balance of probability was in favour of Baldwin. Fulk had arrived by sea with soldiers determined to fight for the cross of Jesus. Hugh de Payens was present with his white mantled knights and all those recruits from the west. What could possibly go wrong?

How the crusaders and Templars turned almost certain victory into defeat was detailed by Al-Qalinisi within the city and years later, on the Frankish side, by William of Tyre. A degree of laxity had descended on the secular knights, emboldened by the intelligence being gathered about the situation within Damascus. Everybody was resigned to a period of siege, but the result was assumed to be a foregone conclusion. However, the Franks let down their guard fatally.

At a place called the Wooden Bridge, Baldwin and Hugh surveyed an enemy force made up of Arab fighters from local tribes and what the chronicles refer to as Turcomen or Turkmens. These were warriors of the same ethnic origin as the Seljuks, originating among the Oghuz Turks of central Asia. Al-Qalinisi describes how they broke up into squadrons surrounding the Franks on all sides in the hope that Baldwin would launch a frontal assault and then be encircled. But frustratingly, Baldwin struck camp and remained in position for several days. Unnerved, Buri sent out scouts to find out what the crusaders were doing and discovered that they had sent out cavalry and infantry to the Hawran region, west of the Golan Heights, to collect provisions for a long siege. Baldwin had resolved not to move an inch until they returned.

In charge of the detachment sent to Hawran was William of Burres. He had led the diplomatic mission, alongside Hugh de Payens, that had negotiated the marriage between Fulk V of Anjou and Melisende. So, he was a trusted pair of hands. Buri calculated that as William's foraging party returned, it would pass through the town of Buraq. What the ruler of Damascus needed was to inflict a decisive blow that would demoralise the invaders. He gambled on wiping out the returning Franks and denying Baldwin his much-needed provisions. To ensure success, Buri sent out an 'overwhelming force', temporarily depleting his ranks.

They found William and his soldiers, as well as several Templars, entirely off their guard. Before the Franks could mount their horses, arrows rained down and very soon the ground was littered with crusader corpses. Frantically, William got his troops into battle ranks and formed a solid phalanx. But this was a temporary respite. The relentless blows of swords and thrusts of lances and showers of arrows, described gleefully by Al-Qalinisi, took their grisly toll. At some point, William fled the scene leaving the others to their fate.

Buri's victorious Arabs and Turcomen headed back for Damascus with seized horses, mules, weapons, and prisoners. It was decided that at dawn the next day, Baldwin's camp would be taken. As the sun rose, a body of cavalry stormed out of the city and made for the crusaders. They could see a multitude of fires and smoke rising so assumed the camp was its usual hive of activity. But on arriving, Buri's men discovered a ghost town. Receiving the terrible news from Buraq, Baldwin had ordered the burning of their baggage and weapons as there were no mules to transport them back to Jerusalem. His army, dejected, had then begun the march home.

This was not an auspicious start for the newly recognised Knights Templar. The *Anglo-Saxon Chronicle* sneered at Hugh de Payens with a waspish aside about him leading his newly found recruits on a fool's errand. What role they played in William's foraging party is uncertain, but it would be fair to assume that they were central to the desperate phalanx formation that attempted to fight back. How many Templars were killed that day is a mystery. But for a brief while, their light dimmed.

The Templars revolutionised the accepted social order by their mere existence. In the Middle Ages, a distinction was made between three types of people with very defined roles: 'oratores' who pray; 'bellatores' who make war; and 'laboratores' who work. The English abbot Aelfric of Eynsham (c.955–c.1010) explained this social division:

> *'Laboratores are those that labour for our sustenance. Oratores are those who intercede for us with God. Bellatores are those who protect our towns and defend our soil against the invading army.'*[24]

He presented the three social orders as entirely dependent on each other. 'The three groups, which co-exist, cannot bear to be separated; the services rendered by one are a precondition for the labours of the two others.' The serfs toiled to create the wealth of a kingdom while monks prayed to ensure God's favour and the nobility defended everybody from external attack. This was a comforting argument from a monastic perspective, justifying the existence of monks who enjoyed a relatively cosy existence in their abbeys compared to a serf in the fields, who even Aelfric referred to as a 'luckless breed', providing food for everybody else. But just in case the serfs should ever get it into their heads that monks were surplus to requirements, Aelfric insisted they were an essential building block of society.

The Templars, however, subverted this model by being both monastic and warlike: oratore and bellatore. And they were not alone. Other military orders would pop up in the twelfth century combining the roles of oratore and bellatore.

The Knights Hospitaller, for example, developed into a rival order to the Templars during the crusades and arguably became their nemesis at the very end, when the Templars were crushed. As Templar assets were seized after 1307, they were divided up among secular nobles and the Hospitallers. The origin of the Hospitallers predated the Templars by fifty years or more. They traced their beginnings to around 1070 when a group of Italian merchants from the Duchy of Amalfi obtained permission from the Fatimid caliph to set up a hospital for sick pilgrims near the Holy Sepulchre at a site dedicated to Saint John the Baptist.[25]

Obviously at this point, under the watchful eye of successive Fatimid and Seljuk rulers, they were not an armed body bent on the destruction of Muslim kingdoms. Instead, the Hospitallers set up a loose network of hospices serving all faiths, admitting both men and women, and overseen by the Benedictine monks from St. Mary of the Latins. They were barely recognisable as a distinct order as they ran their community-based health centres. But all that changed in the year 1099.

After the crusader conquest of the city, the Hospitallers evolved from peaceable medics to sword-wielding knights fully absorbing the call to religious war expounded by Pope Urban at Clermont. They were given operational independence from the Benedictines and by 1113 received Rome's recognition in Pope Paschal II's papal bull, *Pie Postulatio Voluntatis* (The Most Pious Request). Under their grand master Raymond du Puy (1083–1160), they shadowed the development of the Templars, taking up arms after 1118, adopting a similar organisational structure, a rule book, and a distinctive uniform for the battlefield. Their logo was an Amalfi cross, eight-point star on a black mantle as opposed to the pure white of the Templars.

Like the Templars, the Hospitallers went on a recruitment and fundraising drive around Europe but had difficulty firing up the imagination of their target audiences. So, they embroidered their origin story, claiming that the order dated back to the biblical period. John the Baptist's parents had been involved with their work, tending the sick, and Jesus Christ had once paid them a visit performing some miracles on the patients. The first Christian martyr, Saint Stephen, who was stoned to death in the temple of Jerusalem, had in fact been a grand master of the Hospitallers. And for good measure, the Virgin Mary stayed at one of their hospitals for three years before being bodily assumed into heaven.[26]

Another military order also began its existence looking after the sick before reinventing themselves as a military machine: the Order of Saint Lazarus. Outside the city walls of Jerusalem was a forlorn building, the Domus Leprosorum, tending to those stricken by what was then an incurable disease: leprosy. Transmitted through droplets from the nose and mouth, sufferers could be physically disfigured and were forced to wear bells or clappers to announce their presence. Leper Masses were held in villages and towns where a leper would be declared an outcast and dead to the rest of the community. While most people lived in dread fear of those afflicted, some sought to alleviate their suffering.

Two years after recognising the Hospitallers, Pope Paschal II gave his blessing to the Order of Saint Lazarus, which lived by the Rule of Saint Augustine. The crusades had proven to be a super-spreader for leprosy and this order was dedicated to the care of those who society so tragically rejected. However, like the Hospitallers, they too expanded their activities from leper outreach to fighting in battles. It's believed that all members of the order involved in the disastrous Battle of La Forbie in 1244 were killed but nevertheless, they went on to have a presence at the final siege of Acre in 1291 – easily identifiable by their green cross on a white mantle.[27]

The crusades in the Iberian Peninsula gave rise to the military orders of Santiago, Calatrava, Alcántara, and Montesa. Just as the Templars protected pilgrims on the routes in Jerusalem, the Order of Santiago guarded those on the long trek to Santiago de Compostela. This was believed to be the burial place of Saint James, one of the twelve apostles. In various accounts, he either preached the gospel in the Roman province of Hispania and died there or he was martyred in the Holy Land and his body brought to far-off Santiago for burial. In the mid-ninth century CE, at the height of Muslim power in what is now Spain and Portugal, the apostle appeared in the sky to the Christian king Ramiro I before the Battle of Clavijo. Despite the Order of Santiago being heavily outnumbered, the Muslims from the south were routed.

Few modern historians think this battle happened – certainly not in the way described – but it was a legend that inspired Spanish and Portuguese crusaders to take on the caliphate, which ruled over half the Iberian Peninsula. It does seem incongruous today to imagine that an apostle of Jesus ended up buried in north-eastern Spain. But his cult was hugely popular with depictions of Saint James trampling a Moor (the Arab and Berber Muslim rulers of southern Spain) underfoot. He is still referred to as Santiago Matamoros: Saint James the Moor-Slayer.

Possibly one of the tensest cinematic portrayals of a medieval order of warrior monks in action is the 1938 Soviet movie *Alexander Nevsky*, directed and written by Sergei Eisenstein. It depicts the invasion of the Russian medieval state of Novgorod by the Teutonic Knights. The movie title refers to the protagonist, a prince who must lead his countrymen in the decisive Battle on the Ice. Nevsky is fighting for Russian orthodox Christianity against the Teutonic Knights, who were champions of Roman Catholicism.

The two sides met in April 1242 in a clash that took place on a treacherous stretch of ice. The Teutonic Knights, properly known as The Order of Brothers of the German House of Saint Mary in Jerusalem, were one of the later orders of monastic-style knights set up around 1190 in Acre. While they began in the Holy Land, their main arena of activity was in the Baltic states where they undertook the forcible conversion of Europe's last pagans. Then they turned on the orthodox Christians of Russia. At the Battle on the Ice, the knights were defeated despite being an awesome sight as they thundered across the frozen water.

Eisenstein's stunning portrayal of the battle was set to a stirring score by the composer Sergei Prokofiev. In 1938, in the real world, the Soviet Union and Nazi Germany were squaring up to each other as the Second World War loomed. Eisenstein wanted Soviet cinemagoers to view the Teutonic Knights as proto-Nazis against the plucky Soviets led by Nevsky, for which read Joseph Stalin. In early scripts, swastikas were even going to feature on the helmets of the Teutonic Knights, and the mitres of their accompanying Catholic bishops. This rather crude propagandistic twist was dropped.

However, what the war by the Teutonic Knights showed was that the crusades were not only directed against Muslims in the Holy Land and the Iberian Peninsula but could also be turned on Christians who refused to recognise the primacy of the pope. Rome had no qualms about extending the crusading mission to those who, while accepting the death and resurrection of Christ, refused to bend the knee to the supreme pontiff. As a case in point, by the time the Teutonic Knights were defeated by Nevsky, the eastern orthodox Christian city of Constantinople, whose emperor had helped to instigate the crusades, lay in ruins. The destruction of the city of cities by fire carried out by crusaders, not Muslims, in 1204 during the fourth crusade.

The origin of the story of the Knights Templar with nine knights banding together to defend pilgrims on the routes into Jerusalem has proven to be unsatisfactory to many who are fascinated by this order of holy warriors. They are convinced that the Templars were called into being by an organisation operating in the shadows. The most popular of these esoteric theories relates to a clandestine body known as the Priory of Sion, popularised in recent decades by two books. One being *The Holy Blood and the Holy Grail*, a lengthy treatise on the Priory of Sion by Michael Baigent (1948–2013), Richard Leigh (1943–2007), and Henry Lincoln (1930–2022).[28] The other is the thriller novel *The Da Vinci Code*, by the author Dan Brown (born 1964).

So, what is the Priory of Sion? The theory runs that the priory was a clandestine brotherhood founded by Godfrey de Bouillon after taking Jerusalem in 1099. It set up the Templars as its military arm. The priory has its own line of grand masters that continued after the destruction of the Templars in 1307 and has included such luminaries as Leonardo da Vinci and Isaac Newton. It still exists today, under the radar. The priory's mission is the bringing back to power of the Merovingian dynasty that ruled the Franks from 457 CE to 751 CE. Only this time, they will be the Christian kings of Europe. Why? Because they are the direct descendants of Jesus and his wife, Mary Magdalene.

Mixed in with this theory is the centrality of the Holy Grail. Only this is no mere cup, plate, or stone, as described in various tales. No, it is the womb of Mary Magdalene and the sacred bloodline, the 'sangreal', that issued from it. The very existence of this bloodline threatens to rock the Roman Catholic church to its very foundations, overturning Rome's definition of Christ and the idea that it possesses the only direct line to God through his vicar on earth, the pope. Therefore, the church has sought to destroy this bloodline and their guardians. Hence the crusade against the heretical Cathars and the brutal crushing of the Knights Templar. Both knew of the bloodline and had to be annihilated.

Why would the Cathars have known about the bloodline? Well, according to this theory, Mary Magdalene married Jesus and after his crucifixion (which may have been faked), she fled to southern France, finding refuge within the Jewish community. The bloodline was preserved and perpetuated, eventually becoming allied to the Merovingian royal dynasty in the fifth century CE. They were overthrown but the secret continued and was guarded by the Cathars – and the Templars.

One obvious problem with this hypothesis is that the Cathars believed in a wholly spiritual Jesus, divorced from the evil material world, whereas this theory promotes a very human Jesus who marries and has children. Where the theory is on stronger ground is the idea that Jesus was elevated by the church from being a human being to a god. This supernatural Jesus then became the Zeus-like figurehead of the new state religion adopted by the Roman emperor Constantine, which bore little resemblance to the real Christ and his apostles.

It's often conjectured that the Knights Templar knew, by virtue of being an offshoot of the priory, or discovered in the Holy Land, the true nature of Jesus and this led to their destruction by the Catholic church.

As with most of the more esoteric Templar theories, there are many layers of complexity with other conspiracies and myths co-opted to support, or spice up, the argument. The authors of The Holy Blood and The Holy Grail and The Da Vinci Code were not the originators of the Priory of Sion story. That honour goes to the French writer and sometime clairvoyant Pierre Plantard (1920–2000). In the 1950s, he claimed to be the current grand master of the priory, producing a list of grand masters that included himself preceded by the artist Jean Cocteau, the composer Claude Debussy, and the author Victor Hugo. But investigations by historians and journalists have found no evidence of the organisation's existence before 1956 – when Plantard declared it to the world.[29] Yet it has become tightly woven into the Templar story.

There are variations on the Priory of Sion origin myth, with one version claiming the secret society that founded the Knights Templar was in fact an entity termed Rex Deus. This consists of a still existing network of families descended from the hereditary high priests of Jerusalem that includes the family of Jesus and many leading figures of the Middle Ages. Fringe historian Tim Wallace-Murphy (1930–2019) wrote prodigiously on the Rex Deus, which he argued was the real guiding hand behind the Templars. How did he discover them? Well, a member contacted him privately and spilled the beans.[30]

Most mainstream medieval historians have no time for theories like the Priory of Sion and Rex Deus, but elements of these theories have become part of the popular perception of the Knights Templar. That these warriors were not all that they seemed, nor were they shut down in the year 1307. They continue in some form with their mission, which may involve the Holy Grail, whether that is the bloodline of Jesus or a holy relic of untold power. They battle unseen forces – a theme that underscores the hugely successful video game and movie franchise Assassin's Creed. Although in that game, the Templars are very much the bad guys, as will be explained. Disentangling the Templars from these esoteric theories is harder than one might imagine. Especially as so much of what is assumed to be factual history about the knights from centuries past turns out to be nothing of the sort.

Chapter Three

Templar Heroes and Villains

The twelfth century would see the Knights Templar achieve their greatest height in terms of prestige after some stunning victories. Yet this would be followed very shortly afterwards by a crashing low with defeat at the hands of the Saracens under Saladin. However, they would endure for another 130 years until their eventual fall in 1307. It's a staggering story of violence, betrayal, glory, and disgrace. It begins with their main advocate rallying Christendom behind these holy warriors.

Bernard of Clairvaux was the chief ecclesiastical champion of the Knights Templar. The saintly leader of the growing Cistercian order, founder of Clairvaux Abbey, confidante of popes, and propagandist for the crusades. His relentless cheerleading for the knights culminated in a gushing paean to the Templars titled: *In Praise of the New Knighthood.*[1]

Written in the form of a letter to Hugh de Payens, Bernard claimed the Templar grand master had asked him three times to pen such a work. 'You say that if I am not permitted to wield the lance, at least I might direct my pen against the tyrannical foe.' The knights, he declared, were waging a battle on two fronts against enemies of flesh and blood and a spiritual army of evil in the heavens. Monks had been at war with vices and demons for centuries, but the Templars had taken this struggle to a new level, brandishing the sword for truth. Their bodies protected by armour of steel, and their souls by the armour of faith.

Martyrdom was to be welcomed as such warriors would join the Lord up above. 'Life indeed is a fruitful thing and victory is glorious, but a holy death is more important than either.' And to die fearlessly in battle was something to be yearned for. As for killing the enemy, that should not be considered murder in the context of the crusades. Instead, it was the snuffing out of evil and therefore free of the taint of sin. As Bernard explained it:

'If he kills an evildoer, he is not a mankiller, but, if I may so put it, a killer of evil. He is evidently the avenger of Christ towards evildoers and he is rightly considered a defender of Christians.'

Bernard hated ornamentation in churches and illuminated bibles. Not for him the grinning gargoyles to be found in abbeys across Europe. He held the same puritanical disgust of such frippery when it came to the gaudy armour of secular knights. Horses should not be covered in silk, shields painted, and plumes fixed on to helmets. 'Are these the trappings of a warrior or are they not rather the trinkets of a woman? Do you think the swords of your foes will be turned back by your gold, spare your jewels, or be unable to pierce your silks?' Look instead to the Templars with their simplicity and restraint.

For the workaholic Bernard, there was nothing but admiration for the Templar abhorrence of indolence. Not a minute between dawn and dusk was spared for relaxation or idling. The day was punctuated with prayer conducted between drills, repairing worn-out armour and torn clothing, or engaging the enemy in battle. To modern eyes it was a joyless and grim existence. An almost Orwellian nightmare where Big Brother, in the form of the grand master and the hierarchy below him, monitored every thought and deed. Not for the Templars the mindless thrill of sharing gossip or the timewasting that resulted from hours spent playing dice, chess, or hunting. Although in the thirteenth century, long after Bernard's death, there was a depiction of two Templars engaged in a game of chess in a Castilian book titled the Book of Games – *El Libro de los Juegos*. Maybe standards had dropped by then.

In his paean extolling the virtues of the order, Bernard comments on the decision by the knights to be based in what was believed to be the site of the Temple of Solomon in Jerusalem. Solomon's temple had been a grander affair: encrusted with gold, silver, and precious jewels; it had been destroyed by the Babylonians 1,500 years before. But under the Templars, Bernard wrote, the remains of the temple radiated a different kind of beauty – generated by the religious fervour of its occupants and their well-disciplined behaviour. This holy place had been wrested from the control of Christianity's enemies and should never again be 'polluted by pagans' and 'crowded with merchants'.

Why did Bernard support the Templars so vocally? One reason was ties of blood and kinship. This medieval celebrity monk, who advocated a strict asceticism and mortification of the flesh, hailed from an aristocratic Burgundian family. Similarly, many of the early Templars were the scions of wealthy clans in the Champagne and Burgundy regions. Through his mother, Bernard was the nephew of one of the Templar founders, André de Montbard, with whom he engaged in a long correspondence keeping up to date with developments in the Holy Land. It has also been alleged that Bernard was the uncle of Afonso Henriques, the first king of Portugal and staunch ally of the Templars, whose father was a Burgundian noble.

In 1112, Bernard joined the abbey at Cîteaux as a Cistercian monk. He convinced four of his brothers, an uncle, plus twenty friends and cousins to join him. So, Cîteaux became something of a family affair. The abbot in charge was an Englishman, Stephen Harding, who was one of the founders of the Cistercian order, which had split off from the Benedictines. The name Cistercian derives from the Latin for Cîteaux – Cistercium. Bernard stayed for six years until he was offered a site to develop by Hugh, count of Champagne, to whom Hugh de Payens was a vassal.

This was a rather unpromising scrap of land, thirty miles from Troyes, and not far distant from De Payens' ancestral village. Even though it could best be described as a desolate swamp, the industrious Bernard transformed the area into a thriving religious community and renamed it Clairvaux, meaning clear valley. His creation of Clairvaux happened at the same time Hugh de Payens was establishing the Knights Templar and from the outset a strong bond formed between Clairvaux and the knights in Jerusalem. The third grand master of the Templars, Everard des Barres (died 1176), even joined Bernard at Clairvaux as a monk after he resigned from the top job in the Knights Templar. So, there were plenty of interconnections, some undoubtedly now forgotten, linking Bernard to the Templars.

Bernard was bellicose in his support for the crusades and the Knights Templar. He met Hugh de Payens when he was part of Baldwin's diplomatic mission to secure the hand of Melisende for his son, as well as seeking more recruits for the crusades. Some speculate that the two men were related, which is entirely feasible. There's evidence to show the two worked together on defining the Templar mission in line with the vision outlined in Urban's speech at Clermont. Bernard stood alongside Hugh at the Council of Troyes and urged thousands of people across Christendom to join the order and fight for the cross.

The Council of Troyes had given the Templars a rule book and the blessing of Rome, which had reassured donors that they were a credible organisation. But Bernard went a step further. His appeal to the Christian world to support the knights was as much from the heart as the head. It was a raw appeal to the emotions of the medieval nobility. He skilfully combined a theological justification for the Templars with a cry for help. The Templars were in the frontline doing God's work against the pagans and should not be let down in their heroic endeavour.

Hugh de Payens died in May 1136 and was succeeded by a very energetic Burgundian noble, Robert de Craon (died 1149). His family had been enthusiastic crusaders from the moment Pope Urban issued his call, with Robert's grandfather participating in the First Crusade. Robert's strategic objective was to ensure the independence of the Templars from all external control save the pope in Rome.[2] Hugh de Payens had been the founder of the order; now Robert was to be the consolidator. From day one, he pressured the popes to grant the order unprecedented privileges. In the year 1139, he got his wish.

Pope Innocent II issued a papal decree, or 'Bull' to use the technical term, making the Templars directly responsible to the pope alone and exempting the knights from paying taxes. Under the terms of this bull, named *Omne Datum Optimum* (translates as 'every perfect gift'), the knights could collect their own tithes and levy tolls on local fairs and markets, which proved to be a very lucrative source of revenue. Of equal importance, they were entirely free of control from princes and bishops, something that would become a source of growing resentment. Their preceptories, dotted all over Europe, in effect became tax havens for those living and working within their boundaries. Being part of a Templar community meant no longer being taxed by the local noble or church authority.

In September 1143, Celestine II became pope and the Templars found in him an even firmer ally. The following year, he issued the bull *Milites Templi* (Soldiers of the Temple), ordering the Catholic clergy to protect the Templars and enjoining the faithful to contribute to their cause. But the Templars hardly had time to celebrate their good fortune when disaster struck in the Holy Land. On Christmas Eve, 1144, the crusader-held city of Edessa (Urfa in modern Turkey) fell to a Seljuk warlord, Imad al-Din Zengi (c. 1085–1146) after a month-long siege. This snuffed out the northernmost of the crusader kingdoms: the County of Edessa. Although not the most important of the crusader realms – the others being the Principality of Antioch, County of Tripoli, and the Kingdom of Jerusalem – its loss was a huge psychological blow to the Christian world – and an enormous morale booster to the Islamic world.

How could this have happened? Looking at a map of the crusader states in outremer, the County of Edessa looks rather out on a limb. Landlocked and far to the north of Jerusalem, it's hard to imagine it was ever a priority crusader holding. Before the First Crusade, the city of Edessa was ruled by an Armenian Christian, Thoros, who had served as an official under the Byzantine empire but switched his allegiance to the Seljuks when the emir of Damascus permitted him to rule the city. Thoros then promptly betrayed his new masters, declaring Edessa independent under himself.

The furious Seljuks were bent on revenge, so Thoros turned to the newly arrived crusader armies, who were besieging Antioch in the year 1098. Baldwin of Boulogne, who would later be crowned the first king of Jerusalem, entered Edessa with about sixty to eighty crusaders – very much with his own agenda. Thoros mistakenly viewed the crusaders as just another bunch of mercenaries who would do his bidding then leave once paid off. Fatally for him, they did not. Instead, Baldwin insisted on being adopted by Thoros, in an Armenian Christian ceremony, and took an Armenian wife. He then calmly assumed control of Edessa after Thoros, his wife, and children were murdered by a mob – an incident that may have been instigated by Baldwin.[3]

Baldwin and his successors essentially ruled a territory run by Armenian warlords. Occasionally these eastern rite Christians would try to overthrow the Frankish count, and he would react, in true Byzantine style, by imprisoning and mutilating them. This emulated a long and gruesome tradition in Constantinople of blinding and crippling political opponents, even members of the royal family, who posed a threat. Essentially, the western Franks formed an unstable alliance of convenience with the local Armenian Christian elites, cemented by ties of marriage. By the time Zengi turned up with an invasion force, Edessa was ruled by the fourth and last count of Edessa, Joscelin II (1113–1159), who was half-Armenian.

Joscelin spent years forming and breaking alliances with the Byzantines, neighbouring crusader princes, and even Muslim rulers. But in 1143, he was left isolated politically by the deaths of both the Byzantine emperor and King Fulk of Jerusalem. Fearful of the growing power of Zengi, he joined a rebel Muslim force in an attack on Aleppo, one of Zengi's strongholds, hoping to divide the forces of Islam. This was a dreadful mistake. In a display of ruthless tactical brilliance, Zengi responded by marching rapidly on the now defenceless city of Edessa. Its fall on Christmas Eve, 1144, sent shockwaves through the Middle East and Europe, leading directly to the launch of the Second Crusade.

Zengi now loomed large as a Saracen bogeyman for the crusaders. He had outsmarted Joscelin and inflicted a major blow against the Franks. From various Islamic sources, we know that Zengi was born in Aleppo, Syria, between 1085 and 1087 and his father was the Seljuk governor of the city. When Zengi was 10 years old, his father was beheaded by order of the Seljuk emir on charges of treason. One account relates that Zengi's mother was killed by accident when her husband was practising his knife-throwing skills.

As a teenager, Zengi bore witness to the crusader invasion of outremer and a resurgence of the Abbasid caliphate in Baghdad that sought to throw off the yoke of Seljuk military dominance of the Middle East. In adult life, he displayed considerable flair as a military leader and political operator that led to him becoming the governor, or Atabeg to use the Seljuk title, of Mosul in 1127 and then Aleppo in 1128. Although officially a kind of viceroy ruling on behalf of the Seljuk sultan, and very nominally the Abbasid caliph, Zengi began to carve out his own personal fiefdom. He attempted unsuccessfully to annex Damascus and Baghdad, though both cities resisted his forces. Baalbek was less fortunate, falling to Zengi in 1139 with promises of clemency that were broken immediately on capture, with the garrison crucified and the rival Seljuk governor flayed alive.[4]

Zengi and the County of Edessa were content to circle each other for a while, maintaining an uneasy truce as Zengi focused on trying to take Damascus, while Edessa was absorbed in the fractious politics between the crusader states. But Joscelin's decision to join with Zengi's Muslim enemies in attacking Aleppo led the ruthless Seljuk to respond with an audacious siege of Edessa. An army composed of Seljuks, Kurds, and Arabs massed at the impressive fortifications of Joscelin's capital.

Despite its strong walls, there were no soldiers to mount an effective defence. The terrified city relied on three clerics to lead the resistance: the Latin Catholic bishop; the Armenian archbishop, and a Monophysite, Basil bar Shumana. These men represented variants of Christianity, each regarding the other as heretical, now forced to unite in the face of Zengi's forces.[5] Seven mangonels pounded the city and arrows rained down relentlessly while Zengi's sappers dug trenches under the bridge outside the North Gate. Eventually the walls came tumbling down and blood ran through the streets as Zengi stormed in.

According to Arab chroniclers, he spared the eastern Christians, but the Latins, loyal to the pope and Roman Catholicism, were led away in chains to the slave markets. The objective was to show a very religiously mixed population that his policy was anti-Frank but not anti-Christian. Days after the city was taken, Armenian and Monophysite Christians were worshipping again while the Latin churches, where the invading crusaders had attended mass, were boarded up. Within the Muslim world, the triumphant Zengi was showered with gifts and titles by the caliph in Baghdad. However, in the west, outremer, and Constantinople – alarm bells were ringing.

When Edessa fell, the Kingdom of Jerusalem was in the hands of Queen Melisende, the daughter of King Baldwin II of Jerusalem who had also been count of Edessa and married to a local Armenian princess, Morphia of Melitene.

Baldwin recognised the pope as head of Christianity while his wife looked to the patriarch of Constantinople. By virtue of her mixed heritage, Melisende had access to a network of Frankish aristocrats across Europe as well as power brokers in the east. She was groomed to be queen from birth and married to Fulk of Anjou after the diplomatic mission that sought his family's approval to the match, which involved the first Templar grand master, Hugh de Payens.

A year before the fall of Edessa to Zengi, Fulk was killed in a riding accident. At this point, Melisende assumed full regnal powers in the name of her son, Baldwin III. It was in her new elevated role that she wrote to Pope Eugenius III (c.1080–1153) calling for another crusade. Edessa had fallen and Christianity was once more in mortal danger. The queen's letter landed well with the first Cistercian pope, who responded with gusto.

As a young man, Eugenius had become a Cistercian at Clairvaux, under the watchful eye of Bernard, before leading his own community of monks at Scandriglia in Italy and then taking over the church of Saints Vincent and Anastasio alle Tre Fontane in Rome, reportedly a malarial hellhole he converted into a thriving monastic operation. Under his papal robes, Eugenius always wore an uncomfortable Cisterician habit to signal his humility. Yet his election as pope, without having been a cardinal first, displeased his mentor. Bernard wrote an incredibly unpleasant missive to Eugenius sneering that his protégé had been lifted like a beggar from a dunghill to sit with princes. Despite that vindictive exchange, the two worked closely on planning the new crusade.

Far from being cowed by the loss of Edessa, the pope and Bernard drew together the various strands of crusading activity from Portugal to the Baltics and down to outremer to present a narrative that Christianity was on the march. Despite the setbacks in the Holy Land, momentum was on the side of the cross.[6] Damascus still needed to be taken, but so too did the pagan Baltic strongholds of Dobin and Szczecin, east of the river Elbe, as well as the Muslim-held cities of Lisbon, Santarém and Lérida in Al-Andalus (modern Spain and Portugal). The enemies of the Roman church were everywhere, and the work of the magnificent Knights Templar had only just begun. Some historians dispute the notion that Eugenius and Bernard viewed the Second Crusade as an endeavour stretching from Portugal to Syria, thinking it was initially just focused on the Holy Land, but subsequent events suggest that they and many crusader leaders were more than aware of the bigger picture.

Despite the tone of optimism from the pope, it was impossible to ignore the loss of Edessa. From the very beginning, the crusades had been the subject of criticism from the side-lines. It was essential now that those downbeat voices be drowned out with the propaganda of war. Writing to King Louis VII of France, Eugenius reminded him how Pope Urban had sounded 'the heavenly clarion' at Clermont half a century before. The French had been 'inflamed by the power of love' back then and surely could not fail to be moved by the plight of Christians in Edessa at the hands of Zengi.

'They have occupied many Christian castles and they have killed the Archbishop of the city, his clergy, and many other Christians there. The relics of the saints, too, have been given over to be trampled upon by the infidel and have been dispersed.'[7]

After the loss of Edessa, a Syrian bishop – Hugh of Jabala – was sent by Raymond of Antioch to impart the news to the pope. He met Eugenius at the Italian city of Viterbo, from where the pontiff was forced to lead the church as Rome was in a state of revolt against papal rule. Also at this meeting was the German Cistercian historian Otto of Freising, who took copious notes. At some point, Bishop Hugh began to tell the pope about a fantastical Christian kingdom far in the east, possibly India, ruled by a priest-king, Prester John. Here was an ally on the other side of the Islamic world who could join with the Franks in a pincer movement to destroy the Saracens. The gloomy tidings from Edessa were balanced by the prospect of help from this hitherto unknown realm.

Prester John, Hugh explained, adhered to the Nestorian branch of Christianity long condemned by Constantinople, but which had thrived in Persia and further east into China and India. Nestorianism was born out of the almost incomprehensible debates in the early Christian church over the true nature of Jesus Christ and the relation between his human and divine natures. Over such hair-splitting discussions much blood was shed, and the Nestorians were driven eastwards by the Byzantines.

But now, 700 years later, Christian Europe was being asked to forget all that regrettable history and unite with a Nestorian monarch, that nobody was sure existed, to defeat the forces of Islam. Prester John, Hugh continued, was part of that 'ancient race of those Magi who were mentioned in the Gospel', descended from the Three Kings that came to see the baby Jesus in his cradle. Some accounts claimed this mysterious ruler was the direct descendant of one of the Magi and the queen of Sheba.

The story of Prester John took hold, and in the year 1165, the Byzantine emperor Manuel Komnenos, the Holy Roman Emperor Frederick Barbarossa (1122–1190), and the pope all claimed to have received a missive from this entirely mythical king. The letter promised that a very large army would come to Jerusalem to 'chastise the enemies of the cross of Christ and to exalt His blessed name'. In 1177, Pope Alexander III replied thanking Prester John for military support that never materialised, while in 1221, Pope Honorius III was informed by Jacques de Vitry (c.1160–1240), bishop of Ptolemais, that a descendant of Prester John was just fifteen miles from Antioch with an army to defeat the Saracens. It too failed to appear. Christian explorers would continue this fruitless quest to find the elusive monarch well into the sixteenth century, with the Portuguese convinced he was in Abyssinia.[8]

However, Bernard of Clairvaux was not going to leave the future success of the crusade to an imaginary monarch out in the east. With the pope's blessing, he set out on an energetic tour of Europe to drum up support for yet another onslaught against the Saracens in the Holy Land. For fifteen years, he had been cheerleading for the Knights Templar and everything they represented. Now he urged nobles and serfs alike to take the cross and follow their example. The loss of Edessa was to be blotted out in a flood of stirring rhetoric from this hyper-active Cistercian monk.

On Sunday, 31 March 1146, Bernard addressed a monster crowd at the holy site of Vézelay, home to an abbey that claimed to hold the relics of Mary Magdalene. He spoke from a specially erected platform with King Louis VII of France (1120–1180) seated behind him on a throne in his kingly robes. Bernard's soaring oratory drove his audience into a frenzy with cries of: 'The Cross! The Cross!' Crucifixes made of cloth were handed around but soon ran out and so Bernard very theatrically tore up his own cassock and cut it into more crosses for the eager recruits. Among those clamouring for a cross was the then queen of France, Eleanor of Aquitaine (1124–1204), one of medieval Christendom's most formidable women. She would later have her marriage to Louis annulled, marry Henry, duke of Normandy, and be crowned queen of England when Henry became king. Thereby managing in her lifetime to have been queen of both France and England – a unique achievement.

Meanwhile, the Templars were being handed yet more privileges. In 1145, Pope Eugenius issued a new papal bull, *Militia Dei* (Soldiers of God), giving them the right to collect tithes and burial fees as well as interring their dead in Templar-owned cemeteries. It also recognised the order's chaplains who administered the sacraments to the knights. Even though the Templars led a monastic style of existence, the knights were not priests or monks as such – a fact pointed out repeatedly by their opponents. So, they could not administer the sacred sacraments to themselves. They needed a properly ordained chaplain to give communion at mass and administer the last rites.

Combined with previous papal bulls, the Templars now enjoyed a quite unprecedented level of independence from local church hierarchies and were also able to earn revenue from activities previously conducted by parish churches and monasteries, such as burials. Many priests, bishops, and abbots came to resent the loss of fees to the knights. But at that moment, it was all about the Templars being able to operate in such a way that they could finance their military activities from Lisbon to Damascus. Pope Eugenius also sanctioned the inclusion of the red cross to be sewn onto the white mantles of the Templars, creating a brand image for the order, still recognised today.

Bernard's preaching rallied thousands to become crusaders. Sadly, it also sparked another surge in anti-Jewish pogroms. Successive popes had issued a string of bulls, such as *Sicut Judaeis* (As the Jews) in 1120, forbidding Christians from forcing Jews to convert, harming them, seizing their property, or vandalising their cemeteries.[9] But in the years leading up to the Second Crusade, antisemitism had been stoked by the election of a rival pope in 1130 – an 'antipope'.

Anacletus II had majority support in Rome among the people and nobility who were unfazed by his Jewish ancestry. But across Europe, the consensus was that the opposing candidate – Innocent II – was the rightful head of the church. Bernard of Clairvaux sided with Innocent II, writing to the Holy Roman Emperor that 'to the shame of Christ a man of Jewish origin has come to occupy the chair of Saint Peter'. Anacletus was even styled the 'Judaeo pontifex' by his enemies and, as late as the eighteenth century, the French essayist Voltaire referred to him as the 'Jewish pope'.[10] Despite his comments about Anacletus, Bernard toed the line on opposing generalised violence against Jews, believing that they must bear witness to their complicity in the crucifixion and eventually be converted to Christianity.

The Second Crusade would bring the wars against the Islamic caliphate in the Iberian Peninsula, encompassing modern Spain and Portugal, into much sharper focus. Portugal is Europe's westernmost country facing the Atlantic, with Spain at its back. From the eighth century CE, it became the most westerly territory of the all-conquering global Islamic caliphate, which stretched from Portugal to India. Hence the south of the country is still referred to as the Algarve, which is a corruption of the Arabic: Al Gharb (The West). Indicating that this region was the westernmost end of a caliphate extending through north Africa, the Middle East, and on into central Asia. However, the Muslim rulers of the Iberian Peninsula achieved a large degree of independence from the rest of the caliphate in the first hundred years after the Islamic invasion of 711 CE and did not regard themselves as subject to Baghdad.

As with Spain, the northern regions of Portugal saw the Islamic Moors pushed out relatively early on, while the south remained firmly under Muslim rule, with the border between the two faiths roughly corresponding to the mountain ranges that cut across central Iberia, known collectively as the Cordillera Central, culminating in the Serra da Estrela in Portugal. Between the northern crusaders and southern Moors was a no-man's land into which Christian forces increasingly pushed forward.

This Iberian crusade was termed the Reconquista, characterised as the taking back of lands illegitimately conquered by Islam and rightly belonging to the Christians of Iberia. However, by some estimates, through invasion and conversion, most people on the Iberian Peninsula may have been Muslim by the eleventh century, particularly as the major urban centres were in the caliphate.

Nevertheless, in the first decades of the twelfth century, the Knights Templar were making their presence felt. These holy warriors were the shock troops of the Reconquista and as early as 1128, the knights were granted the castle of Soure by a Leonese princess, Teresa (c.1080–1130), who would controversially declare herself queen of the newly emerging country of Portugal, with papal approval in 1116.

Portugal was carved out of both the long-established crusader kingdom of Léon to the north and land taken from the Moors to the south. Initially, it was a mere county, not a country, with Teresa recognised as the countess, obliged to pledge fealty to Léon – a Christian kingdom to the north. Teresa was the illegitimate daughter of King Alfonso VI of Léon, and she was married to a French noble, Henry of Burgundy. This Burgundian link connected her to both Bernard of Clairvaux and the first leaders of the Knights Templar. After her father died, Teresa fought his legitimate daughter Urraca, who had been crowned queen of Léon, but Teresa was eventually deposed by her own son, Afonso Henriques (c.1106 – 1185). He then became the first, more widely recognised, monarch of the independent kingdom of Portugal.

His bond with the Knights Templar was so strong from the outset that it's believed he was a 'co-frater' – a brother of some description. As his armies drove southwards from the river Mondego towards the river Tagus, the Knights Templar established one castle after another, with the Cistercians bringing up the rear with new monasteries. It fell to the Templars to hold the line between Christian Europe and the Islamic caliphate in areas where control by either side was precarious.

By the twelfth century, the golden age of Islamic rule on the Iberian Peninsula was over. The tenth century had witnessed the high point of a glittering Muslim civilisation, centred on the southern Spanish city of Córdoba. But in the eleventh century, the caliphate fractured into smaller 'taifa' fiefdoms, and this growing disunity spurred the Iberian crusader kingdoms – Léon, Castile, Navarre, Aragon, and Portugal – to advance southwards. But progress was not smooth or even. Two Islamic revivalist movements originating in north Africa

– the Almoravids and the Almohads – breathed new life into the caliphate and halted the Christian advance, but this offered only a temporary respite from growing intra-Muslim strife.[11] Ultimately, the momentum was on the side of the crusaders and Templars.

In 1139, Afonso Henriques mustered his forces to take on the Almoravids and remove the threat of a re-energised caliphate. The story of the Battle of Ourique would become the stuff of legend, recited by Portuguese children for centuries. Before the armies clashed, Count Afonso was raised up on a shield and proclaimed king by his soldiers and nobles. During the night, Afonso rode alone and was suddenly bathed in light. In the sky above, Jesus Christ appeared on the crucifix and told the Portuguese leader that he would triumph against the Almoravids by virtue of his faith and courage. Despite being massively outnumbered, Afonso won the day, killing five Muslim kings, according to a contemporary account by Theotonius of Coimbra (c.1082–1162).

At Ourique, fighting alongside Afonso, was a knight called Gualdim Pais (1118–1195). He grew up in the ecclesiastical capital of Portugal – Braga – and was knighted by a grateful king after his great victory. Shortly afterwards, Pais went on crusade in the Holy Land fighting as a Knight Templar. In 1157, he would return to Portugal, becoming the fourth and most notable grand master of the Templars in that country. Initially, he ran the order from his native Braga, but then moved the headquarters closer to the frontier with Islam, building the hilltop fortress of Tomar, with its surrounding town, which today remains arguably the most imposing Templar structure still standing anywhere in Europe. Along the frontline with Muslim Iberia, Pais built castles at Almourol, Idanha, Pombal and other locations, repelling attempts by the Moors to retake lost territory.

After Ourique, Afonso wrote to Pope Innocent II declaring that his new kingdom was a servant of the church, and he was committed to driving the Moors out of the Iberian Peninsula. This was a cunning ruse to place himself directly under papal control, much as the Knights Templar had done, to secure his independence from the neighbouring Christian kingdoms of Léon and Castile. Now he marched south with the Knights Templar determined to take the Moorish-held cities of Santarém and what is now the Portuguese capital of Lisbon, but was then Al-Usbunna.

But how was this to be achieved? The traditional story is that a crusader fleet of up to 200 ships set sail from Dartmouth in the south of England but while making for outremer was forced to shelter in the northern Portuguese city of Porto, in the estuary of the river Douro. This brought soldiers from England, Scotland, France, Flanders, and the Holy Roman Empire to the shores of Portugal. The city's bishop, Pedro Pitões, seemed to be already aware that the fleet was heading towards him and extended generous hospitality to the crusaders, as well as warm greetings from Afonso Henriques. Once the international group of knights was assembled on land, Pitões delivered a stirring sermon to equal that of Pope Urban at Clermont back in 1095.

His voice rang out across the dockside. On their journey along the Spanish coastline, had they not seen the churches and villages despoiled by the Moors? Were they not aware that Christians were being carried away as captives into the Muslim realms and holy relics stolen? They were on crusade, bound for Jerusalem to redeem their souls, but in fact, they could do battle right now, against the same enemy, without travelling much further. Pitões filled the air with his cries for justice:

> 'To you the mother church, as it were with her arms cut off and her face disfigured, appeals for help; she seeks vengeance at your hands for the blood of her sons. She calls to you, verily, she cries aloud. "Execute vengeance upon the heathen and punishments upon the people".'[12]

Echoing Bernard's justification for the creation of the Knights Templar, he told the crusaders that the acts of revenge they would need to commit in the name of Christ were a holy duty. Slaying the wicked was not an act of cruelty. It was the obligation of any servant of the Lord.

> 'Brothers, be not afraid. For in acts of this sort you will not be censured for murder or taxed with any crime; on the contrary you will be adjudged answerable if you should abandon your enterprise.'

But just in case these theological arguments were not landing as intended, Pitões promised the crusaders as much money as the royal treasury would permit after they were victorious. Afonso Henriques would later add that the crusaders could sack Lisbon 'to their full satisfaction' so long as they handed it over once glutted with treasure. And there was no shortage of riches within Lisbon, already a major trading hub with goods exchanged from across Europe, north Africa, and the Middle East.

The encounter between the bishop and this international crusader army was depicted as a happy accident due to inclement weather forcing the fleet to dock – more than likely a sign of divine approval from the heavens. But contemporary accounts make it very clear that there had been previous expeditions by foreign crusaders to Portugal and, in 1142, an unsuccessful attempt to besiege Lisbon. Afonso Henriques was relaying his appeals for help to Christian Europe through the Knights Templar and Bernard of Clairvaux, to whom he may have been related. So, this was no chance event, but something the Portuguese had been agitating for over several years. Now they got their wish – an enormous multi-national force.

Lisbon covered a large hill facing the river Tagus and the Atlantic Ocean. It corresponded roughly to what is now the Alfama and Mouraria districts of the modern city. The lower-level Baixa area, which includes the Rossio square today, was then underwater, yet to be reclaimed. Moorish Al-Usbunna was ringed with a formidable wall inside of which lay a warren of winding streets constituting the medina, or downtown, and above that, a protected citadel for the nobility – the kasbah in Arabic or alcáçova in Portuguese – and finally the governor's castle – al-Qasr or Alcácer – at the centre. In July 1147, a horrified Moorish governor stood on the city's battlements gazing down as Pitões, and the archbishop of Braga, delivered a blood-curdling ultimatum to the Muslim city. Lisbon had been out of Christian hands for 358 years but now an army camped on all sides was ready to take it back. If they refused to surrender, the consequence would be appalling for Lisbon's citizens. Go home, they cried out to the bemused people within the walls, who knew no other home than their beloved Al-Usbunna.

The near four-month siege that followed was brutal. At one point, an attacking force of 500 Moors was vanquished, with eighty of their decapitated heads put on spears and paraded in front of the city walls. Unable to endure this ghoulish spectacle, a gate was opened briefly to rush out and collect the body parts. The Christian chroniclers delighted in the cries of lamentation heard through the night as the families of those slain and mutilated wept in the streets of the medina.

Eventually the walls of Al-Usbunna were breached, and the crusaders swarmed into what would now become Lisbon. This triggered an orgy of looting and destruction that even a contemporary chronicler shuddered when describing. He was especially shocked when Flemish soldiers slashed the throat of the Mozarabic bishop of the city, showing their contempt for the Arabised, eastern rite Christians in Lisbon. The dead bishop was replaced immediately by an English monk, Gilbert of Hastings, who was more to the liking of the Roman Catholic crusaders. Very soon afterwards, the city's great mosque was demolished to be replaced by Lisbon's fortress-like cathedral.

One of the more poignant stories from the siege of Lisbon is an account of an unfortunate Portuguese crusader, Martim Moniz. The Christian army had reached the al-Qasr (now Saint George's castle), residence of the Moorish governor. They heaved against the main gate, forcing it ajar, but from the other side, the Moors expended equal effort to close it again. Seeing that the gate was about to shut, Moniz threw himself, literally, into the breach. His body was crushed under the weight of the thick wooden doors, yet his courageous and suicidal example inspired those present to put their backs into it one more time. Sure enough, they were streaming through the entrance and into castle precincts in no time. Today in Lisbon, one of the metro stations is named after this slain knight.

To consolidate his hold over Lisbon and other nearby cities, Afonso Henriques turned to the Knights Templar. The white-mantled holy warriors threw up a chain of castles and, in 1160, Gualdim Pais founded the city of Tomar as the order's Portuguese headquarters. On a hill overlooking the river Nabão, the Templars constructed a large fortress at the centre of which was a circular tower, referred to still as the 'charola', that mimicked the Byzantine aedicule of the Church of the Holy Sepulchre in Jerusalem, with pillars supporting a dome. One oft-repeated theory is that an altar was placed at the centre of his tower with the knights observing mass on horseback around it, ready to ride out against any approaching enemy. It's also speculated that at some point the Holy Grail, spirited out of Jerusalem by the Templars, was hidden below that altar.

Although the taking of Lisbon was a blow to the Moors, they had not given up on Iberia. Across the Mediterranean in north Africa, a Berber Islamic scholar, Ibn Tumart, launched a reform movement to stiffen the resolve of Muslim believers and thereby resist the forward momentum of the crusaders. He declared himself the Mahdi – the prophesied redeemer of Islam – and with his band of fanatics attacked unveiled women, wine shops, and other signs of religious backsliding. These fundamentalists came to be known as the Almohads, and they seized control of Islamic north Africa and Iberia from the Almoravids.[13]

For them, the loss of territory in Al-Andalus, Islamic Spain and Portugal was due to theological laxness, in particular the toleration of religious innovation – bid'ah in Arabic – which was regarded as heretical by the Almohads. Their interpretation of the Qur'an meant that the relative tolerance and cultural exchange between the Abrahamic faiths (Islam, Christianity, and Judaism) that had been the hallmark of Al-Andalus in the past would henceforth be prohibited.[14] Once fully reconquered, Al-Andalus would be subject to a strict separation of Muslims from non-Muslims and an assertion of Islam's superior position. To display their intention to retake most of the Iberian Peninsula, they moved their capital from Marrakech in Morocco to Seville in southern Spain. In 1190, the fourth Almohad caliph, Yaqub al-Mansur (c.1160–1199), set off with a colossal armed force heading for Portugal.

Al-Mansur felt justifiably provoked. The previous year, the Portuguese had repeated their trick of intercepting passing crusader fleets, with King Sancho I (1154–1211), son and heir of Afonso Henriques, convincing a Christian army, on its way to the Holy Land, to help him take Alvor and Silves off the Moors, extending his kingdom into the Algarve.[15] The Almohads decided enough was enough. In early July 1190, the Templars in Tomar were greeted by the sight of a terrifying host of Moorish warriors advancing from the horizon. They had already destroyed the nearby town of Torres Novas and massacred the Cistercian monastery of Alcobaça.[16] Now they were determined to take out the Templar nerve centre at Tomar.

At this stage of the Reconquista, the Templars were in the Christian vanguard, holding the line along the river Tagus. The Almohads intended as a first step to retake everything to the south of this divide. But far away in Rome, the leader of the Catholic church was determined that the Almohads should not get their way. Successive popes made it very clear that while fighting in outremer was the primary obligation, knights fighting the Moors on the Iberian Peninsula should remain there. That theatre of holy war was as important and sacred a fight as anything happening in the Kingdom of Jerusalem.

Once more it was impressed on the crusaders that the same indulgences applied to fighting in Portugal as in the Kingdom of Jerusalem. These papal indulgences were a transaction between the pope and his flock whereby he promised to cancel out sins in advance of death in return for certain actions being performed in life – like killing a lot of Saracens or Moors. This would reduce the time that one's immortal soul spent in purgatory, thereby speeding up entry to heaven.

Despite the promise of reduced time in purgatory, the Portuguese Templars were badly shaken by the sight of this Almohad host moving rapidly towards them. Addressing his troops as the Almohads approached, Gualdim Pais would have invoked the name of Henry the Crusader, a foreign knight killed during the siege of Lisbon in 1147 around whose tomb a cult had developed. His resting place was venerated in a similar manner to the grave of the Unknown Warrior after the First World War. He became the example that all Christian martyrs should emulate in the fight against the Muslim foe.[17]

Over the five days of the siege at Tomar, the Templars were hopelessly outnumbered. The Almohads eventually broke through the castle's first line of defence and thousands of Moorish soldiers poured into the fortress. Gualdim Pais was over 70 years old, but this crusading warhorse still possessed great reserves of energy. He marshalled the knights and the fighting now centred on one gate. Both sides stabbed at each other frantically in this small area to such an extent that the blood ran down the hill. To this day, this entrance is still referred to as the Gate of Blood, or Portão do Sangue in Portuguese. Incredibly, the wearied Almohads signalled the retreat and Tomar survived in Templar hands. Pais lived another five years, and his statue still dominates the town square today.

There are various esoteric theories about the Templars and Tomar, including claims that secret tunnels connect the castle on the hill with the church of Santa Maria Olival, where the Portuguese Templar grand masters were buried, and the church of Saint John the Baptist in the main square. These tunnels enabled the knights to scurry from one location to another unseen, while others assert that the order's treasure was hidden away in these murky depths. It certainly would have required a significant feat of medieval engineering to construct such tunnels, and the evidence is not overwhelming.

The association of the Knights Templar with subterranean passages is a recurring theme. In 1994, a plumber in the city of Akko, Israel, discovered a 500-foot-long tunnel leading from the Templar commandery to the seashore, passing underneath the old city of Acre. It was carved out underground as a semi-barrelled arch with a ceiling supported by hewn stones. The tunnel's existence had been forgotten since the fall of the city to the Saracens in 1291. In 2019, a *National Geographic* documentary claimed to have found further evidence of Templar tunnelling at Acre used to move gold underground to their 'treasure tower'.[18]

While this example of Templar digging is plausible, other examples of tunnels allegedly dug by the knights have been questioned. For example, the 2021 claim that beneath Sinai House, a timber-framed mansion in England, there is a labyrinth of tunnels and chambers in which both the Holy Grail and the Ark of the Covenant can be found. Attempts to verify this have been reportedly stymied by mysterious fumes emitting from the passageway, which have led to it being bricked up.[19]

For Christendom, the Second Crusade brought mixed blessings. While the tidings from Portugal were well received by the pope in Rome, the news from outremer was far less comforting. In 1146, Zengi was killed by his Frankish slave, Yarankash, who was to have been severely punished for daring to drink from the Atabeg's goblet. If the Templars were hoping for a lighter touch in his successor, they were soon to be disappointed. Zengi's second son, Nur ad-Din (1118–1174), took over Aleppo and wasted no time in attacking the Principality of Antioch and defeating Joscelin II's attempts to take back Edessa. Just to make sure the city of Edessa remained compliant, Nur ad-Din launched a pogrom against the Armenian Christian population, resulting in many deaths.

Meanwhile, the great powers of Christian Europe mobilised for war in the Holy Land, inspired by Bernard's stirring oratory. This was to be a crusade led by monarchs. The king of France, Louis VII, and the Holy Roman Emperor, Conrad III (c.1093–1152), marched their armies overland across the Balkans towards the Byzantine capital, Constantinople. A small detail but Conrad was never crowned by the pope, who traditionally conferred the title on the ruler of the empire so, technically, he was not the Holy Roman Emperor – but few disputed his right to assume the role.

In his preparations for war, Louis worked closely with the master of the Templars in France, Everard des Barres (died c.1176), who went on to become the overall grand master after the death of Robert de Craon in 1149. Des Barres exercised a strong influence over Louis, who seems to have been in awe of the knights, to whom he would hand an extraordinary level of military control over the operation, in part because of his own lack of battlefield experience.

In January 1147, Pope Eugenius III crossed the Alps into France. The former Cistercian monk made his way to the monastery where his clerical career had started: Clairvaux. After a short stay, he moved on to Paris where he attended the chapter meeting of the Templars, presided over by Des Barres, at the Paris Temple. It was within this formidable building, dominating the skyline, that the pope declared that from thenceforth, the Templars could wear the red cross on their white mantles representing the blood of the martyrs. He also instructed the Templar treasurer, Brother Aymar, to take responsibility for gathering one twentieth of all church revenues to pay for the crusades, which of itself was a recognition of the Templars' financial acumen.[20]

Meanwhile, Conrad had two crusades on the go – one against the Saracens in the Holy Land and another, the Wendish Crusade, directed at Europe's last pagans along the German Baltic coast. When Bernard of Clairvaux turned up in Frankfurt on 13 March 1147 to urge people eastwards towards the Holy Land, he found the local knights were far more eager to head north and smash the Slavic non-believers. While Bernard clearly convinced some to head towards outremer, he eventually decided to not only endorse but also sanctify the proposed slaughter of the pagans. By God's help, he declared, they would either be converted or wiped out. Pope Eugenius allowed some of the nobility to head off and fight the pagans, including two German nobles named Henry the Lion and Albert the Bear. However, the majority of Germany's knightly elite accompanied Conrad, with 20,000 troops, for Jerusalem.

Des Barres journeyed ahead of Louis to Constantinople to conduct diplomacy with the Byzantines, who were apprehensive about the western armies heading in their direction, not least because they were currently embroiled in a growing conflict with the Norman kingdom of Sicily, which had just grabbed Corfu from the Byzantines. There was a dream in Constantinople of restoring their control over southern Italy and coming to some kind of rapprochement with the pope, possibly even reuniting the eastern orthodox and Roman Catholic churches. This had a certain appeal for Rome, with the popes imagining the more refined Byzantines as neighbours in Italy as opposed to the warmongering Normans. None of this would ever come to pass.[21]

Louis VII and his army made steady progress through central Europe, but on entering the Byzantine empire found an unfriendly population that refused the crusaders entry to their walled cities, instead lowering down inadequate supplies by rope. The reason was that Conrad's force had preceded the French, looting and burning as they went. According to the French king's chaplain and chronicler, Odo of Deuil (1110–1162), the Germans had even taken grave exception to a jester in a tavern who produced a pet snake, resulting in the frightened, drunk soldiers tearing him to pieces. Presumably they had never seen a snake before. They then went on to massacre many of the local Byzantines, ensuring that the stereotype of crusaders as brutish louts was duly reinforced.[22]

Louis arrived in Constantinople in October 1147 and, like any visitor to this magnificent metropolis, was dazzled by the Hagia Sophia and the Palace of Constantine with its chapel brimming with holy relics. The royal party was received by the emperor, Manuel I Komnenos (1118–1180), at the Palace of Blachernae, decorated throughout with gold and multi-coloured marbles. His dynasty, the Komnenoi, had made this palace their primary residence. A sumptuous banquet was laid on accompanied by witty conversation.

But Odo of Deuil noted the other side of Constantinople, beyond the palace gates. Squalid and fetid with many districts 'afflicted with perpetual darkness' where murder and robberies were commonplace and 'other sordid crimes which love the dark'. Criminals felt neither fear nor shame as crime did not appear to be punished, or even recognised. Even allowing for anti-Byzantine prejudice, Odo's description has a ring of truth. A medieval urban sprawl on the scale of Constantinople was bound to present a sharp contrast between opulence and squalor.

Conrad had already marched out of the reassuringly robust walls of Constantinople, venturing deep into Asia Minor. One part of the army remained within Byzantine territory, but Conrad and his nobles struck out into the Seljuk-controlled areas. This was the height of rashness. What happened next should have been anticipated. The picture that emerges is of a lumbering mass of European soldiers, weighed down by baggage and armour, being picked off by lightning-fast Seljuk archers on horseback displaying the fighting skills developed by their ancestors on the steppe of central Asia. Three days out of the town of Dorylaeum (near the city of Eskişehir in modern Turkey), Conrad's generals advised a retreat as supplies were dangerously low. The Seljuks, detecting weakness, stepped up their attacks and what ensued was a bloody rout that decimated the German forces.

Conrad was lucky to escape with his life, while the remains of his army managed to hook up with Louis VII at Ephesus. However, Conrad was too sick to continue and returned to Constantinople from where the emperor Manuel would eventually transport him by sea to the Holy Land. Louis was determined not to suffer the same outcome. Moving forward more cautiously and sticking to Byzantine territory, he hoped to avoid the same fate. But the Seljuks harried his soldiers – and at Mount Cadmus, the French made a dreadful mistake.

Louis was with the unarmed pilgrims and baggage train at the rear while his queen, Eleanor of Aquitaine, who had taken the cross from Bernard of Clairvaux at Vézelay, rode at the front alongside an army commander, Geoffrey de Rancon. Having reached the summit of Mount Cadmus, De Rancon had been ordered by the king to strike camp – but he knew better. Instead, the commander ordered the vanguard of the French force to continue downhill towards a nearby plateau. This, he decided, was a better spot. His action resulted in the front of the army becoming separated from the back, which was pacing itself on the expectation of stopping soon for the night. The Seljuks, keeping a watchful eye, could hardly believe what they were seeing.

No second invitation was needed to descend on the French and inflict severe losses. At one point in the ensuing chaos, Louis found himself pressed against a tree to avoid the hail of arrows and clash of swords. Nevertheless, despite the horror unfolding around him, the king noticed that one group of soldiers were holding their nerve, protecting their possessions, and even helping others at risk. Louis observed the Knights Templar keeping their cool in the heat of battle and concluded that kind of discipline and strategic brilliance was required across his army.

Utterly humiliated and separated from his own army, Louis was forced to sneak back to the surviving vanguard under cover of night. Radical change was needed. After deciding not to hang De Rancon for insubordination, Louis took a decision that cemented the reputation of the Templars as the military brains of the crusade. He asked des Barres to take control of his army. This was completely unprecedented, but the king had experienced a brush with death that he did not care to repeat. The grand master of France obliged and set to work immediately.

What des Barres evidenced through the decisions he now took was that the Knights Templar really were a different kind of animal to the secular knights. Their ethos set them apart. These were professionalised and highly motivated soldiers, under a rigid command structure, and governed by a rule book. Everything written by Hugh de Payens and Bernard of Clairvaux over the last two decades was translated into action on the march from Mount Cadmus. It was solid proof that a new kind of military was required if outremer was going to remain in Christian hands.

Des Barres organised the army into units of fifty soldiers, each led by a Templar Knight. Everybody swore oaths to obey their new Templar commanders, doing exactly what they were told. There would be no more unilateral decision making, desertion, or confused thinking. The Seljuk attacks were not going to abate, but from now on, the French army would behave as one cohesive block under Templar control. The crusaders would be forced to submerge their own personalities in just the same way that a member of the order was trained to do. In this manner, Des Barres led the armies of France to the city of Attaleia – modern Antalya – saving many lives and allowing the king to continue his crusading mission in the Holy Land.

From Attaleia, Louis sailed for the Principality of Antioch, a crusader kingdom ruled by his wife's uncle, Raymond of Poitiers (1099–1149). He had taken control of Antioch after marrying Constance of Hauteville (1128–1163), the 10-year-old daughter of the previous prince of Antioch, Bohemond II, who died when she was 2 years of age, leaving her to rule through regents.

For Raymond's niece, Eleanor of Aquitaine, this was a joyful reunion. Her husband Louis, in contrast, was battle scarred and broke. Bitter at what had happened at Mount Cadmus, he was blaming the Byzantines for alleged collusion with the Seljuks and for charging him extortionate amounts of money for supplies. Dejected, he turned to Des Barres, realising that the Templars were not only an effective military fighting force, but competent bankers. Louis stuck out his royal begging bowl. The French grand master delivered the required sums while Louis instructed his royal adviser in Paris, Abbot Suger (c.1081–1151), to transfer an eye-watering sum to the Paris Temple as repayment, estimated to have been half the tax revenue of France.

The French royal visit to the prince of Antioch did not go well. Louis suspected his wife was sleeping with her uncle, who in turn wanted to divert the cuckolded king from continuing to Jerusalem, and instead help him take Aleppo and Caesarea. The accusation of incest must be taken with a large pinch of salt. Medieval chroniclers like William of Newburgh (1136–1198) disapproved of the nobility taking their wives on crusade. It was like the old trope of women bringing bad luck on ships. William believed that the French barons had followed the king's bad example, which 'introduced a multitude of women into those Christian camps, which ought to be chaste, but which became a scandal to our army...'.[23]

Eleanor of Aquitaine, as a forthright and assertive woman in medieval politics, had her reputation comprehensively trashed by the chroniclers, especially as relations with her husband soured at their failure to have children, leading the queen to sneer that her husband was more a monk than a king. She had no intention of taking the blame for a childless union. Their marriage would eventually be annulled.[24]

Conrad and the remnants of his army reached Acre and Louis joined him in 1148 with his disgruntled queen in tow. They were met by the international force of crusaders that had just conquered and ransacked Lisbon, with the permission of Afonso Henriques. On 24 June, the crusaders held what was in effect a war council at Acre attended by Louis, Conrad, and Baldwin III, the teenage king of Jerusalem, and his mother Melisende, who had been acting as regent. Also present was the Knights Templar grand master Robert de Craon and the Knights Hospitaller grand master Raymond du Puy, along with a galaxy of medieval nobles including Count Thierry of Flanders, the margrave of Tuscany, and the marquess of Montferrat.

In retrospect, the advice of Raymond of Poitiers to attack Aleppo makes more sense than what happened next. Zengi's son and heir, Nur ad-Din, had his powerbase in Aleppo and invading his capital would have dealt a knock-out blow to the Seljuks. However, Raymond was not at Acre and Louis was in no mood to consider his point of view. Instead, all eyes were fixed on Damascus. The ancient Syrian city, with its biblical resonances, was like an itchy scab for the crusaders – it was impossible to ignore. Even though attacking it would drive its citizens firmly into the hands of the Seljuks, who had been viewed with more fear than the crusaders up until that point.

So, there was to be no attack against Zengi directly at his base of operations in Aleppo. While invading the Fatimid caliphate, centred on Egypt, was out of the question as the city of Ascalon, guarding the roads south of Jerusalem, was still in Fatimid hands. And lingering in the back of many crusader minds was the failed attempt to take Damascus back in 1129. The Syrian city was unfinished business. Confidence ran so high that according to the Arab chronicler Al-Qalanisi, the crusaders had even worked out the division of victory spoils before setting off. Yet, as Karl Marx observed in the nineteenth century, history repeats itself – first time as tragedy and second time as farce. Believing that they constituted an invincible force, the crusaders marched out to the orchards south of Damascus fully expecting a short and victorious siege. What transpired was the exact opposite.

The orchards fast became a killing field as small buildings and mud walls were used by the city's Muslim defenders to fire arrows and stab at the passing crusaders. Nevertheless, they took their positions with Baldwin at the front, Louis and Conrad with their armies, and the Knights Templar in strict formation – a solid square of white mantles and red crosses. The orchards provided food and water as well as wood for building siege equipment. But the constant sniping by Saracens from protected positions, and reports that Saracen reinforcements were on the way to relieve Damascus, led the crusaders to make a fateful decision. To the astonishment of the city's defenders, they relocated to the barren plain on the eastern side of the city, apparently on the pretext that the city's walls were weaker there. However, it also meant there was no supply of water for the Christian troops.

According to the Arab chronicler Ibn al-Athir (1160–1233), the ruler of Damascus sent messages tailored to the Frankish crusaders from Europe and to the local crusaders from Jerusalem.[25] To the former he warned that if they did not depart, he would hand the city over to Nur ad-Din, who was already on his way, and they would live to regret that. While to the latter, he said that the Kingdom of Jerusalem would soon be extinguished once Damascus was under the Seljuk heel. Undoubtedly, some of the local crusaders must have begun to wonder why they were attacking a city that had once been a Muslim ally against the Seljuks. The European nobles, meanwhile, argued on the battlefield about who among them should rule Damascus even though the siege was clearly failing. After just four days, as morale collapsed, the retreat was sounded. The Christian army trudged back to Jerusalem fired on by Saracen archers much of the way.

The aftermath of the failure of the Second Crusade saw an orgy of recrimination. In the resulting blame game, the local Frankish rulers were accused of being in league with Damascus, their former allies, and even taking bribes to abandon the siege. King Louis was sure the double-dealing Byzantines were behind their misfortune and promptly made an alliance with the Normans, the dread enemy of Constantinople. While returning to France on a ship loaned by the Norman kingdom of Sicily, his flotilla came under attack from Byzantine naval forces, who allowed the king to continue home but relieved him of all his possessions, which found their way to Constantinople. As for Conrad, he was in Constantinople by this stage, forging an anti-Norman alliance, with the Byzantine emperor marrying his brother to the niece of Manuel Komnenos.

To some, the failure of the Second Crusade was a result of immorality. Henry of Huntingdon (1080–1160) wrote of the crusader army that 'God despised them, and their incontinence came up before Him; for they abandoned themselves to open fornication, and to adulteries hateful to God, and to robbery and every sort of wickedness'. The Knights Templar had assisted the crusaders at Damascus, but that was not enough as they lacked 'the favour of God'.[26] What a contrast, he noted, between the humble army of crusaders bereft of monarchs and princes that had taken Lisbon compared to the glittering feudal multitude that had made its way to the Holy Land, nosediving so spectacularly.

The Knights Templar did not emerge from the debacle unscathed. They may have rescued the French army in Asia Minor and bankrolled King Louis, but wagging tongues inferred they were a perfidious bunch, pursuing their own interests. John of Würzburg was a German priest who went on pilgrimage to Jerusalem over a decade later and recorded rumours that the Templars had taken bribes to help lift the siege of Damascus. The Bavarian city of Würzburg also gave rise to an anonymous chronicle of the Second Crusade, the *Annales Herbipolenses*, alleging that those who had roused thousands to take the cross had been 'certain pseudo prophets, sons of Belial, and witnesses of antichrist, who seduced the Christians with empty words'. This was clearly aimed at Bernard of Clairvaux, provoking one of his own monks, his biographer Geoffrey of Clairvaux (c.1115-c.1188), to make the rather disingenuous claim that his boss had been 'commanded' by the pope and 'urged' by King Louis to preach the crusade and before that had 'refused to speak or to give his advice on the matter'.[27] It's difficult to imagine that many bought that weak spin emanating from Clairvaux.

The Templars continued to be cast as the bad guys for the next few years. English-born John of Salisbury (1120–1180), who went on to become bishop of Chartres in France, wrote that although King Louis admired the Templars, John heard on the grapevine that their conduct had been decidedly treacherous, though he was short on details. Ralph Coggeshall, a Cistercian abbot in Essex who went on crusade, sustaining a serious head injury, believed the Templars were bribed directly by Nur ad-Din, while Gervaise of Canterbury was more specific, claiming the Templars had received three jars of gold bezants from within Damascus but, on closer inspection, discovered the gold coins were made of copper. In truth, these stories were baseless, amounting to the kind of malicious gossip common among medieval monks and priests.

Likely a broken man, the Templar grand master, Robert of Craon, died not long after the disaster of the Second Crusade and was replaced by the French master, Everard des Barres. This was an astute move by the order, promoting a senior figure still held in the highest esteem by King Louis. With so many ugly rumours circulating, the Templars were in dire need of friends in high places. Especially as their finances and supply of willing recruits in outremer were running low and Nur ad-Din was taking full advantage of the defeat at Damascus.

At the Battle of Inab, his army annihilated a smaller combined force led by Raymond of Poitiers and the Assassins. It may seem an unusual alliance, but the dagger-wielding killers also felt threatened by the emboldened Seljuks. Raymond was captured and beheaded, with his embalmed head placed in a silver casket and sent to the caliph of Baghdad. One wonders how Louis greeted that terrible news. But by then, his marriage to Raymond's niece, Eleanor of Aquitaine, was over and she was on course to become queen of England via her next husband.

The early 1150s saw many of the key figures of the Second Crusade bow out. Conrad died in 1152; Pope Eugenius in 1153; and Bernard of Clairvaux breathed his last on 20 August that year. The last count of Edessa, Joscelin II, was captured by Nur ad-Din in 1150 and transported to Aleppo where he was blinded in public, then thrown into a dungeon where he died in 1159.[28] Everard des Barres took the unusual step of resigning as grand master of the Knights Templar in 1152 and went off to become a monk at Clairvaux, living until around the year 1176. He was succeeded by the fourth grand master, Bernard de Tremelay, a Burgundian whose period in office would come to a grisly end.

The balance of power in outremer in the mid-twelfth century was changing yet again. The century had begun with the First Crusade catching the Seljuks, Fatimids, and Islamic caliphate completely off guard. Four kingdoms had been carved out of the Levant by the crusaders and a city holy to all the Abrahamic faiths – Jerusalem – restored to Christian control. Constantinople heaved a sigh of relief as the fortunes of the Byzantine Empire improved significantly with the threat of imminent extinction removed. Pope Urban's sermon had been fully realised, giving rise to a new order of holy warriors: the Knights Templar.

Fifty years later and the Second Crusade had altered the geopolitics of the region, as well as attitudes and sentiment. The Seljuk empire had unified around Nur ad-Din, adding the County of Edessa to its territory. It was feeling increasingly bullish, whereas uncertainty was starting to grip the crusader kingdoms. The Principality of Antioch, for example, was looking very vulnerable after the beheading of Prince Raymond.

As early success gave way to failure, Europeans wondered if their Christian counterparts in outremer had gone native, lacking any real commitment to the crusading ideal. They heard stories of men from France and the Holy Roman Empire now swanning around in silks, eating dates, refusing to eat pork, and even keeping a harem. These orientalist attitudes bred hatred towards the men of the east who had traded in their Catholic faith for effete eastern luxury.

The Byzantines, meanwhile, had learned to distrust the Franks, treating them with kid gloves and worse, denying them supplies or military assistance. Constantinople's suspicion of the west was only further fuelled by ongoing conflict with the Normans. The crusaders had always been viewed with trepidation as uncouth barbarians brawling their way through the empire's territory, treating Constantinople with little respect, and then refusing advice as they marched off into enemy territory, blaming the Byzantines when things went badly wrong.

And then there were the monastic chroniclers, dipping their sharpened pens in poison and stabbing the Knights Templar in the back, sometimes with insinuation but increasingly with explicit hostility. Many had never bought into Bernard's propaganda about these monks-cum-knights. They were a hybrid creation that caused unease. Added to that were the privileges being showered on the knights by successive popes that enriched their preceptories across Europe, seemingly at the expense of local monasteries and churches. The Templars, it was muttered, were leeching money away from hard-pressed priests and abbots.

As if things could not get any worse, the Assassins killed their first Christian ruler: Raymond II, count of Tripoli in 1152. Up until then, their murderous activities had been focused on Sunni Muslim targets, mainly Seljuks, as the Assassins were a variant of Shi'a Islam. The Seljuks had become intimately acquainted with Assassin daggers from the 1090s with viziers, emirs, governors, and military commanders murdered by the fanatics. To the Frankish rulers of outremer, the Assassins were even regarded as de facto allies, with Raymond of Poitiers fighting alongside the Assassin leader, Ali ibn-Wafa, at the Battle of Inab, where he was killed. But now, the Assassins had shown a willingness to extend their homicidal tendencies to the Christian rulers in the Levant. Their brutal killing of Raymond II, and two knights accompanying him, left a power vacuum in Tripoli at a particularly dangerous moment.

Why did the Assassins murder Count Raymond of Tripoli? The reasons are not at all clear, but some have speculated that they were angered at the decision by the count to give the Syrian city of Tortosa to the Knights Templar, which the order then began to fortify.[29] The Templars constructed an impregnable castle, including a keep surrounded by thick double-concentric walls. There was good reason for the knights to work fast. In early 1152, Nur ad-Din had captured the city and sacked it, but then departed. A shaken populace and local bishop were only too happy for the Templars to effectively take over and run their defences. However, the Assassins may have viewed things differently. A Templar stronghold on their doorstep was very unwelcome.

In 1149, the Templars were tasked with holding the city of Gaza. This was part of a deliberate policy by the Kingdom of Jerusalem to encircle the Fatimid stronghold of Ascalon, ten miles to the north of Gaza. This was the first significant castle, that we know of, granted by the kingdom to the Templars. Over the next century, a growing number of fortresses would be handed to both the Templars and Hospitallers to manage, while the secular authorities were increasingly stretched. Gaza had emptied out in recent years because of its proximity to the border between the Kingdom of Jerusalem and the Fatimid caliphate, centred on Egypt. Nobody wished to live in a permanent war zone. But under Templar control, the city started to fill up with people again, given its location on a key trading route and the knights' protective muscle.

The Templars built a large church on top of the ruins of what had been a sixth-century Byzantine Christian place of worship subsequently transformed into a mosque after the seventh-century Islamic invasion. Going back much further in history, the site was once a Philistine temple to the pagan god Dagon, famously toppled by Samson in the Old Testament. It reverted to being a mosque after the Templars lost control of the city later in the twelfth century. The building went on to have a turbulent history, being bombed by the British in the First World War, as they fought the Ottoman Empire, and then falling victim to the conflict in Gaza in late 2023.[30]

To wipe away the shame of what had happened at Damascus in 1148, Ascalon had to fall. It was the gateway to and from the Fatimid caliphate and taking it would ensure the safety of both the Kingdom of Jerusalem and pilgrims journeying from the port of Jaffa, northwards to the holiest sites in Christendom. Fortunately for the crusaders, court politics at the Fatimid caliph's palace in Cairo had entered an especially murderous and fractious phase.

The caliph, Al-Zafir (1133–1154), was saddled with a vizier (first minister), Ibn al-Sallar (died 1154), who had seized the position after killing the previous vizier and 17,000 of his followers.[31] There was no love lost between Al-Zafir and al-Sallar, both of whom conspired to have the other deposed or murdered. On one occasion, the caliph organised a group of palace guards to assassinate his vizier at midnight, when he had fallen asleep. The plot was betrayed, and the conspirators were ambushed by men loyal to al-Sallar – then massacred.

In between avoiding attempts by the ruler that he was supposed to be advising to have him killed, al-Sallar attempted to deal with the crusader encirclement of Ascalon through attacks by land and sea, as well as reaching out to Nur ad-Din and the rulers of Damascus to form an anti-Frankish coalition.[32] The Fatimid navy inflicted significant casualties on the Franks but on land, al-Sallar was unable to break the growing stranglehold the crusaders were exerting on Ascalon. Matters were not helped by Nur ad-Din having little interest in diverting resources to help as he was still occupied with Damascus and harrying the crusader kingdoms further north.

While the Fatimids were beset by bloody palace intrigues, the Kingdom of Jerusalem had just gone through its own internal upheaval. Baldwin III was the oldest son of Queen Melisende and King Fulk, formerly the count of Anjou, who had been the subject of Hugh de Payens' diplomatic mission years before to convince him to journey to the Holy Land and marry Melisende, thus ensuring the royal succession. Fulk was killed in a riding accident in 1143 and his son, Baldwin, was crowned king, but as he was still a child, his mother ruled as regent. However, Melisende displayed a distinct reticence to step aside as he reached maturity, largely because he had never shown much interest in statecraft whereas she was something of an expert.

The royal council – or Haute Cour as it was called – met and devised a Solomonic solution whereby the kingdom would be divided in half between mother and son. That was never going to last. Within weeks, Baldwin invaded his mother's southern half of the Kingdom of Jerusalem, and she was effectively deposed, though allowed to hold the city of Nablus for life. The two were reconciled as it dawned on Baldwin that medieval geopolitics was not his strongest point. However, the king needed a triumph and Ascalon presented the obvious opportunity. The Templars had now fortified Gaza and the city was surrounded. While the Fatimids in Cairo tore each other to pieces, it was time for the crusaders to act.

The chronicler William of Tyre described Ascalon as a city with a large population bankrolled by the caliph. He claimed that 'even the smallest of its inhabitants, including the children, receive salaries from the Egyptian Caliph's treasury'. This was the price of keeping the city on side and loyal, such was its strategic importance to the Fatimids.[33] If Ascalon fell, then Egypt was open to invasion by the Franks. For this reason, it was graced with thick walls, barbicans, towers, and ramparts as well as being generously supplied with arms and provisions 'beyond all expectation'. The citizenry was also trained to use arms and resist any besiegers.

From January 1153, the siege got underway. The Knights Templar joined the action under their grand master, Bernard de Tremelay, while the Hospitallers were led by Raymond du Puy. Within Ascalon, there was an expectation that Cairo would keep the city well supplied, sending reinforcements to see off the crusaders. The siege dragged on for months. In April, at Easter, a flood of pilgrims arrived from Europe to visit the site of Christ's crucifixion. Instead, they were greeted by Baldwin's representatives offering them cash in return for joining the siege – with the additional bonus of showing your love for God through ultra-violence. According to William of Tyre, many were convinced, and a 'tremendous host of pilgrims' joined the action.

To breach the walls of Ascalon the crusaders took the masts from several ships and began to construct a very tall siege tower. It was protected from fire, inside and out, with wickerwork and animal hides that would shield those within this contraption when the time came to wheel it towards the battlements. The carpenters also created portable sheds – a kind of canopy under which soldiers could move right up to the walls and begin undermining them, despite the city's defenders raining rocks and other projectiles down on the shed roof.

Eventually, the tower was on the move. A stretch of wall was chosen that could be easily attacked. As it lumbered across the sand towards Ascalon, the soldiers roared their approval. In no time, crusaders at the top of the tower were engaged in hand-to-hand combat with Fatimid soldiers defending the walls. The citizens of the city, trained in warfare for such an eventuality, fired with their bows and ballistas but were unable to hit those within the siege machine. This was repeated daily until there were definite signs that the enemy's resolve was weakening.

But then an unwelcome development. A large Fatimid fleet appeared with seventy galleys and other ships loaded to the gunwales with men, weapons, and provisions. From within Ascalon, a delirious cheer went up and hands raised skywards in joy. The new reinforcements were 'fresh and greedy for glory', eager to give the crusaders a beating on the battlefield. Though initially stunned and dismayed, the crusaders soon recovered their spirit and resumed the daily assaults. Huge rocks were catapulted over the walls destroying houses and causing casualties. Then the Fatimid defenders made the kind of mistake that leads to defeat. They resolved to burn down the crusader siege engine.

A large pile of dry wood covered in pitch and oil was assembled on the battlements at the point where the engine usually made contact. As it approached, the fire was lit. However, nobody thought to stick their finger up and check the wind direction. The small inferno was blown back towards the city, causing a conflagration that continued during the night. The next morning, just before daybreak, those who were sleeping among the crusaders awoke with a start as a section of Ascalon's huge walls crashed to the ground. At this point, William of Tyre levelled a startling accusation against the Knights Templar.

In his account, he claims that the Templar grand master, Bernard de Tremelay, got to the breach in the wall first, taking control of the area. 'They allowed no one save their own men to enter'. Why? The reason, William alleged, was so that the Templars could enter the city first and 'get the greater part of the spoils and the choicer booty' as whatever a besieger could physically seize in such circumstances was 'possessed by him and his heirs in perpetuity'. Overcome by greed, the Templars muscled everybody else out of the way, with forty knights entering the city and blocking access to all the other crusaders. Tragically for De Tremelay and his men, the citizens of Ascalon were not quite ready to surrender yet, and butchered the entire party.

Another medieval source claimed that once De Tremelay and his knights got into Ascalon, they were confronted by narrow streets and were assailed from all sides by the populace. The Templars were overwhelmed and killed. Their heads were sent to the caliph in Cairo while their headless bodies were hung from the battlements.[34] Hurriedly, the walls were repaired with large beams and pieces of timber. But the sight of the mutilated corpses provoked a furious response from the crusaders, eventually forcing the city to capitulate. Victory for the Templars was bittersweet. They had lost their grand master and many of their knights. But was there any truth in the claim, repeated in several subsequent accounts, that they had charged in eager to line their pockets?

Underlying these accusations against the Templars were the provisions of the papal bull, Omne Datum Optimum. This was the document issued by Pope Innocent II in March 1139 that among other things, allowed the knights to hold on to any spoils gained from conquering Muslim territory. This must have irked some chroniclers. Combined with the later papal bulls Milites Templi (1144) and Milita Dei (1145), it gave the impression that the Templars were a law unto themselves. This was to form the basis of propaganda against the order right up to its destruction after 1307. Interestingly, the Arab version of what happened at Ascalon makes no mention of the Templars charging through the breach and stealing lots of treasure. It is entirely silent on the matter, which is curious given the hatred and fear that the knights inspired among the Saracens.

The fifth grand master of the Knights Templar was André de Montbard (c.1097–1156), another Burgundian noble who was the uncle of Bernard of Clairvaux and one of the founding members of the order alongside Hugh de Payens. Bernard was the third child of Tescelin le Roux (c.1070–1117), a vassal of the duke of Burgundy, and Aleth de Montbard (c.1064–1106), who was the daughter of Bernard de Montbard, brother of the new grand master. This familial connection was undoubtedly one of many threads connecting Bernard to the order. But the uncle outlived his nephew by a couple of years. In his short tenure as leader of the Templars he was plunged into a series of crises.

First, there was the seizure of Damascus by Nur ad-Din, ending the Burid dynasty. Like the Seljuks, they were of Oghuz Turkic origin but had played a risky diplomatic game to remain independent, siding at times with the Franks and then the Seljuks. In 1151, things had been so cordial with the Kingdom of Jerusalem that the Burids allowed some of Baldwin III's soldiers to enter the city on a shopping trip to the bazaars.[35] This was insufferable to the Seljuks. Nur ad-Din called time on the Burids in 1154, exiling the last emir of the dynasty, Mujir ad-Din (c.1124–1169), to the city of Homs. Now the Seljuks were consolidating their empire, unifying Syria, and posing an even greater threat to the crusader kingdoms of outremer.

Second, Fatimid Egypt was still in turmoil. In April 1154, the caliph Al-Zafir was murdered by his vizier, Abbas ibn Abi al-Futuh (c.1115–1154), who then proclaimed the dead ruler's 5-year-old son as the new, much more compliant, caliph. The trauma of viewing the corpses of his father and two uncles may have contributed to a lifetime of epileptic seizures for the young boy.

Abbas had arranged for the assassination of the previous vizier, al-Sallar, while on his way with an army to relieve the siege of Ascalon. His preoccupation with court intrigues back in Cairo undeniably led to the fall of the city in 1153. In the following year, his son, Nasr, had lured Al-Zafir to the vizieral palace and, closely following his father's instructions, killed the caliph.[36] But Abbas was immediately confronted by a city-wide revolt in which the women of the harem played a leading role. Finding his own troops unwilling to take on this harem-led revolution, Abbas and Nasr fled. They were intercepted by a crusader force who slew Abbas and sold his son back to the royal court in Cairo. Once there, Nasr was mutilated and beaten to death by four widows of the late caliph, and his corpse publicly displayed.[37]

That is an account of what happened to Nasr from an Islamic chronicler. On the Christian side, William of Tyre and Walter Map told the same story, but with added Templar greed and duplicity thrown in.

According to William, the Templars took Nasr captive, taking the treasure he and his father had packed before fleeing Cairo. A desperate Nasr pleaded with the knights, claiming that he wished to convert to Christianity, and had even learned some Latin. This is plausible as it's the reversal of a precedent set in the Qur'an where the life of a captive could be spared if they converted to Islam – and learned Arabic. So, maybe Nasr thought it could work the other way in terms of saving his skin. However, William stated that the venal knights sold him back to the Fatimids for 60,000 gold pieces, knowing full well his fate would be truly grim. They placed Nasr in an iron cage on the back of a camel and sent him on his way. Walter Map endorses all the above with a slight variation, adding that the Fatimids used Nasr for target practice when he got back home, piercing his body with arrows.

William of Tyre was tireless in his criticism of the Templars. Born in Jerusalem, he was very much a creature of outremer, though educated in Orléans, Paris, and Bologna. His career was marked by great success, becoming the archbishop of Tyre and an ambassador for the Kingdom of Jerusalem to the court of the Byzantine emperor. His renowned intellect meant he was an obvious choice to tutor the future king of Jerusalem, Baldwin IV, later claiming to be the first person to diagnose the boy's leprosy.

William is remembered primarily for his burning hatred of the Knights Templar. In his view, they had been a troublesome bunch from the outset. Pride was the signature vice of these knights – their humility having evaporated long ago. Even though the Latin patriarch of Jerusalem had given his full backing to the Templars, they had repaid him with ingratitude and disobedience. Like many in the church, William disapproved of the privileges extended to the knights whereby they were only accountable to the pope in Rome. As for their wealth, it equalled the treasuries of kings and princes. This was not entirely false. William grumbled that they had taken tithes from the church, which again was not inaccurate. Successive popes had allowed the Templars to collect their own taxes, which did in effect take money from local priests and bishops. But what William did was to spin all of this together to create a very damaging narrative that would contribute to the downfall of the Knights Templar.

Walter Map (1130-c.1210) was a Welsh cleric who rose to be the Archdeacon of Oxford and an emissary for King Henry II of England. His only surviving written work is *De Nugis Curialium* (Courtiers' Trifles) in which he portrayed the Templars as having started out with good intentions, but succumbed to temptation as 'their love waned, and their wealth waxed'. Medieval Europe, Map noted, spoilt the knights rotten:

> '…*kings and princes, deeming their purpose high and their life honourable, honoured with the aid of popes and patriarchs, the Templars as defenders of Christianity, and heaped upon them immeasurable possessions. They had what power they would and whatever they wished.*'[38]

Map had to tread carefully as he ladled out the poison. Recognising that prelates and princes still admired the knights, he felt constrained to warn them that their heroes had drifted from the path of righteousness. Like all greedy people, they 'inject avarice and pride from the lake of sins'. He then gave his version of what happened to Nasr, son of the slain vizier of Fatimid Egypt. To Map, Nasr was a 'gentle man' of 'soldierly prowess, letters, and purity of mind'. His intention to embrace Christianity was sincere, Map wrote, yet the Templars put him in chains and refused his request to be baptised. Worse, they sold him back to the 'Babylonians' (Fatimids) where he proclaimed his new faith openly and was tied to a stake and martyred in the manner of Saint Sebastian and King Edmund. Incredibly, to besmirch the Templars, Map transformed a homicidal Fatimid palace operator into a Christian saint.

Both William of Tyre and Walter Map attended the Third Lateran Council held at Rome in 1179 and convened by Pope Alexander III. William represented the church in Jerusalem while Walter was sent by King Henry II of England. The council had a full agenda that included a demand (in canon number nine) that the Knights Templar and Knights Hospitaller fully observe church regulations in just the same way every bishop and priest was required to do. The language was surprisingly strident and suggested that Rome had fallen out of love with the Templars:

> 'Now we have learnt from the strong worded complaints of our brethren and fellow bishops that the Templars and Hospitallers…exceeding the privileges granted them by the Apostolic See have often disregarded episcopal authority, causing scandal to the people of God and grave danger to souls.'[39]

In short, the bishops were annoyed at being circumvented or ignored by the Templars, who had been led to believe that their only line manager was the pope in Rome. The accusations at the Lateran Council came thick and fast. The knights admitted excommunicated people to their ranks and appointed and removed priests without the knowledge of the local bishop. The complaints continued as if a pressure valve had been released, allowing the steam out. If this council was any indication, the mood towards the holy warriors was souring rapidly.

Pope Alexander was in no mood for dissent or freethinking. He had spent the first twenty years of his pontificate fighting off rivals claiming to be the real pope and often supported by the Holy Roman Emperor. By 1179, he was firmly in control of Rome, but decades of conflict had exhausted his patience. He craved a disciplined and united church.

If the Templars and Hospitallers were posing a threat to unity, then they had to be reprimanded. But the pope saw this as a part of a broader onslaught against disruptive and treacherous elements. There were other agenda points tackling lax conduct among monks and priests including relationships with women and homosexuality, 'that unnatural vice for which the wrath of God came down upon the sons of disobedience and destroyed the five cities with fire'. The very vice that some 140 years later, the Templars would also be accused of indulging in, with charges of sodomy.

The other threat to the church, discussed at the council, were two stubborn heresies: the Cathars and Waldensians. The latter were believed to have been founded by a French merchant known as Peter Waldo (c.1140-c.1205), who gave up all his worldly goods. Details of his life are disputed, including whether he really founded the movement named after him. In short, Waldo was said to have commissioned a translation of the bible from Latin into Provençal, making him a proto-Protestant – as the Catholic church forbade the bible to be available in any language other than Latin.

Initially, Rome viewed the Waldensians as an ascetic movement in the tradition of the Franciscans, and Pope Alexander even met Waldo. But when they began to reject the authority of bishops, demanding complete poverty in the church, and allowing women to preach, Rome performed a rapid U-turn and declared them heretics. At the 1179 council, Walter Map was asked to go and argue with them one last time in the hope that they might avoid prohibition and mass execution.

However, there was a far worse heresy bubbling up for which dialogue was not even being considered as an option. Across southern France and into Italy, the 'loathsome heresy' of the Cathars was spreading. A dualist and Gnostic movement that rejected the material world and held the wealth of the Roman Catholic church in utter contempt. Like the Waldensians, they allowed women to preach. The council noted that 'they no longer practise their wickedness in secret, as others do, but proclaim their error publicly and draw the simple and weak to join them'. The Cathars became so powerful and influential that in 1209, Pope Innocent III launched a twenty-year crusade against them using military violence to wipe the Cathars out. Knights who killed Cathars were offered the same papal indulgences that excused their slaughtering of Saracens in the Holy Land.

Despite the growing strength of the papacy, or maybe because of it, there was a proliferation of heresies at this time. The Third Lateran Council also mentioned the Brabanters, who Walter Map described as 'a new and particularly noxious sect'. Based in the Holy Roman Empire, they were of mixed social class, armed to the teeth and included women, 'renegade monks', and unemployed mercenaries. Whether they had a coherent theology, or just enjoyed looting churches, is a grey area. It was in this context of growing revolt against church authority, combined with recent failures in the Holy Land, that one can understand why sentiment towards the Templars was changing. The sunny optimism that characterised the turn of the twelfth century was giving way to something much darker in its closing decades.

André de Montbard died in January 1156, severing the last link to the first generation of Knights Templar. He and his nephew, Bernard of Clairvaux, had corresponded over the years, updating each other on the progress of the crusades. At one point, Bernard realised that the distance between them and their respective ages meant they were unlikely to ever meet again. He told his uncle that they should 'mount above the sun, and may our conversation continue in the heavens, there my André will be the fruits of your labours, and there your reward…' Despite the pleas for his uncle to visit Clairvaux one last time, it was never to be.

The sixth grand master was Bertrand de Blanchefort (c.1109–1169). His time at the top hardly got off to an auspicious start when he was taken prisoner by Nur ad-Din after a battle between the Zengid forces and Baldwin III of Jerusalem near Banyas. Also seized was another Templar, Odo of St Amand, who would be a future Templar grand master. De Blanchefort was imprisoned in Aleppo for three years before being released to the Byzantine emperor Manuel I Komnenos as part of peace negotiations with Nur ad-Din.

De Blanchefort is at the centre of one of the most enduring Templar conspiracy theories in modern times: the alleged treasure found in the French village of Rennes-le-Château. It is a theory that underscores the Dan Brown novel *The Da Vinci Code*, and the 1980s bestseller *The Holy Blood and The Holy Grail*. In a nutshell, the previously mentioned Priory of Sion was set up to protect the sacred bloodline of Jesus Christ from the Roman Catholic church, which feared the threat to its power posed by his descendants. It was established in Jerusalem after the First Crusade and based at the Byzantine Hagia Sion, which subsequently housed the Abbey of Our Lady of Mount Zion.

This holy family tree began with a child conceived by Mary Magdalene from her marriage to Jesus. Her descendants were the Merovingian kings of modern France, Germany, and Switzerland. That dynasty was overthrown in the eighth century, but the Priory of Sion has supposedly been striving behind the scenes ever since to reinstate it as an all-powerful, divinely ordained kingdom to rule the world. The Knights Templar were formed by the Priory of Sion as part of that objective.

Subsequent centuries have seen an under-the-radar war waged between the Priory, Freemasons, Templars, and the Roman Catholic church. At the centre of this conflict is the Holy Grail – which is not a cup that held the blood of Christ but the very bloodline of Jesus: the Sang Real. As for the Templars, they are the Grail Knights referred to in the Arthurian legends, but the Grail they guard is a family.

In the nineteenth century, a French village priest – François-Bérenger Saunière – discovered the truth about the Priory of Sion after being sent to run a very peculiarly designed church at Rennes-le-Château. The church was dedicated to Mary Magdalene who, after the crucifixion of her husband, fled to southern France. How and when Christ died has its own cottage industry of theories. Some claim that the crucifixion and resurrection were staged and Jesus in fact survived, fled, and lived to a ripe old age.[40] Or yet another theory has him committing suicide as an elderly zealot rebel at the siege of Masada in 73 CE.[41]

In a short time, Saunière became very rich, leading to speculation that he had discovered treasure of incalculable value. Evidence of his sudden increase in wealth was that between 1898 and 1905, the priest built a large estate including the Rococo-style Villa Bethania and the Tour Magdala with a nearby orangery. *The Holy Blood and The Holy Grail* pointed out that Rennes-le-Château was close to the ancestral home of Bertrand de Blanchefort, the Templar grand master, and so might the long-dead knight have buried Templar treasure brought from Jerusalem somewhere in the vicinity?[42]

Treasure hunters came looking. Rumours abounded that the Nazis, with their obsessive quest for the passion relics of Christ that they imagined would endow them with immense power, had conducted excavations in the area. It was said that the Third Reich's favourite composer, Richard Wagner, visited Rennes-le-Château shortly before composing his opera *Parsifal*, based on the medieval chivalric romance, *Parzival*, authored by the poet and knight, Wolfram von Eschenbach.

In 1891, Saunière carried out renovations in the church and, inside a Visigothic pillar dating back some 1,500 years, discovered four parchments in sealed wooden tubes from the thirteenth and eighteenth centuries. The 1780s parchments were written by a priest, Antoine Bigou, who was the chaplain to the Blanchefort family in the lead-up to the 1789 French Revolution. They appeared to be texts from the New Testament written in Latin, but were worded rather oddly and clearly contained coded messages. This became the subject of a BBC documentary in the 1970s presented by one of the three authors of *The Holy Blood and the Holy Grail*, Henry Lincoln. One parchment referred to the last Merovingian king, Dagobert II, with the cryptic line: 'To Dagobert II, king, and to Sion belongs this treasure and he is there dead.' Another parchment contained a very enigmatic message:

'*Shepherdess, no temptation. That Poussin, Teniers hold the key. Peace 681. By the cross and this horse of God. I complete this daemon of the guardian at noon. Blue apples.*'

Saunière made the discovery of the parchments known to the bishop of Carcassonne who, realising their importance, sent him to Paris straight away. While there, visiting clerics and mixing with society people, he went to the Louvre to acquaint himself with the Poussin painting *The Shepherds of Arcadia*, long believed to include a Templar-related secret message. The priest then returned to Rennes-le-Château and embarked on a bizarre redecoration of his church that featured a representation of the demon Asmodeus who, in Talmudic legends, built the Temple of Solomon. In Kabbalistic circles, Asmodeus was the offspring of King David and the queen of the demons, Agrat bat Mahlat.

On 22 January 1917, Saunière suffered a stroke and died. The huge estate he had built was passed to his long-serving housekeeper Marie Denarnaud. Unable to afford the upkeep after the Second World War, Denarnaud sold the estate to a businessman called Noël Corbu (1912–1968). She promised to confide a secret to Corbu that would make him rich and powerful, but tantalisingly died before she could impart this knowledge.

The author Dan Brown ran with the tale of these hidden parchments, bringing the story of the Priory of Sion back to public prominence with his book *The Da Vinci Code*. The adventure starts with the murder of a curator at the Louvre called Jacques Saunière (same name as the priest who served at Rennes-le-Château), who also happens to be the grand master of the Priory of Sion. His killer is a Catholic monk under the direction of a 'teacher' who wants to use the secret of the Holy Grail to destroy the Vatican. The real meaning of the Holy Grail is the bloodline of Christ, and it leads the book's hero to the sarcophagus of Mary Magdalene, under the Louvre.

From the 1980s, cracks began to appear in this account of the Priory of Sion; the super-rich French village priest; and the treasure hidden by Bertrand de Blanchefort. It emerged that the Priory of Sion had been invented by a rather colourful character, Pierre Athanase Marie Plantard (1920–2000), who launched the Priory of Sion in 1956 as a pressure group campaigning for better local housing. Somehow, this evolved into a top secret, ancient organisation behind the Knights Templar. As for the story about Saunière, this had first been serialised in a local paper by Noël Corbu, who claimed that the priest had chanced upon millions of gold pieces amassed by Blanche of Castille, wife of King Louis VIII of France (1187–1226) to ransom her husband who had been captured in Egypt while on crusade.

Cynics have pointed out that Corbu was a restaurant owner keen to turn Rennes-le-Château into a tourist trap. Treasure hunters would, after all, need lunch and dinner. As for Saunière's sudden enrichment, church disciplinary proceedings from the early twentieth century showed that the priest had been selling masses, which was against church law. Priests are not supposed to profit from prayer. He was eventually stripped of his priesthood and died in poverty. The real source of his fortune had been gullible parishioners who chanced upon his classified newspaper advertisements. As for the parchments he discovered, this came from the fertile imagination of Plantard and his friends, a mixed bag of conspiracy theorists and bored minor aristocrats.

One of his accomplices, Philippe de Chérisey, later admitted that they had placed fake documents in the Bibliothèque Nationale de France to lend more credibility to the Priory of Sion theory. The late Italian author and academic Umberto Eco (1932–2016) was fascinated by the Knights Templar and the fantasy that surrounds them. He satirised people like Plantard and his friends in his book *Foucault's Pendulum* where three publishers develop an entirely truth-free conspiracy theory only to be sucked into a real one.[43] Yet despite the weight of evidence mitigating Bertrand de Blanchefort's treasure being buried at Rennes-le-Château, the myth of the Priory of Sion, and its connection with the village, has endured.

Fatimid Egypt was tottering on the verge of collapse as the 1160s dawned. Taking a keen interest in the political crisis that racked the country were the region's three superpowers: Syria under Nur ad-Din; the Kingdom of Jerusalem; and the Byzantine Empire. Destined to play a key role in the upheaval were the Knights Templar, for whom Egypt would become an ongoing theatre of combat.

Within the Fatimid palace, factional in-fighting drew in external forces. The vizier for most of the 1160s was Shawar ibn Mujir al-Sa'di (died 1169), who allied, at different times, with the crusaders, and then Nur ad-Din, in a desperate bid to retain power. Both the Sunni Muslim Zengids and the Roman Catholic Kingdom of Jerusalem became intimately involved in the Shi'ite Muslim politics of the Fatimids. This led to fighting on Egyptian soil between the crusaders and one of Nur ad-Din's Kurdish generals, known as Shirkuh (died 1169). The ambitious general took his nephew with him on campaign to Egypt, a young man called Sal ad-Din Yusuf ibn Ayyub who would be known to posterity as Saladin, the unifier of Egypt with Syria – and scourge of the crusaders.

In February 1163, King Baldwin III of Jerusalem died suddenly aged 33 in Beirut, with William of Tyre inferring heavily that poison, administered by a local doctor, may have been involved. He was succeeded by his younger brother, Amalric (1136–1174). Under Baldwin, relations with the Byzantines had been improving, and this policy of rapprochement with Constantinople continued under Amalric. The new king's gaze was fixed on Egypt, which he dared to hope could be annexed in its entirety to the Kingdom of Jerusalem.

In 1163, Amalric launched the first of several attempted invasions of Egypt on the pretext that the Fatimids had not paid the tribute that the crusaders were demanding. Faced with an advancing army of crusaders, Templars, and Hospitallers, the Fatimid vizier literally opened the flood gates and unleashed the river Nile at the enemy. The Christian force wisely retreated. Amalric was forced to pause his Egyptian operations the following year as Nur ad-Din scored a devastating victory to the north against both the County of Tripoli and the Principality of Antioch, taking prisoner the leaders of both realms at the Battle of Harim.

Bohemond III of Antioch was released a few months later because Nur ad-Din, according to the Arab chronicler Ali ibn al-Athir, fretted at the thought of the Byzantines seizing his crusader kingdom: 'To have Bohemond as a neighbour I find preferable to being a neighbour of the ruler of Constantinople'. Raymond III of Tripoli, on the other hand, whose father had been killed by the Assassins, was kept in a dungeon for several years – during which time he developed a superb command of the Arabic language. About sixty Templars were killed at the Battle of Harim and it's thought this caused a great deal of anger within the order. They had fought in a disciplined manner while the princes of Antioch and Tripoli had been impetuous, lacking any understanding of the enemy. From now on, the Templars would be more assertive in giving their view of how to proceed on the battlefield.

From 1166 to 1168, Amalric was in Egypt attacking Cairo while the vizier, Shawar, frantically swung like a weathervane, playing Amalric off Shirkuh and vice versa. Amalric's advisers counselled that this was the moment to annex Egypt, leaving the Kingdom of Jerusalem as the most important power in the region, eclipsing Nur ad-Din. This must have been intoxicating for the crusader king. However, opinions were divided on the Frankish side. The Knights Hospitaller, according to William of Tyre, relished the thought of carving a piece of Egypt out for themselves, possibly because they were in dire financial straits and needed to take some territory, and treasure, as a matter of urgency. In contrast, the Knights Templar were more reluctant. Bertrand de Blanchefort had just seen many of his finest knights killed in the north at the hands of Nur ad-Din's forces and was in no mood for any rash adventures. Also, there is a suggestion that growing rivalry between the Hospitallers and Templars meant that whatever the former wanted, the latter would oppose.[44]

In November 1168, so terrified were the Fatimids of an imminent crusader invasion of Cairo that Shawar, the vizier, decided to burn down his own capital city. The ancient district of Fustat, which had been the Muslim capital since the Islamic invasion of Byzantine Egypt in the seventh century CE, was set ablaze. The Arab chronicler Al-Maqrizi (1364–1442) described 20,000 clay pots of inflammable material being placed around Fustat and then ignited. He claimed the inferno raged for fifty-four days. 'In the panic and chaos of the exodus, the fleeing crowd looked like a massive army of ghosts.' The fires spread out of control, accidentally consuming the wooden ships of the Fatimid navy.

This was the last hurrah for Shawar. Once more he had asked the Zengids to come to his assistance and Shirkuh, accompanied by his nephew Saladin, duly obliged. He drove Amalric out but this time, decided not to leave Egypt. Shawar went to his camp with his official retinue to pay his respects to Nur ad-Din's top general, which he had done many times before. Only Shirkuh now instructed his soldiers to cut the vizier down in cold blood. 'The ministers of death ran up to him and carried out the execution which had been ordered: they threw him to the ground, stabbed him with their swords, and cut off his head.'

Shawar's sons fled to the caliph in Cairo begging for their lives. The young caliph said he would spare them on condition they did no secret deals with Shirkuh – but showing they were truly chips off the old block, that is exactly what they attempted to do, and were then executed. Duplicity, it seems, ran in the family – like father, like sons.

Within a couple of months, Shirkuh was dead after over-indulging himself at a banquet. He was immediately succeeded by Saladin, the son of his brother, Najm ad-Din. Described by William of Tyre as 'a man of keen intelligence' who was 'vigorous in war and unusually generous'. He soon faced a joint operation by the Byzantines and the Kingdom of Jerusalem to take the Egyptian port city of Damietta. Rapid action by Saladin halted their advance but ultimately the failure of that expedition came down to mistrust and bickering between the Byzantine commander, Andronikos Kontostephanos (c.1132–1183), and Amalric. The window of opportunity to take Egypt was closing.

Saladin declared that Egypt was once more a part of the Sunni Muslim Abbasid caliphate, which landed well with a Muslim population in the country that was majority Sunni. For 200 years, Egypt had been ruled by a Shi'ite empire that rejected the overlordship of Baghdad. But now, it was back in the caliphal fold.

However, Saladin's seizure of Egypt was not so warmly welcomed in Aleppo where Nur ad-Din had to contend with the fact that the nephew of one of his generals had just become a major power player in the region. How could the Zengid ruler construe that development in any other way than a flagrant challenge to his authority? As for the last Fatimid caliph, he limped on for another two years, nominally in charge, until dying suspiciously young at 21 years of age. The chroniclers had a field day wondering if it had been suicide or murder. One account even had Saladin personally striking him dead with his stick.

There is evidence of growing tension between the Knights Templar and the Kingdom of Jerusalem in the decades after the Second Crusade. Amalric certainly displayed a degree of resentment over his lack of control over their decision making. In 1166, the king hanged twelve Templars on a charge of having surrendered a fortress to Nur ad-Din, believed to be impregnable. Two years later, Bertrand de Blanchefort was telling Amalric to his face that his knights would not be participating in the planned invasion of Egypt. Then in 1172, the Templars were accused of deliberately scuppering peace negotiations between the Kingdom of Jerusalem and the Assassins.

Events in Egypt had not landed well with the Assassins. They were Shi'ites, as were the overthrown Fatimids. What they were witnessing was an extension of Sunni Muslim power from Cairo to Aleppo and Damascus. The very people who had dominated the Assassin hit list since their formation were now taking over the entire Middle East. Only the crusaders were left to resist this unwelcome tide. Diplomatic overtures were made by the Old Man of the Mountain, the Assassin leader Rashid al-Din Sinan (c.1131–1193), to Amalric offering peace on condition that the tribute they were paying to the Knights Templar at their fortress in Tortosa be cancelled. Amalric was amenable.

The chronicler Walter Map claimed the Old Man of the Mountain requested a bible from the Latin patriarch of Jerusalem, which was sent to him along with an interpreter. According to William of Tyre, the Assassin leader was so blown away by the gospels that he rejected Islam, pulled down mosques, and ordered his followers to eat pork and drink wine. He then sent an envoy who William referred to as Boabdelle, but was more likely called Abdullah, to go and meet Amalric and the patriarch in Jerusalem. On arrival he assured his hosts that the Assassins were serious about converting to Christianity and becoming loyal allies – just so long as the financial demands of the Templars could be stopped. Amalric agreed. The party then returned home, believing they were under royal protection on their journey.

However, a one-eyed Templar, Walter de Mesnil, intercepted the Assassins and together with his fellow knights hacked them to pieces. Why? Walter Mapp depicted a military order bent on war and destruction for its own benefit. William of Tyre claimed the Templars did not want to forego their annual tribute from the Assassins of 2,000 bezants. Peace was not in their interests. But as ever with these chroniclers, one must take their version of events with a pinch of salt. Nevertheless, the argument that the Templars sought war when others strove for peace, and vice versa, would become a growing refrain over the next century. It insinuated that the knights were not pursuing the same objectives as everybody else in outremer.

Amalric was incandescent with rage at news of this slaughter. The Old Man of the Mountain immediately broke off all negotiations, so the king rounded on the Templars and demanded they hand over Walter de Mesnil to face justice. Nobody doubted that would involve a tree and a rope. The grand master in 1172 was Odo of St Amand (1110–1180). In his frostiest tone of voice, he pointed out to Amalric that under the terms of the papal bull Omne Datum Optimum, the king's jurisdiction did not cover the order. Odo was not in any way obliged to hand over the errant knight.

That was the final straw for the king. The Templars were behaving like a law unto themselves, which strictly speaking they were, and something had to be done about it. Amalric rode for the city of Sidon where he knew a Templar chapter meeting was in progress presided over by Odo. Barging in, he seized Walter de Mesnil and threw him into a dungeon at Tyre. Having imprisoned the offending Templar, Amalric contacted the Assassins to beg their forgiveness. In 1172, seven years before the Third Lateran Council at which the Templars and Hospitallers had their wings clipped, Amalric was minded to approach Pope Alexander III and demand the Templars be disbanded, so it was a lucky break for the order that he died two years later in 1174.

Both Nur ad-Din and Amalric died in 1174. The death of Nur ad-Din cleared the path for Saladin to eventually take power in both Egypt and Syria. Amalric was succeeded by the 13-year-old Baldwin IV, who was afflicted with leprosy, though managed to reign with great fortitude. However, he was precluded from marrying because of his condition and so there was no heir to the throne. In a world that lacked any sympathy for leprosy, he was at least a little fortunate to be part of the nobility. Any ordinary person with leprosy in England, for example, was subjected to a special mass where a priest officially excluded them from the community with these chilling words:

'I forbid you ever to enter churches, or to go into a market, or a mill, or a bakehouse, or into any assemblies of people. I forbid you ever to wash your hands or even any of your belongings in spring or stream water of any kind: and if you are thirsty, you must drink water from your cup or some other vessel…I forbid you to touch infants or young folk, whosoever they may be, or to give to them or to others any of your possessions. I forbid you henceforth to eat or drink in any company except that of lepers. And know that when you die, you will be buried in your own house, unless it be, be favour obtained, in the church.'[45]

Baldwin's medical condition had been spotted by his childhood tutor, William of Tyre. He described how the 9-year-old child, years before he became king, often played with other boys of noble birth. They would pinch each other with their fingernails on the hands and arms. But while the other children yelped in agony, William noticed that Baldwin 'bore the pain altogether too patiently, as if he did not feel it'. At first, the chronicler thought it was a sign of his endurance but on closer examination, discovered that about half of his right hand and arm were numb. Physicians were consulted and prescribed a range of cures including 'poisonous drugs', but in vain. Tearful, by his own admission, William watched as the boy advanced into his teenage years and began to be more affected. Yet he was 'adept at literary studies', quick to learn to ride horses, and had a tenacious memory. He also loved to talk. Despite everything, he had the makings of a future monarch.

One of his first challenges as king was to address a growing divide between those Franks who were now second or even third generation in outremer and the newcomers who continued to arrive from Europe. Both Christian and Muslim commentators observed the difference in outlook and manners between the two groups. Those who had been in the Middle East longest had the more refined manners and exquisite taste, while the recently arrived Franks were boorish and narrow minded.

An illustration of this was given by the Arab chronicler Usama ibn Mundiqh (1095–1188), who held the Knights Templar in high esteem. Though it was exactly this kind of inter-faith friendship that would contribute to their undoing over a century later. The knights were accused at their trials in the early fourteenth century of being far too close to the Islamic world, for which read – engaged in treasonable activity. Ibn Mundiqh visited the Temple Mount while in crusader-held Jerusalem, and approached what had been the Al-Aqsa Mosque but was now the headquarters of the Templars. He was keen to pray at this holy site and the knights allowed him to use a small chapel just outside.

Hardly had he recited the first line of prayer, when a newcomer accosted him. This bullying Frank spun him round from facing south to east – Mecca to Jerusalem – demanding he pray in the proper (for which read, Christian) direction. To their credit, the Templars intervened and told the Frank to back off – not once but twice. Eventually, the Frankish newcomer, surrounded by well-built Templar knights, apologised profusely, and went away. What this indicates is that Latin Christians in the Holy Land became acclimatised to the many variants of Christianity as well as the presence of Muslims and Jews. In a medieval sense, they accepted diversity.[46]

This division between the Frankish old guard and the newcomers impacted the political scene. Newcomers arrived expecting to grab territory and riches in short order and were angered by the old guard who seemed more concerned with retaining their own lucrative holdings, freezing the newcomers out, while dressing and eating increasingly like easterners, as well as focusing on their diplomatic relations with certain Muslim power brokers. All of this seemed a world away from the stirring rhetoric of priests and bishops in France and England exhorting their flocks to take the cross.

In the first years of Baldwin IV's rule, Raymond III of Tripoli – fresh out of several years in an Aleppo jail – claimed the right to be the king's regent as the closest male relative. But the newcomers were not impressed by Raymond. In 1180, Baldwin's widowed sister Sibylla (c.1159–1190) married Guy de Lusignan (c.1150–1194), who was more of a newcomer – brash and vulgar. The couple persuaded Baldwin that Raymond did not have his interests at heart. William of Tyre, born in outremer, took an instant dislike to Guy, who he felt was keeping Raymond far away from Baldwin so that he could exert maximum influence over him and 'turn the king's infirmities to their own profit'.

In the year 1177, a large force including Knights Templar and Hospitallers marched north from Jerusalem to help Raymond III retake the fortress at Harim. From Egypt, Saladin coolly observed the reduced military manpower in the Kingdom of Jerusalem combined with the dreadful politicking at court. It was surely time to invade. With a 26,000-strong force, Saladin moved northwards through Sinai. The Knights Templar at Gaza, led by Odo of St Amand, braced for a bloody onslaught. But their wily opponent simply bypassed Gaza and headed directly for Ascalon where Baldwin was stationed with just several hundred soldiers. There was only one thing to do. The king resolved to take his chances and move straight towards Saladin. He messaged the Templars at Gaza to join him.

Saladin had every reason to be confident of wiping out Baldwin's kingdom. Not only was it riven with division, but the crusaders were bereft of powerful external allies. Henry II of England was faced with rebellions by his own children and wife – Eleanor of Aquitaine. Her former husband, Louis VII of France, was also in bitter conflict with Henry II. Meanwhile the Byzantine empire had suffered a catastrophic defeat in 1176 at the Battle of Myriocephalon, where the Seljuks finally ended all hope for Constantinople of ever regaining Asia Minor. After that loss, Byzantine influence in the Middle East slowly diminished.

As Saladin progressed towards Jerusalem, he allowed his army to fan out over a large area, pillaging and foraging. A certain complacency took hold. Christian chroniclers described how Baldwin led his troops at speed to intercept the diminished military presence around Saladin. But Muslim chroniclers attributed what the Franks did next to a combative crusader: Raynald of Châtillon (c.1125–1187). A veteran of the siege of Ascalon; a former prince of

Antioch; and a man who once tortured the Latin Christian patriarch of Antioch by tying him up outdoors then covering his body in honey in the expectation he would be stung by furious bees – all because the patriarch refused to lend him some money.

The crusaders caught up with Saladin at a place referred to as Montgisard. Its exact location is disputed but it was somewhere near the town of Ramla, possibly the mound of Al-Safiya. It was Saint Catherine of Alexandria's day – a very popular saint in the Middle Ages. As the crusaders sped towards their target, they carried with them the enormous crucifix-shaped reliquary for the True Cross. This Christian symbol shimmered in the sun. Meanwhile, Saladin's baggage train had become mired in marshy ground when from seemingly nowhere, Raynald of Châtillon, Odo of St Amand, and King Baldwin descended on the Egyptian army.

Speed and precision would be critical, and this is where the Templars displayed the superiority of their tight formation and discipline. Their squadron charged in a box formation tightly packed with lances and swords at the ready. The chronicler Ralph of Diss (c.1120-c.1202) was full of admiration for the impact the Templars had on the Saracens:

'Spurring all together, as one man, they made a charge, turning neither to the left or right. Recognising the battalion in which Saladin commanded many knights, they manfully approached it, immediately penetrated it, incessantly knocked down, scattered, struck, and crushed.'[47]

Saladin's bodyguards melted away along with many of the Egyptian troops. Those who decided to withstand the Templar onslaught were massacred. Supplies and weapons were thrown to the ground as the Saracens took flight back to Egypt. Trekking through the Sinai, the survivors were attacked by Bedouins, contemptuous at their defeat. Others who begged for food or water were slain or handed back to the Franks as captives. For his part, Saladin was reduced to fleeing for his life while sending messages back to Cairo to assure the palace and his subjects that he had survived.

This was an ignominious defeat – and for somebody in Saladin's position, highly dangerous. He was still consolidating his power in Egypt and Syria and any other ruler might have expected to be assassinated in a palace coup after such a humiliation. But Saladin was made of sterner stuff. The memory of defeat at Montgisard could only be blotted out by stunning victories against Baldwin and the Knights Templar. His newly founded Ayyubid dynasty, which had now replaced the Fatimid empire and absorbed Syria, needed to look successful if it was going to endure. Very soon, Saladin would be back.

From 1178, the Knights Templar, under Odo of St Amand, began constructing the imposing fortress of Chastelet at a place known as Jacob's Ford, or Bayt al-Ahzan, between Lake Huleh and the Sea of Galilee. The Templars were experts at frontier defences and recognised this site as being of strategic importance if entry routes into the crusader states were to be blocked to Saladin.

However, Saladin twisted Baldwin's arm by promising not to attack his kingdom if the Templars would desist from their building work at Jacob's Ford. Initially, the king relented, but then Odo of St Amand prevailed on Baldwin that this was not a good idea. Whatever respite might be gained would be more than offset later if Saladin decided to invade. Given his track record, it was reasonable to assume that the Saracen leader was just buying time to muster his resources and resolve other issues, before striking out at the Kingdom of Jerusalem.

William of Tyre presented the Templar activity at Jacob's Ford as a naked land and power grab, but it reflected the way they operated as frontier guards both in the Holy Land and on the Iberian Peninsula. After six months of intense activity, the fortress was still not completed, though by April 1179 it was already taking shape. Saladin's chief counsellor, Al-Qadi Al Fadil (1135–1200), wrote a letter describing the Templar castle:

'The width of the wall surpassed ten cubits; it was built of stones of enormous size of which each block was seven cubits more or less; the number of these dressed stones exceeded 20,000, and each stone put in place and sealed into the masonry did not come out at less than four dinars, and even more. Between the two walls extended a line of massive blocks raised up to the proud summit of the mountains.'

Within the castle, enough provisions had been stocked to withstand a siege lasting several years, according to Al-Fadil, and there was a cistern so large that after the castle fell, the victorious Saracens filled it with a thousand crusader bodies, with room to spare. The eighty knights were well equipped with squires, blacksmiths, and armourers as well as horses. Saladin had made an offer of 60,000 dinars to dismantle the castle, but this was refused. So much for the venal Templars as demonised by William of Tyre and Walter Map. They were not prepared to be bribed into removing their fortification. Unable to take the castle, Saladin ravaged the surrounding countryside, destroying crops needed to feed the Templars and their servants.

At this point in June 1179, the Templars resolved to strike at Saladin's troops to halt their raids. King Baldwin and Odo of St Amand managed to defeat a group of Saracens led by one of Saladin's nephews at Marj Ayun (Marjayoun in modern Lebanon), near the Litani river. But in a subsequent engagement, they were badly defeated, and the Templar grand master was captured along with up to 270 knights. This was an unmitigated disaster for the Templars.[48] Odo disappeared into one of Saladin's prisons and was never seen again, believed to have died some months later. True to form, William of Tyre blamed Odo for his own predicament:

> 'Among our men captured there was Odo of St Amand, the master of the Knights Templars, an evil man, full of pride and arrogance, "in whose nostrils dwelt the spirit of fury". He neither feared God nor had any respect for man. In the opinion of many he was responsible for the aforesaid disaster and the eternal shame; he is said to have died in chains in the squalor of prison in the same year he was captured, mourned by no one.'

With the grand master locked away, Saladin assembled a force so huge that the plain overflowed with troops. Mangonels, stone-throwing machines, were erected to pound the thick walls of Chastelet. While below ground, Saladin's sappers set to work undermining the walls. On 29 August, the castle was stormed with an orgy of killing by the Saracens, who took a huge number of arms and wiped out the garrison. Those who survived were either executed or killed while being marched out of the castle. Al-Fadil claimed that the Templar commander, on losing all hope, 'threw himself into a hole full of fire without fear of the intense heat and from this brazier, he was immediately thrown into another (hell fire in the afterlife)'.

After Montgisard, the Knights Templar felt they had validated their existence. Their discipline on the battlefield had overwhelmed a far superior enemy force and protected King Baldwin. On the back of that success, they had flexed their political muscles, insisting on having a decisive say on the protection of the frontiers and deciding on the future territorial ambition of the crusader kingdoms of outremer. But this had backfired spectacularly, to the malicious glee of the medieval chroniclers who wanted a return to control by church and state. The military orders – especially the Templars – were an unholy aberration. Now, their failures showed God's displeasure as Saladin claimed a great victory. Their castle at Chastelet lay in ruins and their grand master languished in jail. What more evidence was required that they were the devil's work?

Chapter Four

Getting Rich Quick

After the crushing of the Knights Templar in 1307, sheriffs all over England were ordered to make a detailed inventory of Templar assets in every county of the kingdom. The value of their land and property was impressive enough, though not by modern standards. But when it came to movable goods including rich armour, vestments, and expensive trappings, the cupboard was bare. In terms of spare cash, about thirty-six pounds (roughly £25,000 today) was found in various chests at Templar preceptories. Royal officials were soon convinced the Templars had hidden their wealth away from prying eyes. It's a suspicion that has lingered to the present day.[1]

The truth is that the Templars appeared frugal, living in spartan conditions, not because they lacked money but because they furiously channelled their wealth into the war effort in outremer, and other theatres of combat like the Iberian Peninsula. In fact, they were handling huge amounts of money throughout their existence, but it was not for their personal enrichment. Their enemies assumed that senior Templars must have been leading the medieval equivalent of a Rolls Royce lifestyle. But the reality was self-denial. Medieval abbots and bishops might live like kings, but the Templars were governed by their rule book and ethos.

This made them an attractive home for donations and bequests. Donors knew that their money was going to the frontline where it was needed most. The land and treasures they handed over were translated into horses, shields, and lances to defend the holiest sites in Christendom. Some of the donations made were extraordinarily generous. For example, a massive gift to the Templars in the year 1134.

On 8 September 1134, Alfonso I, king of Aragon and Navarre, known as 'The Battler', died. Thirty years before, he took over a feisty mountainous fiefdom determined to push back the frontiers of the Islamic caliphate in central and southern Spain. After seizing the city of Zaragoza in 1118, Alfonso opened the Ebro valley to Christian conquest and Muslim-controlled towns duly fell to his armies one after another. During his reign, the kingdom of Aragon doubled in size, becoming a credible state and a superpower of the eastern Mediterranean. Even though, to the south, great cities like Seville and Córdoba remained part of the caliphate. But momentum was on the side of the crusaders.

Alfonso's death was therefore a grievous loss to the crusades in Iberia – termed the Reconquista. Yet his last will and testament horrified the nobility of Aragon. The dying Alfonso, who had no children, bequeathed his entire kingdom to the Knights Templar, the Knights Hospitaller, and the Order of the Holy Sepulchre. The latter began as a group of church canons looking after the Holy Sepulchre in Jerusalem, but like the Templars and Hospitallers, evolved into a military order. So, in effect, the kingdom was split three ways between these three orders.[2]

However, the Aragonese barons had no intention of honouring the late king's wishes. They dragged his younger brother Ramiro out of a monastery, where he was just about to become a bishop, and married him to Agnes, the duke of Aquitaine's sister without bothering to get permission from the pope. With that formality out of the way, they popped a crown on his head, informing the military orders that their promised inheritance had been cancelled. They had a new king, and he would be ruling every inch of his late father's territory.

While that bequest vanished, other rulers on the Iberian Peninsula showered gifts on the Templars. They realised the potential of the knights as shock troops in the frontline against the Islamic rulers, the 'Moors', ruling to the south. Ramon Berenguer III (1082–1131), count of Barcelona, gave the castle of Grañena to the knights while pledging himself as a brother to the Knights Templar. His barons agreed to the gift. The count's son and heir, Ramon Berenguer IV (c.1114–1162), handed over a string of castles in perpetuity to the Templars and welcomed the decision by the second Templar grand master, Robert de Craon, to expand the order's military activities on the Iberian Peninsula.

Ramon also declared that he would 'not henceforth make peace with the Moors except on your recommendation'. That represented a trend for the Templars, with growing respect for their institutional expertise, becoming military, financial, and political advisers to kings and popes. Rulers like Ramon genuinely valued the insights and knowledge of the knights. They would also turn to the Templars to run state finances as the order developed incredible financial acumen.

From the Templars' 200 years of operation to the present day, commentators have wondered just how the knights got so rich, so quickly. Could it just have been from the farms and estates they owned or was there something they got their hands on in the Holy Land that propelled them to prosperity? Sceptics counter that the supposed wealth was on nothing like the scale imagined. But critics of the order have argued for centuries that their vow of poverty and image of frugality was a sham. So, who is telling the truth?

To get to grips with how the Templars created their wealth, we need to understand their structure. The order was a highly centralised organisation directed from the very top by a grand master, initially based in Jerusalem (until the city was retaken by Saladin in 1187), who had supreme decision-making power. He was selected by a group of senior Templars and held that position for life, sometimes dying in battle. A couple of the grand masters opted to resign but that was unusual. The only person to whom he was ultimately answerable was the pope. He exercised his authority through a kind of inspectorate called the visitors-general, who reviewed performance in the provinces and rooted out any malpractice.

The grand master's right-hand man was the seneschal, who took on many administrative duties and helped oversee the provincial masters running the order's affairs in areas like England, Castile, Aragon, Portugal, France, Lombardy, Hungary, and so on, sometimes referred to as 'tongues' in reference to the majority language in each region. He both deputised for the grand master and acted as a close advisor. His secular equivalent was the head servant or steward in a noble's household, managing the servants and daily tasks.

The marshal was a key figure after the grand master, as he oversaw war preparations, and below him was an under-marshal. Then the draper, who, as the name suggests, had special responsibility for Templar garments and linens. His job was not regarded as trivial. Making sure that the knights dressed and acted strictly in accordance with the rule, established at the Council of Troyes, was seen as crucial to the order retaining its credibility.

Within outremer, the grand master had to take note of the views of the Templar Commanders of Jerusalem, Antioch, and Tripoli who were actively engaged in crusading activity. In Europe, there was a network of provincial masters and grand priors running their respective regions and entirely subordinate to the grand master. In places like Portugal and Castile, the provincial master might be involved in direct combat against a neighbouring Muslim enemy whereas in England, the master was removed from the theatre of combat while in his allotted country.

These provincial masters attended chapter meetings and reported back on their affairs directly to the top. Below them were masters and commanders of individual Templar estates, from England to Hungary, referred to as preceptories or commanderies. These were hives of wealth-creating activity that comprised pasture for grazing, enclosures for animals, fishponds, mills, a buttery, and workshops as well as living quarters and a chapel. Agri-businesses creating the wealth that bought equipment for knights on crusade.

Three ranks of Templars were found in a preceptory: knights, sergeants, and chaplains. Knights were usually from the nobility, wearing the distinctive white mantle and equipped as heavy cavalry. Later, a red cross would be affixed to their mantles. They had three or four horses and a squire. Sergeants were from non-noble families and carried out the daily tasks in the preceptories or commanderies. They wore a black surcoat with a red cross on the front and a black or brown mantle. Many fought alongside the knights in battle, but not all. The chaplains were ordained priests and administered the holy sacraments. Important to note that despite taking monastic-style vows, knights could not act as priests themselves.

An under-appreciated body of men within the Knights Templar were the Turcopoles, local Arab and Turkic recruits who understood Saracen fighting techniques. Western combat style had been developed on very different terrain to the deserts and steppe of the Middle East and central Asia. The European knight was heavily armoured with a lance and sword powering into battle like a one-man tank. In contrast, the Turcopoles understood the more lightly armoured, high-speed approach of the enemy with the ability to fire arrows while on horseback. The Seljuks were this type of warrior and they had overrun the region. The Templars took note.

Turcopoles could carry out reconnaissance, hit-and-run raids, and provide protection in battle to the knights as they formed up for a thunderous charge. The Templars appreciated that riding in the style of a Turcopole was something grasped from the youngest age. It was not something a western knight could learn on a crash course. Regarding their religion, to have been fully integrated into the Templars, it seems most likely that the Turcopoles were Christians – but of the eastern variety. Some may have acknowledged the pope as supreme leader of the faith, for example the Maronites, who can still be found in modern Lebanon, but others would have been loyal to the orthodox patriarchs in the east. Whether any of the Turcopoles were Muslim is a moot question.[3]

There is something of a fog surrounding Templar finances because of the secrecy of the organisation. All those working within a preceptory from knights to chaplains, sergeants to servants, understood that the order's internal affairs were not for public discussion. Much of what we know comes from the inventories that were put together when the order was crushed. These were lists of assets for the king, secular nobility, and the Hospitallers to survey, as they carved up Templar wealth between themselves.

However, we can paint a fairly accurate picture from contemporary records. Take for example the level of Templar wealth in England. In 1137, Queen Matilda (c.1105–1152), wife of King Stephen, donated the manor of Cressing in Essex to the Templars. The magnificent barley barn and wheat barn they built are still standing today. Over the years they added a chapel, hall, brewhouse, dairy, dovecote, bee hives, and a blacksmith's forge, as well as a large range of livestock including peacocks. Cressing was one of the earliest preceptories in England and further bequests followed with King Stephen giving the knights the nearby town of Witham while King John (1166–1216) handed over land at West Bergholt and Newland in 1199 and 1214 respectively.

This resulted in an estate at Cressing and Witham covering 1,400 acres worked by eighty-five people. Not all of them were peasants in the fields. Medieval surnames indicate trades and the names that show up on this estate included farmers, but also a merchant, mason, and thatcher.[4] This evidences the range of activity on Templar properties, extended from pig and sheep rearing to trade and building. Indeed, the Templars rapidly expanded Witham from a dozy ancient settlement to a fully fledged town. They did this to create a market venue that would attract custom from as far afield as the city of London, enabling the Templars to sell more produce and thereby generate more wealth.

While Witham was taken from being a hamlet to a town, Baldock in Hertfordshire was built entirely from scratch. This was, in effect, a Templar new town. There is no mention of it in the Domesday Book (the great survey of England completed by the year 1086), so likely, it was conjured into existence by the knights in the twelfth century. Baldock sprang up on land given to the Templars by Gilbert de Clare (c.1115–1152), who had been made first earl of Hertford by King Stephen. His generous donation in 1148 may not be unrelated to his ill-judged decision the year before to rebel against the king, leading to the seizure of all his castles by the crown.[5] Whatever the earl's motives for his gift to the knights, by the year 1185, the town of Baldock was a bustling centre of commerce and in 1199, it received a market charter.

There is a curious and disputed theory that the Templars gave Baldock its name in reference to the gilded and opulent Islamic city of Baghdad. Baldock being an English corruption of that city's name. In deepest Hertfordshire, therefore, a newly created town's name reminded the Templars of their mission in the east as well as associating Baldock with that rich, distant metropolis. No doubt the knights dreaming that their urban creation would become similarly wealthy. But sceptics counter that it's merely a reference to a bald oak.

England is dotted with references to the Templars in place names. For example, Carnaby Temple in Yorkshire; Temple Balsall in the Midlands; Temple Bruer in Lincolnshire; and Temple Cowley in Oxfordshire. But the extent to which the Templars shaped both urban and rural life, not only in England but across Europe, has only recently been studied in more depth. What records remain paint a picture of an order that was incredibly efficient and made maximum use of the gifts it received.

For example, by 1308, just after the Templars were crushed, their preceptories owned 300,000 sheep producing 29,000 pounds of wool a year, which was half the entire income for England and Wales.[6] They were super-wealthy manorial landlords active in nearly every county, producing huge harvests and managing a vast number of livestock. Most of their rural and urban centres of activity were close to a preceptory. Unlike the imposing abbeys of the Benedictines and Cistercians, dominating the surrounding countryside, the Templar estates more closely resembled the manors of the secular nobility with much more modestly sized buildings. This made them cost efficient and meant more of the wealth created on farms and in markets could be sent off to the Holy Land.

The Templars were very active in the English capital, London. The old city once had a ceremonial entrance that took travellers under a gateway leading from the City of Westminster into the City of London. This entrance was known as Temple Bar given the proximity of a preceptory nearby. The area is still known as Temple and has its own tube (metro) station. It's to the south of where Fleet Street meets the Strand and amid a network of ancient streets, the church built by the Templars is still standing. Although the buildings that once surrounded it have long gone.

As with Baldock, this land in London may have been donated by yet another earl who rebelled against King Stephen, the earl of Essex, Geoffrey de Mandeville (died 1144). He was active during a turbulent period known as The Anarchy (1138–1153) when Stephen was forced to defend his throne against the previous king's daughter, the Empress Matilda (c.1102–1167), who felt she had been usurped. The war between Stephen and Matilda was vicious and at one point, the king nearly lost power after being captured. The English barons struggled to know which side to support, as neither side achieved a decisive victory during the constant violence of those years.

The earl switched sides twice, had his castles seized by Stephen after he regained his freedom, and then became an outlaw. He was killed, shot through with arrows, at Burwell Castle in 1144. Geoffrey died excommunicated from the church because he had raided an abbey. One account has his body being taken in a lead coffin to the Templar preceptory in London where it remained unburied for a while, possibly hanging from the branches of a tree. The knights must have felt obliged to take the body of their disgraced benefactor, suspending his remains in mid-air to reflect the condition of his sinful soul, stranded between heaven and hell. At some point, the church relented, and Geoffrey got a Christian burial. An effigy of the hapless earl can still be seen in eternal repose in the Templar church.

To access the church today, the visitor pushes through a wooden door on Fleet Street and walks down an ancient alley flanked by the offices of barristers. Now sunken beneath the modern street level, one encounters a circular church modelled by the knights on the design of the Holy Sepulchre in Jerusalem, which was replicated in other Templar churches across Europe. This place of worship has suffered ill-considered renovations but worst of all, took a direct hit from a German bomb on the night of 10 May 1941, during the Second World War. The incendiary device landed on its roof, destroying wooden furnishings that post-dated the Templars and splitting the chancel's columns. But incredibly, the walls built by the knights stood firm.

For nearly 200 years, the Templars generated wealth in this corner of London that funded their activity in the Holy Land. Just a year before they were crushed in 1307, there was a complaint from the earl of Lincoln that the knights had diverted water from the river Fleet to their mill to such an extent that boats could no longer navigate this waterway through the city.[7] They were also accused of polluting the river, which did eventually become an open sewer. Today, it's been diverted into an actual sewer underneath Blackfriars Road. But this paints a picture of Templar industriousness that on occasion irked their neighbours.

The knights provoked a degree of anger from the religious orders and parish churches because of the perception that they were diverting money that might have gone to them.[8] Basically, parishes formed around preceptories, and local people increasingly attended mass given by a Templar chaplain in one of their chapels instead of going to the longer-established village church or abbey. An added attraction for the faithful was the Templar ownership of relics, which could be venerated. Some of those saints' bones recently arrived from the Middle East. Something a medieval Catholic simply could not resist.

What has fascinated people for centuries is the extent to which the Knights Templar were involved in medieval high finance and whether it's true that they developed the beginnings of our modern banking system. The usual image of the Templars is of knights in their white mantles emblazoned with red crosses charging into battle against the Muslim foe. But many in the order could be found instead in counting rooms engaged in bookkeeping and accounting, pouring over ledgers, and totting up figures. Managing deposits for wealthy clients. Paying out monies on receipt of a verifiable credit note (a cheque basically). In fact, the Templar involvement in finance was so extensive that in Europe, it sometimes seemed to overshadow their military mission.

The twelfth and thirteenth centuries saw the need for a more complex financial infrastructure in society. The English and French kingdoms were forced to raise vast amounts of money to fight each other, while not always having the means to make repayments any time soon. Soldiers and pilgrims departing for the Holy Land were unwilling to carry their wealth physically with them in chests only to be robbed by brigands on the way. How could they travel light? There seemed to be no obvious answer. Nobles wanted somewhere to deposit their precious metals and jewels, often to raise money on those assets to meet a short-term requirement. Basically, people's financial challenges were getting more complicated, and they yearned for solutions that were flexible and trustworthy.

Enter the Knights Templar. The network of thick-walled, well-guarded preceptories and commanderies turned out to be part of the answer. These buildings were clearly safe places to leave valuables without fear of theft. But there was more to the Templar financial proposition than a well-constructed vault. They developed the internal expertise within the order to manage money in many ways. So much so that in England and France, they were engaged in managing the state's financial affairs, even down to gathering taxes, paying ransoms, securing large loans, etc.

The Templars are most recognised for developing an early form of bank cheque, though the idea was not entirely original and may even have existed at the great medieval fairs, such as the two held at Troyes every year. But the knights added the network of preceptories that functioned like medieval bank branches. So, in practical terms, a noble from Flanders going on crusade could deposit some of his assets in a preceptory in the home country and then on arrival in the Holy Land, make a withdrawal from a preceptory in Jerusalem or Acre. All he had to do was produce a Templar credit note to make the transaction.[9]

The knights also branched out into money lending, which had traditionally been the preserve of Jewish merchants because of the papal prohibition on charging interest. The Templars sidestepped the thorny theological issue of charging interest by levying what the modern financial services sector would term handling fees and management charges. To pay off a loan, the debtor would assign to the Templars the revenues on their holdings until the loan was cleared.

This is evidenced by a loan taken out by Robert II, Count of Artois, who was first cousin of King Philip III of France. The count took out his loan with a Templar called John of Tour, Treasurer of the Paris Temple – a formidable building. This was the order's unmissable headquarters in the French capital, dominating the city skyline and only finally demolished in the nineteenth century. In illuminated books throughout the Middle Ages, depictions of Paris often include the tall edifice with its five conical towers.

To deter unwelcome visitors, the Temple was surrounded by ditches, pits, and water, with drawbridges for access. Absolutely nothing remains today after its demolition was ordered by Napoleon in 1808. After the French revolution, it was briefly used as a prison for King Louis XVI and Marie-Antoinette before they were guillotined in 1793, then becoming a place of pilgrimage for French royalists, hence the decision to flatten it. By that time, it had not been occupied by the Templars for 500 years.

The Paris Temple arranged the loan for the count of Artois against future earnings from his estates. He obviously needed the money badly. This included all 'rents, proceeds, and income' deriving from 'woods, waters, pannage, ovens, mills, pastures, hay, hens, capons, wheat, and whatever else exists'. The count's servants would collect these revenues and pass them on to the Temple treasurer until the loan was completely paid. It was sufficient for the count to make a public declaration and oath using his seal in the year 1281. Neither side doubted that this transaction would be honoured.[10]

The financial acumen of the Templars was so recognised at their height that kings and popes trusted the knights to handle royal and church revenues as well as the payment of large ransoms and other significant amounts. For example, in 1235, King Henry III of England ordered regular payments of 200 pounds sterling from his treasury to the London Temple, which then transferred 800 livres tournois (the French currency) to the Paris Temple, which in turn paid the count of La Marche a sum that had been agreed in a peace treaty between France and England. In exchange for getting his money, the count let England keep the island of Oléron near La Rochelle, which it had invaded. The Templars were therefore an effective way of paying large amounts in very delicate, diplomatic situations given their reach across borders.[11]

So professional and advanced in their thinking for their time were the Templar treasurers in Paris that they effectively ran the state finances of France. They were even asked to collect taxes on behalf of the French king and gather church tithes. Three times a year, the order submitted financial reports to the king, who was then told whether he was in credit or debit to the Templars. However, the condition for wielding this kind of financial power was that the king demanded more oversight over the Templars. This must have created a simmering tension over time and certainly compromised the religious integrity of the order. Were they royal bankers and tax collectors or the pope's warrior monks? Was their loyalty still to Rome or Paris? It is easy to see how this all boiled over in the early fourteenth century when the French king came to feel he had insufficient sway over the knights.

A similar use of the Templars to manage royal accounts happened in England under King Henry III (1207–1272). The king had two pots of money to draw on for spending: the Exchequer and the Wardrobe. The second pot referred to the financing of the royal household as opposed to a piece of furniture for clothes. Unlike the Exchequer, the Wardrobe could be used as the king's personal piggy bank out of reach of the barons. At times, it accounted for more public spending than the Exchequer. This wealth travelled around with the monarch but in 1225, King Henry decided to deposit much of it in the London Temple where it stayed until it was moved to the Tower of London in 1291. The Templars, then, oversaw half the kingdom's budget during the thirteenth century.

Having mastered current accounts, loans and credit, money transfer, and tax collection, the Templars added safe deposits to their financial product range. Plenty of nobles wanted to hide their riches away from prying eyes. But there was always the risk that ill-gotten gains would have to be handed over by the knights to the authorities. Fawkes de Bréauté, for example, was an Anglo-Norman knight who loyally served King John of England in the early thirteenth century and was showered with honours. But his manner of putting down rebels was especially brutal and earned him many enemies, leading to his eventual downfall. In the year 1226, the English and French Temples were ordered to hand over his deposits to pay damages to his victims.

King John, one of the least popular kings of England, deposited the crown jewels with the Templars as he faced a revolt from the barons and an invasion from France. As his reign slipped into chaos, John came to rely on the Templars not just for money but political advice and even a bed for the night. In his last four years, he became a rather forlorn and beleaguered guest at the London Temple. While there he was counselled by the English provincial master, Aimeric de St Maur (died c.1219), who told the monarch to sign the Magna Carta, a document of rights foisted on him by the barons. Aimeric was also an executor to John's will, along with Fawkes de Bréauté.

The crown jewels were eventually withdrawn from the London Temple as the king was forced to go on the run from his enemies. As he fled across the Wash, a tidal estuary in eastern England that included treacherous quicksand and whirlpools, his baggage train fell into the murky water and the jewels disappeared. This included several priceless royal crowns; the great sceptre; ornate swords; luxurious tunics and other embroidered regalia. The loss undoubtedly contributed to the king's death shortly afterwards.

The wars between England and France kept the Templars busy lending money to the English king, which does raise the question of whether the knights always regarded themselves as part of a supra-national order or were they loyal to their respective monarchs? In England, the Templars in London were lending to the king down the road in Westminster. In France, the Templars in Paris were lending to the French monarch. How did that work internally for the knights? The answer seems to be that business was business. Ultimately, the obedience of all Templars was to the grand master and above him, the pope. Whatever dealings they undertook at the provincial level to enrich the order and fund the crusades was reported upwards and approved – or not.

The knights felt able to lend money to monarchs across borders even when two neighbouring kingdoms were at war. When the English king Henry III was ruined in 1242 by his abortive attempt to seize back the province of Gascony (in south-west France), the Paris Temple helped bail him out with a huge loan that year.[12] There seemed to be no issue with Paris being the capital city of Henry's dread enemy, King Louis IX of France. Henry even sent his crown jewels to the Paris Temple who acted like a pawnbroker, giving the king some ready cash in exchange for the regalia of state. The transaction was negotiated by Henry's queen, Eleanor of Provence.

While the Christian monarchs of Europe were united in their support for the crusades in the Holy Land, they nevertheless continued to fight among themselves. This imposed severe pressure on their treasuries. In effect, the Knights Templar offered a solution to the ongoing financial crunch faced by Europe's medieval kings using the fees and charges raised on loans to fund their military activities in outremer. Thereby profiting from trouble at home to do God's work in Jerusalem, Acre, Tripoli, and Antioch in the east.

The late thirteenth century saw the emergence of Italian banking as a potential competitor to the Templar financial services machine. England's King Edward I (1239–1307) made increasing use of this new source of funding. However, he continued to use the services of the knights at the same time. Indeed, monies related to the king, nobles, and clergy shifted around from one group of financiers to another and there was a good reason. The Italian merchants who arrived in London, setting up their money-lending operations, quickly saw the advantage of a working relationship with the knights. The Templars had a form of security that the Italians lacked with a Europe-wide network of thick-walled preceptories guarded by trained knights who were honour bound to be honest in their dealings.

There are indeed examples of the Templars acting as intermediaries, almost heavies, for the Italians. In 1252 an abbot in St Albans, England, recorded that he had borrowed 115 Marks from a foreign merchant, most likely Italian, but was told to repay it at a fixed time to the Templars in London, who would then pass it on. The unarmed abbot was in no position to mess with the knights, acting as agents for the Italians. Fulk Basset (died 1271), the archbishop of Dublin, borrowed money from Florentine lenders and again, payments were made to the London Temple. In effect, the Templars were acting as debt collectors with the added menace of swords, shields, and chain mail at their disposal.

Inevitably, in the murky world of medieval high finance, the Templars did business with some unsavoury characters. The Caursine (or Cahorsin) userers were a widely loathed group of lenders from Italy and France who came to England to collect revenues due to the pope. Their base of operation was the town of Cahors in France, and they were notorious for their strongarm tactics and obscene wealth. The medieval writers Dante Alighieri (c.1265–1321) and Giovanni Boccaccio (1313–1375) both made disparaging remarks about the Caursines in their works. But their unpopularity did not deter the Templars from collaborating with them. They were, after all, papal agents and the pope was the ultimate boss of the Templars. The Caursines trusted the Templars ordering their debtors to make payments directly to the London Temple. However, this must have made the Templars hated in some quarters.

Aside from the Knights Templar and the emerging Italian bankers, Jewish moneylenders were the other major source of finance for those in need of money. However, Jews were in a permanently insecure social position: denied the rights of other citizens; banned from the professional guilds; and prohibited from engaging in most trades. So, they funnelled their talents into a commercial activity barred to Catholics by the church – usury. The earning of interest on a loan was deemed an offence in the eyes of God.

From the first church councils in the fourth century under the Roman Empire, usury was viewed as so sinful that those engaging in it could not be given communion or receive a Christian burial. In 1179, the Third Lateran Council, presided over by Pope Alexander III (c.1100–1181), reconfirmed excommunication as the punishment for moneylenders. Therefore, Catholics were unable to lend money for interest. Jews, however, could make these loans, although the church's position varied from tolerance to capping the rate of interest, but then eventually banned Jews from earning any interest on loans as well.

Medieval kings needed to borrow money, so up until the twelfth century, they protected Jewish moneylenders. But this started to unravel in the late twelfth and thirteenth centuries. Ironically, just at the time that the Knights Templar and Italian merchants were engaging in financial activities that looked suspiciously like usury.[13] Looking back through modern eyes, it's difficult to understand how the Templars could have engaged in every conceivable area of financial services for 200 years without any sanction or penalty, yet Jewish lenders were abused, robbed, exiled, and murdered without consequence.

Before looking at the relationship between the Templars and Jewish communities, we must humanise these medieval moneylenders who were so often demonised and worse. Jews were ostracised by the church as the killers of Christ. Worse, they were subjected to lurid stories, today referred to as blood libel myth. Jews were accused of murdering Christian children to use their blood in secret religious rites. One of the most notorious examples of this libel was the death of a child, William, in Norwich in 1144. His death was unexplained until a monk, Thomas of Monmouth, spread the baseless allegation that the city's Jews had tortured and killed him. Similar tales were told elsewhere with terrible consequences.

The lives of two Jewish moneylenders operating in England are known to us in some detail: Aaron of Lincoln (c.1125–1186) and Licoricia of Winchester (died 1277). They exemplify the success that a minority of Jewish businesspeople experienced in medieval Europe alongside the ever-present threats to their property and person. They also show how both Jewish men and women conducted financial operations, even having access to the royal household in their dealings.

Aaron lived and worked at a time of frantic monastery building. But donations from the Christian faithful were insufficient to cover the costs of a soaring nave, stained glass windows, and accommodation for the monks. The abbots and bishops had to borrow money and Aaron positioned himself as a leading source of finance for the church. Nine abbeys built by the Cistercians between 1140 and 1152 were in debt to him at this death: Rievaulx, Newminster, Kirkstead, Louth Park, Revesby, Rufford, Kirkstall, Roche, and Biddlesden. When the abbot of St Albans decided to revamp his Norman cathedral in the Gothic style, he turned to Aaron for the funds. While Robert de Chesney (died 1166), bishop of Lincoln, pawned the church ornaments to Aaron as he sunk into financial difficulties.

When Aaron died, his estate passed to the king, rivalling the amounts in the Exchequer and Wardrobe. The records showed that Aaron's clients included the king of Scotland, earls of Northampton, Leicester, Arundel, and Chester plus the abbot of Westminser, the prior of the Knights Hospitaller, and the Archbishop of Canterbury who owed money on land in Kent.[14] Many of his debtors were eager to avoid paying back their loan and resorted to antisemitism to achieve this aim. For example, a knight named Roger de Estreby pawned his chain mail to Aaron but then claimed it was miraculously returned to him by angels who urged him to see the king and demand that all Jews be driven from his land.[15]

The king's Exchequer took fifteen years to sort through Aaron's affairs after his death. During this time, in 1190, a noble in York who was in debt to Aaron's estate decided to take matters into his own hands. Richard Malebisse was determined to destroy the records relating to his debt. He believed that an agent of Aaron in York possessed them and incited a mob to attack the city's Jewish community, forcing some to be baptised while murdering others. In this confused atmosphere he hoped to steal the paperwork and torch it. Instead, he provoked a crazed pogrom that came to an appalling denouement as York's Jews took refuge in Clifford's Tower, a round stone keep that can be visited today.

A contemporary chronicler, William of Newburgh, who was an Augustinian canon and native of Yorkshire, described what happened next. His account gives us a bleak insight into the twelfth-century mind. A new king, Richard the Lionheart (1157–1199), had been crowned and he was known for his commitment to the crusades and fight for the cross. So, with Richard on the throne, mobs took to the streets around England believing they could attack Jewish people with impunity. They were fired up by strange visions such as a crucified man, presumably Jesus, who appeared in the sky at the town of Dunstaple. This wave of brutality swept through Lynn, Stamford, and Lincoln, before arriving in York. The city's Jews knew perfectly well what was in store for them at the hands of these rioters and holed up in Clifford's Tower but then found themselves accused of illegally occupying crown property.

Outside the walls, a priest from the Premonstratensian order roused the crowd with a cry of: 'Down with the enemies of Christ!' Meanwhile, the Jewish families within dislodged stones from the battlements and threw them down, with one striking the bigoted priest dead. Siege engines were wheeled up to the walls. It was now very clear that the situation was hopeless for those inside. A Jewish physician, visiting from abroad, turned to the forty or so families around him and delivered a terrible message:

'…if we should fall into the hands of the enemy, we should die according to their pleasure, and amidst their mockery. Therefore, let us willingly and devoutly, with our own hands, render up to Him that life which the Creator gave to us…'[16]

It was a call to commit mass suicide, emulating the example of those who had taken their own lives at the fortress of Masada a thousand years before, rather than be captured by the Roman legions. William of Newburgh makes this comparison explicit, referencing the Romano-Jewish historian Josephus. Men cut the throats of their wives and children and then turned the blade on their own necks. Truly one of the most shameful episodes of English medieval history.

In the wake of this atrocity, Malebisse had some land confiscated as a punishment while the leading nobles of York were fined sixty-six pounds. Incredibly, just four years later, England's Jews were ordered to contribute towards a ransom demand for the release of Richard the Lionheart, who had been taken prisoner by Leopold, Duke of Austria (1157–1194), while returning from the crusades. Jews in London and Lincoln gave generously but York registered nothing as the city's Jews had only recently been wiped out.[17]

Another prominent Jewish moneylender was Licoricia of Winchester, an enterprising woman who took over the family business after being widowed. Her unusual name reflects a fashion in early thirteenth-century England among both Christians and Jews for giving girls exotic names like Saffronia, Preciosa, and Almonda.[18] For Jewish parents it had the bonus of not being a saint's name. Licoricia's home city had once been the English capital and every year, St Giles Fair brought Jewish and Christian traders together, although the Jews had to record their transactions with the authorities. From 1253 onwards, all Jews aged over 7 were required to sew two pieces of yellow felt to their clothing resembling the tablets of stone carried by Moses bearing the Ten Commandments.

Licoricia was at one point imprisoned by Henry III in the Tower of London (a castle whose expansion was paid for, ironically, by Jewish financiers) and only released after a sizeable sum was extorted by the king towards the building of Westminster Abbey. Licoricia decided to overlook this unpleasant episode, developing a profitable relationship with the king. However, on a spring day in 1277, her body was found alongside a servant with multiple stab wounds. Nobody was ever convicted of her murder.

So, what, if anything, was the relationship between the Knights Templar and the Jewish communities across Europe? On the downside, it's recorded that the Templars were ordered to hold money at the London Temple extorted from England's Jews in 1274. This was a very large sum that King Edward I intended to be passed on to his Italian merchant creditors. The money had been taken during one of several repeat raids on Jewish moneylenders by the king through an arbitrary tax the monarch could levy at a whim called the 'tallage'.

A century earlier in 1188, the Saladin tallage was levied by King Henry II of England (1133–1189) after crusader-controlled Jerusalem fell to the armies of the Muslim Ayyubid ruler, Saladin. This royal tithe to fund the crusades was applied across the whole population but at a higher percentage of assets on Jews. The king tasked the Templars with collecting this punitive tithe, which can hardly have endeared them to the country's Jews.[19]

The author at the Templar fortress in Mogadouro, a town in north-east Portugal. (*Author*)

The Palatine Chapel in the Norman palace at Palermo in Sicily shows the fusion of Islamic art in the ceiling and Byzantine mosaics on the walls. (*Author*)

Medieval re-enactors process in the annual Viagem Medieval at Santa Maria da Feira, Portugal. (*Author*)

The author in the ruins of Fountains Abbey in Yorkshire, one of the richest Cistercian abbeys in England before the Protestant Reformation. (*Author*)

Hugh de Payens, first Grand Master of the Knights Templar. (*Public domain*)

Seal of the Knights Templar. (*Public domain*)

The claimed site of the crucifixion of Jesus in the Holy Sepulchre, Jerusalem – venerated by the Templars. (*Author*)

Praying at the Western or "Wailing" Wall in Jerusalem – part of King Herod's second temple. (*Author*)

Temple church in London with the distinctive circular shape mimicking the Holy Sepulchre rotunda in Jerusalem. (*Author*)

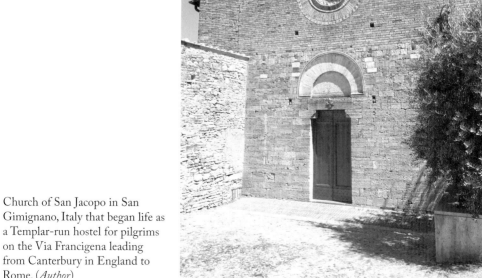

Church of San Jacopo in San Gimignano, Italy that began life as a Templar-run hostel for pilgrims on the Via Francigena leading from Canterbury in England to Rome. (*Author*)

The Hagia Sophia in Istanbul – vandalised by crusaders during the Fourth Crusade. (*Author*)

Byzantine emperor makes donation to the church – mosaic in the Hagia Sophia in Istanbul. (*Author*)

William of Tyre discovers that the future King Baldwin IV has leprosy. (*Public domain*)

The author at the gateway into the Templar fortress at Tomar, Portugal where a bloody battle was fought against the Almohads. (*Author*)

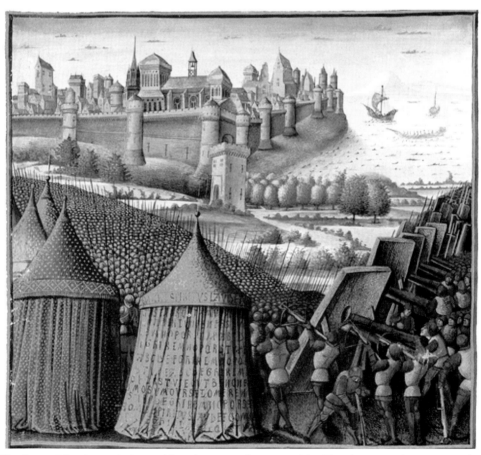

The Siege of Ascalon 1153 from a fifteenth-century depiction of this Templar victory. (*Public domain*)

Third Reich stamp depicting the Wagner opera Parsifal and the Holy Grail. (*Public domain*)

The crypt at Saint Seurin church in Bordeaux dates to the fifth century, with medieval claims it was consecrated by Jesus Christ himself. Bordeaux was the seat of the dukes of Aquitaine. (*Author*)

Nineteenth-century romantic image of
Saladin as invincible hero. (*Public domain*)

Dark passageways under Kerak castle in Jordan, once the stronghold of Raynald of Châtillon – a knight
executed by Saladin. (*Author*)

The remains of Ajlun castle in Jordan, built by the Ayyubids on the site of a Byzantine monastery. (*Author*)

The author at Sainte-Chapelle in Paris, built by King Louis IX of France to house the Crown of Thorns. (*Author*)

Genghis Khan founded the Mongol Empire, an ally and enemy of the crusader states. (*Public domain*)

Klis fortress in Croatia, held by the Knights Templar and stormed by the Mongols. (*Author*)

King Philip IV of France, known as "the Fair", who set out to destroy the Templars. (*Public domain*)

A bizarre but untrue story that Pope Boniface VIII went mad before dying, gnawing off his own hands. (*Public domain*)

French medieval monarchs on the exterior of Notre Dame Cathedral in Paris. (*Author*)

Papal palace at Avignon from where Pope Clement V crushed the Knights Templar. (*Author*)

The Knights Templar were accused of worshipping a demon called Baphomet, portrayed here in a nineteenth-century drawing. (*Public domain*)

Templars burned at the stake in France. (*Public domain*)

The site where Jacques de Molay, the last Templar grand master, was burned at the stake in Paris. (*Author*)

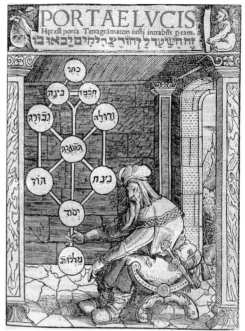

Knights Templar were said to have knowledge of mystical philosophies including the Jewish Kabbalah. (*Public domain*)

Bernard-Raymond Fabré-Palaprat – claimed to be the Templar grand master in the nineteenth century.

Augustin Barruel – anti-masonic Jesuit priest who wrote anti-Templar tracts. (*Public domain*)

Though the Knights Hospitaller must have been held in even greater contempt after their grand prior, Joseph of Chauncy (c.1213–1283), acting as royal treasurer to King Edward I, ordered all Jews to report to the main towns in the English counties to be assessed for yet another tallage, on pain of death. This is an uncomfortable image for us in the modern era given the twentieth-century history of Jews being rounded up during the Nazi Holocaust.

Subsequently, in the 1270s, a scare was whipped up over alleged coin clipping (fraudulent debasement of the currency by literally shaving silver off coins), leading to 269 Jews being executed in London alone. Eventually, the king banned Jews from engaging in usury and then exiled them from England completely. Jews were only invited back to England nearly four centuries later under Oliver Cromwell in 1656.

The Knights Templar may have had a more complex relationship with Jewish communities across Europe than other groups in society who were more prone to antisemitism. Their spiritual mentor, Bernard of Clairvaux, condemned the massacres of Jews that accompanied each surge in crusading activity and called for them to be protected as they were, he said, living symbols of the Passion of Christ. Or put another way, they had been complicit in the killing of Christ but needed to be given the chance to convert. Interestingly, while offering the opportunity for Jews to adopt Christianity, he did not extend the same to Muslims. They were expected to either submit to the cross or die.

There is evidence for Templar tolerance towards the Jews. The city of Tomar in central Portugal once sat on the dividing line between the Christian north and Muslim south on the Iberian Peninsula. It was a buffer zone where control shifted constantly from the cross to the crescent and vice versa. Dangerous badlands where the Templar Knights were expected to hold the line. Even today, Tomar is dominated by its Templar fortress featuring a circular tower modelled on the Holy Sepulchre circled by impressive fortifications. Down below in the valley, by the Nabão river, is a warren of medieval streets in which one can find the oldest synagogue in the country. A large meeting space in an otherwise nondescript house where the faithful once congregated to hear their rabbi preach. One curious feature are the amphorae set into the walls to improve the acoustics.

In Tomar, there seems to have been no friction between the Templars and the Jews who operated side by side. When the papal order went out to destroy the Templars in 1307, a strange thing happened in Tomar. The Portuguese king rebranded the knights as the Order of Christ and allowed them to continue in the city, retaining their fortress. As for the Jews, they prospered even more under the new order with an influx from nearby Spain seeking refuge from the inquisition. Sadly, this was a brief respite from torture and execution. The inquisition eventually arrived in Tomar, turning the synagogue into a prison for local Jewish families and conducting burnings at the stake in the main square. The peaceful cohabitation with the knights was over.

Why would the Knights Templar have enjoyed cordial relations with Jewish people? The simplest explanation is that the Templars were super rich so had none of the big debts with Jewish moneylenders racked up by kings, bishops, princes, and abbots. There was no imperative to attack the Jews and destroy loan records. Quite the contrary. The Templars were also in the financial services business and appreciated good bookkeeping. Like their Jewish counterparts, they too fell victim to unwelcome visits by the king demanding money with menaces. On one occasion, the monarch and his retainers barged their way into the London Temple, smashing open safe deposit boxes and emptying them. Jewish moneylenders would have empathised with the knights over such an incident.

In 1307, King Philip IV of France (1268–1314) dealt the death blow against the Knights Templar. It was obvious that the cash-strapped ruler of France coveted the wealth within the walls of the Paris Temple. What is less appreciated is that before Philip turned his attention to the Templars, he had already shaken down the Jewish communities and the Catholic monasteries. He drew up secret plans with his minsters to strip the Jews of all their wealth and on 22 July 1306, over a year before the Templars were arrested, issued orders to arrest every Jew in France. This eerily foreshadows what he would later mete out to the Templars.

The idea that the Knights Templar became super-wealthy through their smart business practices does not convince everybody. There is a widespread view that the Templars became exceedingly rich because they had discovered sacred artefacts of incalculable value under the Temple Mount in Jerusalem. These included the Ark of the Covenant, Holy Grail, the Spear of Destiny, the Crown of Thorns, the head of John the Baptist, and the shroud in which Jesus was buried. Relics were hugely valued in the medieval period and the Templars got their hands on the very best. Items that had been in direct contact with the Messiah, unearthed at the site of his death and resurrection: Jerusalem.

The Ark of the Covenant and Holy Grail have long provoked the most excitement among Templar conspiracy theorists. The Ark was a biblical weapon of mass destruction taken into battle by the Jewish priests and possessing the power to level cities. At the siege of Jericho, it was paraded around the city walls with the priests sounding their shofars, a ram's horn used for ritual purposes.

On the seventh day of resistance, Jericho's walls tumbled down, unable to resist the power of the Ark, and the Jews duly triumphed.

The Ark was made to be a portable temple containing the tablets of stone bearing the Ten Commandments, the rod of Aaron, and manna from heaven – the bread that fell from the skies sustaining the Jews during their long exodus from Egypt, as recounted in the Old Testament. It was constructed to rigorous specifications outlined by God to Moses with exact measurements and materials to be used. In short, the Ark was a large chest made of acacia wood and covered in gold leaf topped by a solid gold lid with two cherubim, wings outstretched, facing each other. This lid is referred to as the Mercy Seat, or 'kaporet' in Hebrew.

After the Temple of Solomon was built in Jerusalem (usually dated around the mid-tenth century BCE), the Ark was housed in an inner sanctum where God was believed to dwell. A space that came to be known as the Holy of Holies where nobody except the leading priests could enter. However, the Babylonian destruction of this temple in 587 BCE saw the Ark disappear and the original Holy of Holies reduced to rubble. Herod reconstructed the temple on a grander scale without the Ark but after the First Jewish Revolt of 66–70 CE, this opulent structure was also levelled.

So, where exactly had the Holy of Holies been and what had happened to the Ark of the Covenant? Jews, Muslims, and Christians were convinced that the Ark once rested on the sacred stone covered by the Dome of the Rock, known as the Foundation Stone or Noble Rock. Underneath that rocky mass is a man-made cave that Muslims in the medieval period named the Well of Souls (Bir al-Arwah), based on the belief that the dead wait there for Judgment Day. To the Knights Templar, this very space was the Holy of Holies that had once housed the Ark.

The task then was to find the Ark. To do this, the knights would have needed clues or even better: a treasure map. The theory runs that the knights discovered a scroll written by the Essenes, a desert-based religious sect during the Roman period, detailing the location of the Temple treasure in code. They then found the treasure, including the Ark of the Covenant, and became exceedingly rich. A far more exciting explanation of Templar wealth than bookkeeping and bank cheques.

Chapter Five

The Holy Grail, Knights Templar, and King Arthur

Millions of people have watched the 1989 movie *Indiana Jones and the Last Crusade*, in which the main protagonist goes in search of his father, a scholar of the Holy Grail, who has been kidnapped by the Nazis. The movie features the notion of the Knights Templar as keepers of the grail and plays on the Third Reich's obsession with finding it. Towards the end of the movie, chased by Nazis, our hero, Indiana Jones, encounters an ancient Templar knight who has inexplicably lived for centuries. He invites Indiana to choose from several cups, one of which can guarantee eternal life. An evil American businessman working with the Nazis, Walter Donovan, grabs an ornate cup and drinks from it, ageing instantly and crumbling to dust. 'He chose…poorly,' the knight remarks drily. Indiana picks a simple cup – the Holy Grail – and can save his father's life, who had been shot earlier.

The association between the Knights Templar and the Holy Grail has been strong since the Middle Ages. Yet there is no evidence the Templars ever possessed this holy artefact. Let alone that they were grail keepers, directed by God to guard a vessel that once held the blood of his own son, Jesus. So why is it that for most people, there is a link between the grail and the Templars?

The answer lies in the legends surrounding a king who may, or may not, have existed: King Arthur. The most important question is not whether he was a Roman general, or a post-Roman fifth-century CE warlord, but why medieval writers, who told his story, inserted the Templars into the tale. Who were these writers and what motivated them to cast the knights as the protectors of the grail? And furthermore, what exactly is the Holy Grail?

The most common explanation is that the Holy Grail is a cup from which Jesus drank at the Last Supper and that was then used by a man called Joseph of Arimathea to collect blood from the dying Jesus at the crucifixion. The blood of Jesus is hugely symbolic. It is, after all, what he literally shed for the salvation of humanity. Add to that the Roman Catholic belief that in every mass, the Eucharist wine miraculously transforms into the blood of Christ during the sacrament of communion. This is termed the doctrine of transubstantiation but has been rejected by Protestants since the Reformation in the sixteenth century. They see the bread and wine at communion as symbols of the body and blood of Jesus as opposed to the real thing. For Catholics though, there has been a belief for centuries that somewhere out there is a vessel that once indisputably held the blood of Christ. By virtue of that amazing fact, it must possess awesome power.

Joseph of Arimathea, who caught Christ's blood in the Grail cup, is mentioned in all four gospels of the New Testament as a rich man from a town called Arimathea who approached the Roman prefect of Judaea, Pontius Pilate (died c.36 CE), asking for permission to bury the dead Jesus. Normally, crucified criminals (who were typically guilty of sedition and riot) would be left to rot in public as an example to others. But Joseph appears to have been very persuasive. He took down the body, wrapped it in a shroud, placed it in a cut rock tomb and finally rolled a stone across the entrance, thereby enabling the miracle of the resurrection to take place. We learn nothing else about Joseph of Arimathea from the gospels. No mention of him collecting blood in a cup at the crucifixion or its use at the Last Supper. In fact, he comes across as nothing more than a plot device enabling Jesus to return from the dead looking presentable, as opposed to a mouldering corpse with its eyes pecked out by crows.

In medieval England, there were stories that Joseph of Arimathea was a wealthy tin and lead merchant who came as a trader to the British county of Cornwall, where tin had been mined for centuries. On one visit, he was accompanied by the teenage Jesus. They landed at a place, appropriately called Paradise Farm, and made their way to Glastonbury.[1] Later, the two men got down to some lead mining near the town of Priddy, before returning to the Holy Land.[2]

After the execution of Jesus by the Roman authorities, a forlorn Joseph travelled to Gaul accompanied by the apostle Philip, Mary Magdalene, and twenty-two other Christian followers.[3] That included Lazarus, whom Jesus had raised from the dead. He and Mary stayed in Marseilles while Philip and Joseph continued to Burdigala, the modern south-west French city of Bordeaux. There, Philip assigned eleven followers to go with Joseph to England and convert a land only recently invaded by the Romans under the Emperor Claudius: Britannia.

Back in England, Joseph rested his ageing bones at a place still called Wearyall Hill. Angered at what had happened to Jesus, he plunged his staff into the ground whereupon it burst into flower, becoming the eternally blossoming Glastonbury Thorn. This miraculous plant thrived for 1,700 years until the English Civil War. Puritan soldiers fighting for Oliver Cromwell took a more jaundiced view of this superstition and duly chopped the ancient tree down. Joseph had on his person the Holy Grail and, realising his death was near, hid it at Glastonbury while also founding the first Christian church in the world that would develop into a massive abbey, destroyed in the sixteenth century by King Henry VIII during the Protestant Reformation.

So, who associated the Holy Grail with Jesus Christ, Joseph of Arimathea, King Arthur, and the Knights Templar? The source for all this is a group of writers during the crusading period, with noble patrons who had taken the cross and done a tour of duty in outremer. Authors like Chrétien de Troyes (c.1160–1191), Robert de Boron (active in the thirteenth century), and Wolfram von Eschenbach (c.1160/80 – c.1220), who depicted the act of crusading as something sacred. In real life, the behaviour of their patrons did not always live up to the sacred ideal and we see that reflected in the Arthurian romances. The knights are shown to be fallible, treacherous at times, and subject to temptation.

Far from being a quest for the truth about a mythical king called Arthur, these stories reflected the real lives of the patrons of these writers, all of whom were linked to the Templars. Even if the Arthurian legend is completely spurious, the point is that it served a propaganda purpose. The question is not whether the Templars had anything to do with a real King Arthur, but why they were linked to the story. What was this supposed to achieve?[4]

Chrétien de Troyes, as his name suggests, hailed from the capital of the counts of Champagne, a city with great resonance for the Knights Templar. The first Templar grand master, Hugh de Payens, had been the vassal of the first count of Champagne, also called Hugh. Troyes had a large Jewish population and this writer's name suggests he may have been a Jewish convert. It's also been speculated that scenes in his five stories on King Arthur reference Jewish ritual and belief.[5] However, Chrétien's Arthurian romances also contain a shocking antisemitic diatribe, which gives us an unfortunate insight into the times, delivered by one of the knights on Good Friday. It blames the Jews, in highly derogatory terms, for the death of Jesus.

In Chrétien's short life (he died at just over 30 years of age) Henry I and Henry II were the counts. The first Henry joined the second crusade, inspired by Bernard of Clairvaux, while the second Henry reigned as King of Jerusalem from 1192 to 1197, when he accidentally fell from a balcony and was killed.[6] Chrétien served at the court of Henry I's wife, Marie of France, countess of Champagne (1145–1198), who ruled while her husband, and then her son, were absent on crusade. She picked up her political skills from her mother, Eleanor of Aquitaine.

Chrétien dedicated his romance *Lancelot* to Marie while *Perceval* was dedicated to Philip, count of Flanders, whom he later served. That count's life was intertwined with the Templars, as he served extensively in the Holy Land, fighting alongside the knights. He was the cousin of the leper king, Baldwin IV, and was at the siege of Acre in 1191. Philip was a larger-than-life character, to put it mildly. He was a regular feature at tournaments but also renowned for his appalling cruelty. On discovering, for example, that his wife was having an affair with a noble called Walter de Fontaines, he got his revenge by having Walter beaten with clubs, hung upside down in a sewer, and suffocated to death.[7]

Philip combined an outward display of chivalry with all the ultra-violence characteristic of medieval warlords. Even his time spent on crusade featured alcoholic binges and 'the pleasures of the flesh' as well as complaining endlessly that he was homesick.[8] There can be little doubt that Philip gave Chrétien plenty of material to work with in his writing.

In Chrétien's account of the Grail myth, a knight called Perceval encounters the Fisher King who takes him to a castle, run by a bedridden man, where he sees a curious procession that includes a spear dripping blood while a young woman carries the 'graal'. Sadly, for Perceval, the castle and all its occupants disappear as he rides away. He is no wiser about the nature of the Grail because he failed to ask the question: Whom does the Grail serve? Infuriatingly, Chrétien died before completing his fictional account of the Grail. Its description, and purpose, was somewhat vague.

In his *Roman de l'estoire du Graal*, De Boron introduced the idea of the Grail being a sacred vessel drunk from at the Last Supper and then used to collect Christ's blood at the crucifixion. De Boron drew on 'apocryphal' gospels rejected by the church and the writings of others, especially Geoffrey of Monmouth (c.1095-c.1155) and Wace of Jersey (c.1100-c.1174), to construct his tale. He introduced a character called Bron, brother-in-law of Joseph of Arimathea, and known as the Fisher King. It was this person who brought the Grail to Britain for safekeeping. To guard the Grail, Bron founded a line of Grail keepers that would include the Arthurian knight Perceval.

In another work, De Boron wove in the character of Merlin who creates the Round Table, which is clearly intended to evoke the table at the Last Supper. The story then relates the birth and upbringing of the future King Arthur, his drawing of the sword from the rock, proving that he was the true king of Britain. A third book on Perceval has been lost but was used as material by others and it very likely featured Perceval's quest for the Grail and how he came to succeed his grandfather, the Fisher King. But he would be the Grail's last guardian as it disappears at his death along with the Holy Lance (Chrétien's bleeding spear) that pierced the side of Jesus on the cross.

De Boron's patron was Walter of Montbéliard (died 1212). Again, we have a patron heavily involved in the crusades and rubbing shoulders with the Knights Templar. From 1205 to 1210, he was regent of the Kingdom of Cyprus, which had been briefly owned by the Templars before they gave it up. He joined the Fourth Crusade, as part of a Flemish contingent, that sacked the city of Constantinople.

Wolfram von Eschenbach took Chrétien's uncompleted work and ran with it, writing *Parzival*. Wolfram went through several patrons including Hermann I, landgrave of Thuringia, who also went briefly on crusade. His court became a meeting place for German poets, such as Wolfram. He claimed that his version of the Arthurian legend was fed to him by an elusive figure known as Kyot of Provence. This Provençal poet had discovered the truth about the grail in a manuscript he discovered in Toledo, Spain. Kyot was one of thousands of Christian scholars who descended on the libraries of this highly cultured city after it was conquered from the Moors.

Kyot's manuscript revealed that the secret of the Grail could be found in the stars. Armed with this knowledge, he set out to find the secret brotherhood that protected this holy treasure – whatever it was. In the French city of Anjou, he chanced upon the story of Parzival, which he then recounted to Wolfram. The identity of Kyot remains a mystery – he may never have existed at all – but Parzival states that the Grail can be found at Castle Montsalvat, guarded by the 'Templeise'. Etymologists have got very upset about the word Templeise being taken to mean Templars, but it seems more than likely that Wolfram had the holy military orders in mind when he conjured up these Grail keepers. As for his definition of the Grail, it could best be described as a magic crystal in Wolfram's story.

In the centuries that followed, the Knights Templar and the Arthurian knights came to overlap in popular consciousness through the writings of a succession of authors and poets. Who else, after all, could truly guard the Holy Grail other than an order of monastic knights, selflessly devoted to Christ?

Chapter Six

Accusations of Treachery

Jerusalem was under crusader control for just under a century. For about seventy years, the Knights Templar were headquartered on the Temple Mount, the remains of the second Jewish temple built by King Herod over a millennium before. Successive kings and patriarchs of the city allowed them to occupy what had been – and would become again – the Al-Aqsa Mosque. Every feature of the Temple Mount had been rebranded by the crusaders and Catholic religious orders to remove the association with Islam. The Al-Aqsa became the Templum Salomonis (Temple of Solomon) and the Dome of the Rock was renamed the Templum Domini (Temple of the Lord).[1] Though neither of these sites had ever been Christian places of worship.

This veneration of the Temple Mount by the crusaders contrasted with the view of the Byzantines when they ruled Jerusalem before the Islamic conquest. To them, control over the raised platform and its buildings was symbolic of the victory of Christianity over Judaism – Ecclesia over Synagoga. It was even referred to dismissively by Saint Jerome in the fifth century CE as the dungheap of the new Christian Jerusalem. For the Byzantines, the religious focus of the city was fixed on the Holy Sepulchre – the site of the crucifixion and entombment of Jesus. A mighty structure built by the emperor Constantine, the first Christian ruler of the Roman Empire.[2]

However, in crusader-held Jerusalem, the Temple Mount vied for importance as the assumed location of the temple built by King Solomon that once housed the Ark of the Covenant. In 1172, a German monk, Theoderich of Würzburg, went on pilgrimage to the Holy Land and penned a guide to Jerusalem.[3] He described the Temple of Solomon, where the Templars were based, as an oblong-shaped building supported by columns like a church with a great dome. Below it could be found stables 'built by King Solomon himself in the days of old', comprising an endless sequence of arches and vaults that he estimated could accommodate 10,000 horses with their grooms. 'No man could send an arrow from one end of their building to the other, either lengthways or crossways, at one shot with a Balearic bow.' He has been accused of exaggerating, but the space was certainly large.

These stables beneath the Al-Aqsa are where it has been speculated the Templars were digging furiously for ancient treasure. Artefacts often cited include the Holy Grail, head of Saint John the Baptist, the Spear of Destiny, and even the embalmed head of Jesus Christ. The most elusive item of all is the Ark of the Covenant, once in a sacred hall known as the Holy of Holies within the temple built by Solomon. To enter without permission meant certain death. The Ark disappeared after the Babylonian conquest of Jerusalem in 587 BCE, but some have wondered if the Templars discovered its location. The many tunnels and chambers below the Temple Mount, observed since the medieval period, have fuelled the rumours and theories.

If the knights were seeking holy relics of incalculable value in the 1180s, then the clock was ticking. As Saladin's strength grew, the leadership at Jerusalem changed. By the middle of the decade, the leper king Baldwin IV had died, in March 1185, leaving the kingdom to his nephew, Baldwin V (1177–1186), with Raymond III of Tripoli as regent. But the reign of this boy king was brief as he died of unknown causes, though of course the chroniclers whispered – poison. Baldwin's mother Sibylla then took the reins of power alongside her husband, Guy of Lusignan (c.1150–1194). Meanwhile, from 1184, the Templars had a new grand master, Gérard de Ridefort (died 1189), whose name would forever be associated with the oncoming calamity that was about to hit outremer. In contemporary accounts and modern popular culture, De Ridefort comes across as arrogant and vindictive with an obsessive hatred of Raymond III of Tripoli that clouded his judgement.

Up until the rise of Saladin, the crusaders had been able to play off rival Muslim rulers – particularly the Shi'ite Fatimids and Sunni Seljuks, as well as the semi-independent city of Damascus, and the weakened caliph in Baghdad. But the Muslim world was now far more united with Saladin recognised by the caliph, a vital step to being accepted by Muslims across the region. In sharp contrast, the Christian Middle East was mired in political bickering. Raymond in Tripoli was fuming as he was no longer regent of neighbouring Jerusalem. The barons in Jerusalem were annoyed because Sibylla had promised to divorce Guy as a condition of becoming queen but then promptly crowned him king.

At the coronation yet another division among the Franks emerged. There were two keys to the strongbox containing the royal regalia – one held by the grand master of the Knights Templar and the other by the grand master of the

Knights Hospitaller. While De Ridefort backed Guy and Sibylla, the Hospitallers preferred Raymond, and their grand master threw his key out of the palace window. Dutifully, the Templars retrieved it, and the coronation went ahead. But this revealed an increasingly fractious relationship between the two orders.

As if things could not be any worse for the Franks, they had a loose cannon in the form of Raynald of Châtillon (c.1125–1187). Undeniably committed to the crusades and a veteran operator, having been in outremer since the Second Crusade, he had not mellowed one bit. Not for him the diplomatic airs and graces that some crusaders adopted when dealing with their Muslim neighbours. His rudeness and belligerence seemed to be a way of evidencing his intention to remain pure to the crusading ideals formulated by Pope Urban at Clermont and Bernard of Clairvaux. Others might go soft in outremer – consorting with Muslims, Jews, and eastern rite Christians – but not Raynald.

If there was an opportunity to poke the Saracens, Raynald did not hesitate. For example, most Christian princes chose to turn a blind eye to the caravans plying the ancient trade routes that ran through the crusader kingdoms from Egypt to Syria, or simply levied tolls on them as an easy source of revenue. But Raynald developed a track record for stealing Saracen property, even ending up in an Aleppo prison two decades before having plundered deep into Muslim-held territory but been caught red handed. In 1186 he attacked a caravan in which the sister of Saladin was travelling – a crime that was neither forgiven nor forgotten by the Ayyubid ruler.

Raynald, Guy de Lusignan, and Gerard de Ridefort were essentially a pro-war party, up for an aggressive policy towards Saladin. They cast the strategically more subtle Raymond as a traitor, dealing under the table with the Saracens. The fact that Raymond agreed a truce with Saladin to protect his kingdom bolstered that view. Meanwhile, Raymond and Bohemond of Antioch could not accept the upstart newcomer, Guy de Lusignan, as king of Jerusalem, and had no intention of bowing to his assumed authority. This polarisation between the two camps created a fatal fissure in outremer that Saladin was only too willing to exploit.

De Ridefort and the Templars urged Guy to march on Raymond and bring him to heel. However, a crusader noble, Balian of Ibelin (c.1143–1192), the fictionalised main protagonist in Ridley Scott's 2005 movie *Kingdom of Heaven*, prevailed on Guy to turn the heat down and go for some forceful diplomacy face-to-face. The king agreed. Gritting his teeth, De Ridefort rode north for a parley with Raymond. Their initial destination was the Templar castle at La Fève, in what is now northern Israel. At the same time, Raymond had yielded to a demand from the Saracens to allow Saladin's son, Al-Afdal ibn Salah Ad-Din (c.1169–1225), to lead a group of troops on a foray through his territory.

Raymond felt obliged to agree to what in effect was a looting expedition, but he highlighted their presence to his officials, and beyond them his subjects, as a warning to stay indoors.[4]

De Ridefort heard the news and in typical bellicose form, decided to engage the Saracen party in combat. Raymond might tolerate Saracens rampaging through his kingdom, but De Ridefort would not. As they moved north, Balian stopped off at his castle, leaving De Ridefort to continue north with his Templars, the Hospitallers, and Joscius (died 1202), the archbishop of Tyre. On the first of May 1187, the Templars, with the accompanying party from Jerusalem, came upon Saladin's troops at a place referred to as the Springs of Cresson, north of Nazareth. On the Christian side, there were about ninety knights from the Templars and Hospitallers, forty local knights, 300 soldiers, and the two grand masters. They looked down from a hilltop at a Saracen force that the chroniclers numbered at 7,000.

The Hospitaller grand master, Roger de Moulins (died 1187), remonstrated with De Ridefort that launching themselves into this enemy force would be suicidal. The two men rarely agreed on much by this stage. Not only had De Moulins clashed with De Ridefort over the coronation of Guy and Sibylla, but had an appalling relationship with De Ridefort's predecessor, Odo of St Amand. So poisonous in fact that Pope Alexander III forced De Moulins and St Amand into an arbitration process. But this had failed to remove the underlying friction between the two orders.[5] De Ridefort was content to shrug off the objections of De Moulins but then his own marshal, James de Mailly, piped up insisting that they leave the area. Some battles were best avoided.

Far from giving De Ridefort pause for thought, he now doubled down on his determination to sally forth and slay the Saracens. He taunted the marshal for his cowardice saying he was too fond of his pretty blonde head to lose it. A furious De Mailly assured De Ridefort that he would die in battle if required but could not say the same for his boss. This was an unusual example of Templar insubordination. To assert his authority, De Ridefort ordered an advance and the whole party was forced to follow him into the thick of it. In the ensuing bloodbath, the knights were almost wiped out, with De Moulins killed by a lance to the chest and De Mailly also slain. Four survivors, including De Ridefort, sped on horseback from the scene of carnage.

While the Hospitallers looked for a new grand master, the Templars were stuck with De Ridefort. The only benefit that accrued from this insane incident was that Raymond and Guy, now realising the gravity of the situation, patched up their differences. Meanwhile, Saladin's troops headed home joyfully with the heads of Templar knights impaled on their lances. The Ayyubid leader smelt crusader defeat in the wind and mustered a huge army from Egypt, Syria, and Iraq to cross the river Jordan and annihilate the Franks once and for all. Guy responded by gathering troops from all over outremer at Acre to meet the invaders and save Jerusalem. The stakes could not have been any higher.

Saladin now amassed the biggest army he had ever commanded drawn from across his empire, comprising Arabs, Turkomen (of Oghuz Turki origin), and Mamluks. The latter were enslaved mercenaries or freed slaves of diverse ethnic origin from Turkic to Slavic.[6] Armed with a bow, lance, and mace, they could be found near the Saracen leader as well as forming the elite cavalry on the battlefield. Like the crusaders, they wore metal armour. In contrast, the Turkomen were more lightly armoured, with speed and the ability to shoot arrows on horseback being their main strengths. The greatest weakness of the Saracen armies was the absence of large-scale infantry, but its strength lay in greater mobility. The exact opposite could be said of the crusaders, who, it could be argued, failed to adjust their military tactics sufficiently to the landscape of outremer and the operational approach of their enemy.

Guy now gathered his forces at Acre as news arrived that Saladin was besieging Tiberias, a port city on the Sea of Galilee. Every able-bodied Frank was to assemble in the city and take up arms for the defence of outremer. The Templars, now recognised as the backbone of the Frankish defence, also brought funds supplied by King Henry II of England as part of his penance for being complicit in the savage murder of the Archbishop of Canterbury, Thomas Beckett (1118–1170), in his own cathedral. That money was used to not only buy more weapons but also hire additional Turcopoles – the local eastern Christian mercenaries who provided valuable auxiliary muscle. They also fought in a similar manner to the Turkomen, lightly armed and on horseback.

Once more, the True Cross was wheeled out to inspire the troops. Initially, the crusader leadership resolved to remain behind Acre's defences until unexpected news arrived that Raymond of Tripoli's wife and queen, Eschiva of Bures (died 1187), was within the walls of Tiberias. Her husband, meanwhile, having temporarily patched up his differences with Guy, Raynald of Châtillon, and Gerard de Ridefort, was sitting pretty in Acre. A council of war was summoned, chaired by the king, with the Templars and Hospitallers flanking him. Fully aware of his wife's plight, Raymond ungallantly suggested that they should stay put as the weather was very hot and water supplies were insufficient. The council agreed. The first lady of Tripoli would have to endure the siege without any help from her husband.

But during the night, the ever impulsive De Ridefort made a beeline for Guy's tent and exploded, denouncing Raymond as a traitor. Citing the defeat at Cresson – a disaster of his own making – De Ridefort insisted that it had to be avenged by taking Tiberias. Guy gave way. So, on a baking hot July day, the heavily armed crusaders, Templars, and Hospitallers began the march from Acre to Tiberias. Raymond rode at the front while the Templars brought up the rear. All the way, Saladin's soldiers harried the crusaders, firing arrows into their flanks.

Meanwhile, in Tiberias, Eschiva was convinced by now that her husband was not coming to the rescue. The question was whether to stay or flee. In 2017, the Israel Antiquities Authority identified a short tunnel in the city that connected the crusader fortress with the Sea of Galilee.[7] Historians have speculated that Eschiva very likely tried to escape via this underground passageway without Saladin's forces noticing. However, having arrived at the shoreline, she reflected on her dire situation and decided to return, surrendering the fortress to Saladin on 5 July 1187. The Ayyubid ruler allowed her to return to Tripoli, possibly because of the reasonably cordial (or treacherous from Raynald's point of view) relations he had enjoyed with Raymond.

Exhausted by the heat and Saladin's arrows, the Franks decided to strike camp at a place known as the Horns of Hattin, an extinct volcano with two peaks overlooking the plains of Hattin. It soon became clear that the hoped-for source of water had run dry. According to William of Tyre, who saw treason everywhere, five of Raymond's knights deserted, riding to Saladin and saying: 'Sir, what are you waiting for? Go and take the Christians for they are all defeated.' The delighted Saracen prepared for battle.

Realising that his enemy was parched, Saladin decided to make things significantly worse. His soldiers were ordered to set fire to the desert brush, wafting hot smoke across the crusader ranks. This would choke the already thirsty troops and weaken their horses, making conditions intolerable. Balian of Ibelin had a squire, referred to as Ernoul, who wrote a history of the fall of Jerusalem. He described the grim scene faced by the crusaders:

As soon as they were encamped, Saladin ordered all his men to collect brushwood, dry grass, stubble, and anything else with which they could light fires and make barriers which he had made all round the Christians. They soon did this, and the fires burned vigorously and the smoke from the fires was great; and this, together with the heat of the sun above them caused them discomfort and great harm. Saladin had commanded caravans of camels loaded with water from the Sea of Tiberias to be brought up and had water pots placed near the camp. The water pots were then emptied in view of the Christians so that they should have still greater anguish through thirst, and their mounts too. A strange thing happened in the Christian host the day they were encamped at the spring of Saffuriya, for the horses refused to drink the water either at night or in the morning, and because of their thirst they were to fail their masters when they most needed them.[8]

Then Saladin ordered his soldiers to fire arrows through the smoke, killing many Franks who were unable to see their assailants. Guy was now desperate and called out to De Ridefort and Raynald of Châtillon, demanding they advise him on what to do next. Predictably, they insisted he stand and fight. The whole thing started to look distinctly suicidal to Raymond, confirming his worst fears about the pro-war party. What he did next has been characterised as an act of desertion, saving his own skin as defeat loomed. Raymond charged at the Saracens but was soon overwhelmed. He managed to wriggle out of the deadly encirclement with his sons then simply carried on riding off the battlefield towards the city of Tyre.[9]

All day the Templars, Hospitallers, and secular knights fought a confused and hopeless battle with Saladin's forces until defeat was acknowledged. Ernoul detailed how Saladin captured the king, Gerard de Ridefort, Raynald of Châtillon, and a galaxy of crusader nobles. 'So many barons and knights that it would take too long to give the names of all of them.' The bishop of Acre, who had brought the True Cross to the battle, was mortally wounded. Some years later, a Templar knight met Henry, the count of Champagne (King of Jerusalem from 1192 to 1197), and told him that he had managed to bury the True Cross as the Frankish leaders surrendered. Sadly, he was unable to remember exactly where he had put it. With Henry's permission, he spent three nights digging before returning empty handed.

The most famous incident in the aftermath of the battle was when Saladin graciously offered a cup of iced water to Guy – a courtesy to a fellow king. Having taken a sip, Guy passed it to Raynald of Châtillon, which angered Saladin. He had not intended to pass the cup of mercy to this boorish villain. The exchange went as follows, according to eyewitness accounts:

Saladin: Drink, for you will never drink again!

Raynald replied that he would never drink or eat anything offered to him by Saladin anyway.

Saladin: Raynald, if you held me in your prison as I now hold you in mine, what, by your law, would you do to me?

Raynald: So help me God – I would cut off your head.

Saladin: Pig! You are my prisoner, yet you answer me so arrogantly.

At which point, Saladin took a sword and ran Raynald through. His Mamluks then rushed forward and decapitated Raynald. Saladin scooped up some of Raynald's blood and sprinkled it on his head as recognition that he had now taken vengeance for this knight's many slights – not least the attack on his sister, and the caravan in which she had been travelling. The Ayyubid leader had nursed that grievance for long enough – now this execution calmed his rage.

On the crusader side, ordinary soldiers and the Turcopole auxiliaries had been decimated by Saladin's onslaught but hundreds of Templars and Hospitallers survived – but not for long. The Ayyubid leader offered his troops a reward of fifty dinars for every knight from these two orders that they could bring to him. Soon after, 200 knights were paraded before Saladin. While he spared Gerard de Ridefort, Saladin ordered the beheading of all of them. They fought as one on the battlefield – so they would die as one. These knights, in Saladin's view, were as ideologically committed to the crusading ideal as he was to the destruction of outremer. In no time at all, hundreds of Templar heads littered the ground.

The day of reckoning for Jerusalem was now at hand. Cities across the crusader kingdoms fell rapidly to Saladin, who swallowed them into his new Ayyubid empire. Though the cities of Tyre, Tripoli, and Antioch resisted him, as did the fortress of Raynald of Châtillon at Kerak, which had repelled Saladin previously. Guy's queen, Sibylla, was left to defend Jerusalem as her husband was being held captive along with most of the nobility. Balian of Ibelin was allowed to return to the city to retrieve his mother, Maria Komnene (c.1154–1217), second wife of the late king, Amalric. Maria was part of the Byzantine royal family, a grandniece of the emperor Manuel I Komnenos. Balian had to promise not to take up arms against Saladin but on arriving, a fraught Sibylla demanded he take charge of the defences.

Jerusalem was soon under siege with arrows falling like raindrops, 'so that one could not show a finger above the ramparts without being hit', as the chronicler Ralph Coggeshall put it. Hospitals filled up with the wounded and dying while beyond the walls, Saladin circled like a determined predator, seeking a weak point to strike. On occasion, the beleaguered inhabitants dared to imagine he was retreating. But then he would reappear with newly constructed siege engines and ballistas. By the end of September 1187, a section of the wall had been undermined and collapsed. On 2 October, Balian surrendered Jerusalem to Saladin, paying a huge ransom to allow the city's Latin Christians to leave in peace, led by the Templars and Hospitallers.

Then the Ayyubid troops poured in. They tore down the golden cross that had been placed on top of the Dome of the Rock and for two days abused it in the streets. The Al-Aqsa was retaken and sprinkled with rose water to cleanse it after which Muslim prayers were recited. The Holy Sepulchre was permitted to remain in Christian hands, shared by different sects from Armenian to Syrian and Greek. Jerusalem's eastern rite Christians reached a rapid accommodation with Saladin, continuing to worship as before. Over in Constantinople, the Byzantine emperor Isaac II Angelos (1156–1204) sent a letter of congratulation to the Ayyubid ruler, expressing his wish that the city's Christian churches should now revert from the Latin to the Greek rite and with the Latin patriarch gone, the eastern Orthodox patriarch would once more be recognised as the only legitimate leader of Christians in the city. Saladin saw no reason to object and duly enforced the emperor's request.[10]

In Rome, it was reported that Pope Urban III collapsed and died on news of the defeat at Hattin. If he had survived that medical incident, the fall of Jerusalem would undoubtedly have finished him off. On 29 October, his successor – Pope Gregory VIII (1100–1187) – called for a new crusade with the papal bull *Audita Tremendi*. The mood music around this document was more gritty determination than the exuberance of a century before. There were calls for fasting and penitence, with a prevailing sense that God had looked with disfavour on the conduct of the crusader kingdoms and lessons had to be learned for future success. The papal bull began:

> *'When we heard of the severity of the awesome judgment that the hand of God visited on the land of Jerusalem, we and our brothers were disturbed by such a great horror, afflicted by such sorrows, that we scarcely knew what to do or what we should do, save that the psalmist laments and says, "O God, the gentiles have invaded your inheritance, they have sullied your holy temple, they have laid waste Jerusalem; they have left the dead bodies of your saints as meat for the beasts of the earth and food the birds of the air ..."'*

The pope detailed how the Templars had been beheaded in Saladin's presence and so many bishops slaughtered. Only a few places now remained in Christian hands and the church was right to openly mourn such a loss. But there had been sinfulness and the pope had heard 'from every direction of scandals and conflicts between kings and princes, among cities, so that we lament...'. Everybody had to reflect on recent events and purge their souls – but not for too long. Because Pope Gregory was offering 'full remission of their sins and eternal life' to those who would take up the cross once more. There were also economic benefits on the table, with interest on debts abolished for the duration of the crusade and protection of goods from any legal claim.[11]

Three European monarchs took leadership of the Third Crusade: The Holy Roman Emperor Frederick Barbarossa (1122–1190); Richard I of England (1157–1199), known as the Lionheart; and Philip II of France (1165–1223), also referred to as Philip Augustus. Barbarossa was a European elder statesman, in his mid-sixties, when he heeded the call to go on crusade. One of his first acts on announcing that he was leaving for the east was to prohibit any attacks on Germany's Jews on pain of death or mutilation.[12] He viewed the Jews in his realm as his personal serfs to whom he extended royal protection, though this was a double-edged sword. In exchange for increased safety, their movements and rights were heavily restricted, subject to Barbarossa's whims.

On entering Byzantine territory with his army, Barbarossa discovered to his dismay that the empire was openly hostile to the Franks. Isaac II Angelos even calling on Saladin to help him remove this large German force heading towards his capital, Constantinople. Not for Barbarossa a state banquet at the Blachernae palace, as was thrown for the leaders of the Second Crusade. Things had changed.

In those far-off days, the Byzantines had perfected their poker face and plastic smiles when dealing with crusader visitors. But in 1190, the two emperors were at loggerheads. They knew exactly how to needle each other with barbed words. Constantinople wrote to Barbarossa addressing him as the 'King of Germany' – instead of the Holy Roman Emperor. In response, Isaac was called the 'King of the Greeks', or just the King of Constantinople. The Byzantines had long baulked at the Germanic kingdom in central Europe daring to call itself 'Roman', insisting they were the continuation of the imperium of Augustus and Constantine. Though, they were a much-reduced power and Barbarossa rubbed it in, even contemplating an invasion of the Byzantine empire, as did his son and successor, Henry VI.

Barbarossa was in a militarily superior position and forced Isaac to the negotiating table, resulting in the Treaty of Adrianople and safe passage across the Hellespont into Asia Minor. By 10 June, the army had defeated the Seljuk Sultanate of Rûm (the rulers of Asia Minor who were not part of Saladin's new empire) at the Battle of Iconium and were then required to cross the river Saleph (now called the Göksu). Even though he could not swim, the emperor rode in to the fast current and was either swept away or suffered a fatal heart attack, according to different accounts.

In death, Barbarossa was not treated with the dignity he might have expected. His corpse was subjected to a process termed 'excarnation' where the flesh was boiled off while the bones were transported homewards. This made sense in a hot climate. However, there were stories that his skeleton went amiss at one stage, although his flesh does appear to have been interred at Antioch while the bones were eventually entombed at Tyre. Saint Paul's Church in Tarsus (in modern Turkey) received his heart and other organs.[13]

Barbarossa became the focus of many strange legends after his death. One was that Kaiser Rotbart, as he is known in German, sits in a mausoleum deep in the Kyffhäuser mountain in central Germany. His seemingly lifeless body is watched over by a group of knights and ravens, who circle the mountain continuously. But when the ravens cease their flying, this will be the signal for Barbarossa to come back to life, after a thousand years of sleep, and claim back his kingdom. The first Kaiser of a united Germany in the nineteenth century, Wilhelm I (1797–1888), lionised Barbarossa, building the huge Kyffhäuser monument, while Adolf Hitler (1889–1945) titled his disastrous invasion of the Soviet Union – Operation Barbarossa.[14]

The death of the Holy Roman Emperor was an early blow to the Third Crusade. It meant that on the Christian side, the coming war would be dominated by Richard the Lionheart and Philip Augustus. History has tended to depict this crusade as a battle of wills between Richard and Saladin but there were other players involved including the French king, the grand masters of the Knights Templar and Knights Hospitaller as well as the princes of outremer. In July 1190, Richard and Philip met at Vézelay, setting out jointly on crusade. The two then made their way by sea to Tyre, where the bulk of the crusader armies were now holed up following the defeat at Hattin and loss of so many cities including Jerusalem.

Richard eventually set sail from Sicily in the spring of 1191 but in stormy weather, part of his fleet ended up diverting to Cyprus. One of these ships ran aground off Cyprus, which was part of the Byzantine empire, and those on board were arrested by the authorities on making it to shore. Among the passengers was Berengaria of Navarre (c.1165–1230), who was betrothed to Richard and had joined him on crusade. She would eventually become queen of England, though never set foot in the country. Once Richard, who had made it to Rhodes, discovered that his future wife was being held against her will, he sped towards

Cyprus demanding an explanation from the Byzantines. They were in no mood to apologise, being on friendly terms with Saladin, so Richard took Limassol castle where he married Berengaria and then annexed Cyprus.

However, the idea of ruling the place had little appeal, so the English king sold it to the Knights Templar for an eye-watering 100,000 bezants. They in turn endeavoured to recoup their investment through high levels of taxation, which did not endear the knights to the local people. At one point, the knights – who were relatively few – faced a full-scale rebellion by the Byzantine population. One account has the twenty or so Templars begging the mob not to be killed. These events were relayed to the grand master, and it was decided to give Cyprus back to Richard in return for the money they had paid. The English king agreed to the first part of the proposal, and retook Cyprus, but refused to hand back the cash. So, the Templars were left badly out of pocket.

At which point, Guy de Lusignan stepped forward pointing out that he no longer had a kingdom to govern and would rather like to purchase Cyprus. Not only had the city of Jerusalem been taken by Saladin but the barons of outremer had stripped Guy of the nominal kingship and handed it to Conrad of Montferrat (died 1192). Richard cheekily offered the same price to Guy as he had demanded from the Templars. The English king was intent on selling the island twice and doubling his money. Guy spent a month approaching wealthy Franks in the region who stumped up 60,000 bezants, which Guy handed over to Richard. He was given the island but very soon the Lionheart, like a modern bailiff, was knocking on his door demanding the other 40,000. Guy, like so many debtors, pleaded poverty – and the king relented.[15]

Richard received a message from the French king urging him to move on from Cyprus and join him at Acre where Christian forces had been trying to regain the city from Saladin for two years, since 1189. In that year, Gerard de Ridefort finally came to grief. After Hattin, he had been released by Saladin on condition that he hand over a Templar fortress. Having gained his liberty, he did nothing of the sort – instead heading to Tortosa and leading its defence. While in Tyre, Gerard grabbed what was left of the money donated to the order by King Henry II, Richard the Lionheart's father, in penance for killing Thomas Becket. This went down very badly with Conrad de Montferrat, who had been put in charge of Tyre's defences.

Conrad was the match of De Ridefort as a larger-than-life character. While holding Tyre, Saladin paraded his captured father – William V, marquis of Montferrat – before the city walls, threatening to kill him. Unmoved by this spectacle, Conrad aimed a crossbow at his own father declaring that the old man had lived a long enough life. A shocked Saladin moved William out of harm's way, noting that Conrad was 'an unbeliever and very cruel'. Before going on crusade to outremer, he had been in Constantinople where some historians believe he committed a murder and ran off to the Holy Land as a fugitive from justice.

His family had been allied to the Byzantines for a while and during this time, he fought the armies of the Holy Roman Empire, on one occasion taking the archbishop of Mainz prisoner and binding him in fetters until a ransom was paid. Despite his unorthodox behaviour, Conrad was very much part of the European aristocracy and related to most of the royal families. Between 1190 and 1192, he would assume the title of King of Jerusalem, even though the city of that name was no longer under his control.

De Ridefort joined the siege of Acre, which was well underway in October 1189, but was killed. One Christian chronicler claimed he died heroically in the thick of battle, while the Muslim chronicler Al-Athir wrote that Saladin had him beheaded as unfinished work from the aftermath of Hattin. The lesson for the Ayyubid leader being – never trust a Templar. De Ridefort had exemplified the Templar reputation for limitless courage, but he lacked cool calculation in battle conditions. He also dragged the order into the swamp of Jerusalem court politics.

When Richard the Lionheart arrived at Acre in 1191, it was to a scene of immense military activity on both sides. The city was surrounded by armies from every Christian kingdom. Yet despite this encouraging appearance, the long siege had seen outbreaks of disease, food shortages, and battle fatigue.[16] Opposing them was a huge Ayyubid force led by Saladin. Philip Augustus greeted Richard and insisted they get on with attacking Acre. But the English king was ill and wanted to wait for more of his troops to arrive. Peeved by this hesitancy, Philip ordered his army to go on the attack. There was 'a terrific assault, firing stones and missiles without interruption from their ballistas and engines'. However, this provoked a furious response from Acre's Ayyubid defenders who 'made such a tumult with their shouting and the sounding of their trumpets that their yells must have reached the stars…'.

Aside from the shrieks and cries, Saladin unleashed the not-so-secret weapon of the Byzantines: Greek Fire. This was an incendiary mix of pine resin, naphtha, quicklime, sulphur, and other ingredients fired out of tubes and usually directed at enemy ships. Though in this case, it was directed at Philip's beautifully constructed siege engines, reducing them to charred embers. The French monarch was apparently so distraught that he 'fell into a fit of melancholy' and found himself quite unable to even mount a horse in his depressed state. In what starts to look like one-upmanship between the kings, Richard then decided that his illness did not preclude him from being carried within sight of the walls of Acre on a 'silken litter, so that the Saracens might be awed by his presence'. He also wheeled out his state-of-the-art ballista to terrify the city's defenders and offered an escalating number of gold pieces to sappers who could undermine the foundations of the walls, especially the towers.

As the siege wore on, intervals between fighting saw a degree of fraternising between the two sides. Scenes reminiscent of the Christmas Truce of 1914 during the First World War when British and German troops played football matches. At the officer level, emirs defending Acre invited knights of high rank to banquets, according to the Muslim chroniclers.[17] Baha ad-Din ibn Shaddad (1145–1234), a biographer of Saladin, described a game between children from both sides of the conflict:

> 'One day, the men of the two camps, tired of fighting, decided to organise a battle between children. Two boys came out of the city to match themselves against two young infidels. In the heat of the struggle, one of the Muslim boys leapt upon his rival, threw him to the ground, and seized him by the throat. When they saw that he was threatening to kill him, the Franj approached and said: 'Stop! He has become your prisoner, forsooth, and we shall buy him back from you.' The boy took two dinars and let the other go.'

Saladin consulted his advisers and decided to withdraw from Acre. Richard bargained hard on the surrender terms with an agreement that the defenders would leave without any weapons or food and that Saladin would release 2,000 'noble Christians' and five-hundred lesser captives being held throughout his domains. He was also told to hand back the True Cross. As the surrender proceeded, Richard became convinced that Saladin was not honouring the terms of the deal, especially regarding the ransom amounts to be paid in exchange for Ayyubid prisoners. In an act that we find chilling today, the English king ordered the slaughter of about up to three-thousand Muslim captives from Acre.[18,19]

It is hard to imagine the scene as this mass execution was carried out and historians have been divided for years over the reasons. Was it revenge for the execution of the Templars and Hospitallers at Hattin or did Richard simply have no intention of letting the prisoners go? Under normal circumstances, if Saladin had not paid the ransom, these prisoners might have been sold into slavery or force marched to a chosen destination. As it was, Saladin prevaricated repeatedly and something inside the Lionheart snapped.

After consulting with his council of war, the executions commenced, verified by chroniclers from both sides. Baha ad-Din wrote that the victims were roped together and then set upon by a large body of men with daggers and swords. One Christian chronicler claimed the number executed was 16,000 (almost certainly a wild exaggeration) and they were beheaded in front of the walls of Acre so that Saladin could witness the gruesome scene and fear what might happen to him.[20] In our time, this would be classified as a war crime and Richard would have faced the International Criminal Court at The Hague.

Philip Augustus had seen enough crusading and on the pretext that Acre was now restored to Christian control, as well as suffering from an unspecified illness, he announced his departure. Richard approached Philip as he prepared to exit seeking assurances that while the Lionheart remained on crusade, the French would not invade his European territories such as Normandy. Through gritted teeth, Philip agreed. However, he would not stick to this promise. The increasingly fractious relations between these two monarchs contrasted with their younger days when Richard, as a mere prince, before he became king, enjoyed a very close relationship with the French monarch. They shared meals and slept at a proximity that the chronicler Roger de Hoveden (died 1202) felt was worthy of note:

> 'Richard, Duke of Aquitaine, the son of the king of England, remained with Philip, the King of France, who so honored him for so long that they ate every day at the same table and from the same dish, and at night their beds did not separate them. And the king of France loved him as his own soul; and they loved each other so much that the king of England was absolutely astonished and the passionate love between them and marveled at it.'

The nature of the relationship between Richard and Philip excites more passion among historians than they may have experienced between themselves. But it does seem to have been remarkably close, followed by a long thaw and freezing winter of growing animosity. Anybody who has witnessed a couple moving towards divorce will find it a familiar scenario.[21]

The crusaders now moved south along the coast heading for Jaffa, the port where pilgrims usually disembarked. Taking Jaffa would afford a great base of operations for an attack on Jerusalem. The Knights Templar, riding alongside the English king, were now led by the eleventh grand master, Robert de Sablé.

Like Richard, he was an Angevin – from a noble family in Anjou. His ancestral home was part of the domains of the Angevin kings that encompassed cities in modern France like Chinon, Nantes and Caen, extending northwards to include London, Chester and York then jumping the Irish Sea with recently conquered Dublin. Richard is referred to as the King of England but in fact he also governed half of modern France and an eastern chunk of Ireland, together forming the Angevin Empire. A patchwork of counties and duchies extending from the Pyrenees (after acquiring Aquitaine through his marriage to Queen Eleanor) up to the Scottish border. Richard's ancestral roots were in Anjou and notoriously, the 'English' king spent only a small fraction of his reign in England.

How had he come to rule England then? It was all due to the marriage of Geoffrey Plantagenet, count of Anjou (1113–1151), to the Empress Matilda (c.1102–1167), daughter of King Henry I of England, that their son was able to claim the English throne, becoming Henry II and beginning 300 years of Plantagenet rule. Though it took a civil war in England, known as The Anarchy, fought from 1138 to 1153, for Henry to inherit the throne after the death of King Stephen (1096–1154). Richard the Lionheart was the son of Henry II and grandson of Geoffrey Plantagenet.

It's very likely that Robert de Sablé was Richard's preferred choice for Templar grand master because of their shared Angevin connections, even though he was not a member of the order when Gerard de Ridefort was killed. It was during the lengthy deliberations among the Templar leadership over who should be the next grand master that he joined and experienced a very rapid rise. After the chaos of the De Ridefort years, they wanted the right man for the job. De Sablé was related to other top Templars and had seen service in the Reconquista in Portugal when in 1190 he had to rein in a group of rogue crusaders who had gone rampaging through Lisbon attacking the city's Jews and Muslims. He was essentially a safe pair of hands.

As Richard the Lionheart, Robert de Sablé, and the crusader force marched along the coastline, they were being shadowed by Saladin's forces. It was an army that was hard to miss or ignore. A long, lumbering chain of heavily armoured crusaders marching in the heat. Despite the ignominy of Hattin and the loss of Jerusalem, the Templars and Hospitallers were increasingly viewed as the backbone of the crusader army. Secular knights came and went with the seasons, while the flow of recruits from Europe was unpredictable. But the Templars were present all year round. In addition, their reputation for discipline and strategic insight on the battlefield was as strong as ever, despite the best efforts of De Ridefort to undermine it.

As they advanced, the Templars were on the right flank with Guy of Lusignan while Richard the Lionheart's troops made up the centre with the Hospitallers bringing up the rear. There were estimated to be about 1,200 knights while the infantry numbered about 10,000. They followed a line of coastal towns still under crusader control while most of the inland area of what had been the Kingdom of Jerusalem was now in Ayyubid hands. Peace overtures were still being made between Richard and Saladin but after the massacre of captives at Acre, this was going nowhere. As they got closer to Jaffa, the Saracens chose to engage the crusaders at a place known as Arsuf. Saladin decided to focus his initial attacks on the Hospitallers in the hope of goading them into an ill-advised charge. The tactic had the desired effect with the Hospitaller grand master, Garnier of Nablus (1147–1192), begging Richard for permission to charge:

> *'My lord the king, we are violently pressed by the enemy, and are in danger of eternal infamy, as if we did not dare to return their blows; we are each of us losing our horses one after another, and why should we bear with them any further?'*

Richard urged patience but Garnier and another knight, Baldwin de Carreo, buckled under the pressure and made for the Saracens. The rest of the Hospitallers followed and at that point, Richard was forced to join in. Fortunately, the Saracens were taken aback by the sudden onslaught. Whereas the Hospitallers had shown indiscipline, the Templars evidenced their tight control and devastating impact on the battlefield. Bearing down on the enemy, they forced Saladin's soldiers to scatter. This victory and the taking of Acre served to erase the shame of Hattin.[22]

Richard wanted Guy to resume the title of King of Jerusalem while Philip of France sided with those barons in outremer who preferred Conrad of Montferrat. They had never come round to the idea of Guy being a legitimate monarch and events under his brief rule had borne out their worst fears. As a compensation prize, Richard sold Cyprus to Guy, but he still thought that Conrad should move aside for the former ruler of the city. However, Conrad was already planning his coronation at Tyre alongside his intended queen, Isabella (1172–1205), the daughter of King Amalric. Then something rather unexpected happened.

Rather unwisely, Conrad seized an Assassin-owned ship and requisitioned its goods to help fund the defence of Tyre. The Old Man of the Mountain got a message to Conrad informing him that if his property was not returned, he would fall victim to one of his trained fanatics. Conrad chose to ignore the warning. This was not a good move. Two assassins were duly dispatched. Posing as Christian Franks, they wormed their way into the entourages of both Conrad and Balian of Ibelin who, along with his wife, Maria Komnene, was living in Tyre.

One day, Isabella went to the baths and Conrad waited for her return. These bathing and washing facilities were more common in the east than in Europe – a legacy of Byzantine and Islamic rule. Realising his wife would not be back soon, Conrad decided to get something to eat. Famished, he rode off with two knights to dine with the bishop of Beauvais. But on arrival, the bishop announced that he had already enjoyed a meal, so a disgruntled Conrad rode back home. As he passed along a narrow street, the two undercover Assassins greeted him and one of them handed Conrad a letter. As he bent down from his horse to receive it, the killer slipped his dagger between his victim's ribs. The other Assassin then joined in, and Conrad was assassinated.

Almost immediately, Richard the Lionheart was accused of having plotted with the Old Man of the Mountain to murder Conrad and so clear a path for Guy to resume the kingship of Jerusalem. Furthermore, it was whispered, Richard was even sending Assassins to France to kill King Philip. No matter how far-fetched this might seem, the French king reportedly doubled his personal guard. Other wagging tongues pointed to Guy as the culprit. Alternatively, it cannot be ruled out that the Assassins were framed by partisan chroniclers for a murder plotted and carried out solely by Frankish hands. They were convenient scapegoats.[23]

Conrad was barely cold when Richard prevailed on his pregnant widow to marry Henry, the count of Champagne. Ernoul claimed the count was a bit squeamish about marrying a woman bearing Conrad's child. But the Lionheart breezily dismissed this concern, promising that Henry would end up ruling not only the city of Jerusalem but also the Byzantine Empire and Cyprus, as Guy had failed to cough up the outstanding 40,000 bezants. Henry found this very persuasive and married Isabella, with the barons of outremer pledging to acknowledge their children as future monarchs of Jerusalem.

Having won the day at Arsuf, the crusaders took Jaffa as a base to reconquer Jerusalem. But Richard, worn down by illness, was seeking an exit strategy from outremer. He wanted to head back home. News from Europe confirmed his worst fears about Philip Augustus and his own brother, John (1166–1216) – the future King John of England who would prove to be one of the worst monarchs ever, being forced in 1215, by his own barons, to sign the Magna Carta, a document restricting his legal powers. To leave on the best terms, Richard needed some kind of peace treaty with Saladin recognising the new borders between the Frankish and Ayyubid realms. But Saladin persisted in attacking Jaffa, which he had no intention of allowing Richard to retain.

Over the winter of 1191 to 1192, the crusaders had taken back Ascalon and refortified it. By the spring, Richard returned to Acre gathering his forces for the journey back to his Angevin empire in France and England. But then letters began to arrive from the garrison at Jaffa announcing that Saladin's forces had broken through the outer walls and were poised to take the citadel. Help was needed urgently. Richard consulted with his advisers who uniformly agreed that Jaffa could not be allowed to fall. The knights rode by land towards the beleaguered city while Richard decided to surprise Saladin, arriving by sea.

Richard left Acre while Vespers was being sung – the evening prayers – and arrived at Jaffa the next morning. As he approached the besieged city, great cries of jubilation could be heard. The English king asked a local man what was going on. He informed Richard that Saladin had won and Christians were being rounded up as captives. The Lionheart 'armed himself with his hauberk, hung his shield at his neck and took a Danish axe in his hand'. He then jumped into the sea, climbed up to the castle, and ensured not a single Frank was taken prisoner. 'Thus did the king keep his oath'.

Jaffa and Ascalon were back in crusader hands with Gaza once more run by the Knights Templar. Saladin was faced by rumours of internal plotting while Richard needed to deal with King Philip of France's incursions into his realms. The Third Crusade had consolidated the much-reduced area ruled by the Franks, ensuring they would remain in outremer for another century. Jerusalem remained out of reach, though pilgrims were assured safe passage to the Holy Sepulchre and other biblical sites. The reputation of Saladin was cemented in Europe as a worthy leader who defended the interests of his people with utmost courage. What a shame, many Franks pondered, there were not more Saladins on the Christian side. While in the Muslim world, Richard became a bogeyman. It was said that when a horse took fright for no reason, the rider would exclaim: 'Do you think the King of England is in that bush?'

In October 1192, Richard left for England. He asked the Templar grand master, Robert de Sablé, to give him ten of his knights and four brother sergeants to be his bodyguards as he feared being taken captive by agents working for Philip Augustus. This was to be done in complete secrecy. Richard specified exactly which Templars he wanted by name, and they sneaked onto the ships and galleys unnoticed. So paranoid was the king that during the voyage by sea, he transferred repeatedly from one ship to another. However, according to the chronicler Ernol, there was a spy reporting back all his moves.

Due to bad weather, his ship was forced to dock at Corfu, then in Byzantine hands, where the king disguised himself as a Templar. He then set sail again only to be shipwrecked at Aquileia, an ancient Italian city at the top of the Adriatic. Continuing overland towards Vienna, the spy in Richard's entourage gave his location away to Leopold V, Duke of Austria (1157–1194), who took him hostage, imprisoning the king at his castle in Dürnstein. Apparently, Richard had been apprehended disguised as a kitchen scullion turning capons over a fire – rather a demeaning ruse for the Lionheart. The spy identified him telling the duke's soldiers: 'See, here is the king. Seize him.'

Why did the duke despise Richard? Ernoul wrote that Leopold had been thrown out of his lodgings in Acre to make way for Richard and had never recovered from this grievous slight. But there was also the killing of Conrad of Montferrat. Leopold was a cousin of Conrad, so took this personally. The murder had become the subject of chatter across Europe. It was a medieval whodunnit that got tongues wagging, with Richard and Guy as the main suspects. Few believed the Assassins had acted on their own. This was a view shared by the Holy Roman Emperor, Henry VI (1165–1197), another cousin of Conrad, who demanded that Richard be transferred to one of his castles. As Europe's most powerful ruler, he got his way.

Henry had a gift for extorting vast amounts of money from other kingdoms. He forced the Byzantine emperor Alexios III Angelos (1195–1211) to pay a tribute of 1,600 pounds of gold, which was raised by a special tax on Byzantine subjects known as the Alamanikon, or German tax, in return for which he promised not to invade Constantinople. Now he demanded from England a ransom of 200,000 silver marks for Richard's release. The collection of this money meant using similar tactics to the levying of the Saladin Tithe of 1188 that funded attempts to recapture Jerusalem.[24] The hefty tax to free Richard was gathered by priests and bishops the length of the country, backed up by the muscle of the Knights Templar and Knights Hospitaller. 'Allegedly there was not a single chalice or censer left in any church in England as they were all taken as part of the ransom.' The Holy Roman Emperor's demand was met, and the king was released.

Richard was crowned king of England a second time at Winchester on 11 March 1194 before leaving for France to reclaim those lands in his empire taken by Philip while he was held hostage. In March 1199, he was besieging the castle at Châlus in western France when a crossbow bolt hit his shoulder. Initially regarded as a minor injury, it became infected, and gangrene took hold. The crossbowman, a boy, was captured and Richard forgave him. But on the king's death, the child was flayed alive. Richard's rival, Saladin, had succumbed to a fever six years before in 1193 and was buried in Damascus. The two giants of the Third Crusade were dead.

Robert de Sablé died in September 1193 and the next grand master was Gilbert Horal, from the Kingdom of Aragon and therefore a knight steeped in the

Reconquista. Like many who rose to the top, he was first a provincial grand master in the provinces of Provence and Aragon, then became grand preceptor of France, before being chosen for the top role. His elevation shows that despite the strong French roots of the Templars – especially from the Champagne region – it was an order operating throughout Christendom. During his tenure between 1193 and 1200, Pope Celestine III (c.1106–1198) extended yet more privileges to the knights.

At the end of the twelfth century, the crusading ideal originally outlined by Pope Urban II was subverted into three crusades directed not at the Muslim world – but other Christians. First, there was the Fourth Crusade ending with the disgraceful scene of Latin crusaders breaking through the walls of Constantinople; burning a large part of the city to the ground; and desecrating the Hagia Sophia, the most magnificent Christian place of worship in the world. Second, there was a crusade launched by Rome against the Cathars in southern France, whose version of Christianity was anathema to the papacy with its rejection of the sacraments and the authority of the church. Third, the Teutonic knights were unleashed against the orthodox Christians of Russia. All this happening as the power of the popes reached its high point under Innocent III (1161–1216).

In 1198, Pope Innocent launched the Fourth Crusade that should have been bound for the Holy Land but would end up in the Byzantine capital. This war would reveal the basest motives of many of those leading crusaders who had taken the cross.

Innocent needed an equivalent of Bernard of Clairvaux to rouse the masses to join the Fourth Crusade. His choice was an eloquent French priest, Fulk of Neuilly (died 1201). This silver-tongued moralist once chided Richard the Lionheart for having three imaginary daughters – Superbia, Luxuria, and Cupiditas (pride, avarice, and lust). The king, Fulk declared, would never receive the grace of God so long as they were by his side. In the medieval equivalent of a 'mic drop' moment, Richard sarcastically replied that he would marry them off to the Knights Templar, the Cistercians, and the prelates of the church.[25]

Boniface of Montferrat (c.1150–1207), brother of Conrad allegedly murdered by the Assassins, ended up taking the leadership of the crusade. He was related through his late brother's wife to the Byzantine court as well as being well-connected to the Franks of outremer. Years before, he had entertained the idea of diverting the next crusade to Constantinople to interfere in its habitual dynastic chaos, but the pope had slapped him down. Now he would get this wish.

The Venetians agreed to bankroll the new crusade, which was why it started in Venice, but there were early indications that the crusaders might not be able to pay back the huge loans. The Doge (ruler) of Venice, Enrico Dandolo

(1107–1205), already in his nineties, used this financial leverage to strongarm the crusaders into attacking the Hungarian-ruled, and Christian, city of Zadar (in modern Croatia). This was an early indication that the Fourth Crusade was going to be blown badly off course. The official aim had been to head for Egypt, now the centre of Muslim power in the Levant, but the operation was repeatedly side-lined in favour of getting involved in the affairs of Christian states.

Both Boniface and Dandolo took a keen interest in the turbulent political situation in Constantinople that seemed to echo the end times of the Fatimid caliphate years before. For Dandolo, the wealth still in that city gave him hope of getting his loans repaid as well as removing a regional maritime trading rival. This culminated in a siege of the Byzantine capital followed by its capture, an orgy of violence, and the incineration of much of the ancient metropolis. In Venice today, it's still possible to see the Horses of Saint Mark and a porphyry sculpture of four Roman emperors from 300 CE looted from Constantinople during the Fourth Crusade.

Even the city's main place of worship was not spared. The sacking of the Hagia Sophia was a low point for Roman Catholic Europe. The church dated back to the early Christian Roman Empire of the fourth century, but it was the sixth-century Byzantine emperor Justinian (482–565 CE) who built the bulk of what can still be seen and visited today. The exterior was originally clad in white marble, which has long been stripped away, while the interior was a glorious mix of polychrome marbles, porphyry, and shimmering gold mosaics. It had suffered during the iconoclast policies of past emperors who had banned icons and statues, plus the ravages of earthquakes. But it was still impressive enough for a visitor from the Kievan Rus to exclaim on entering that he wondered whether he was now 'in heaven or on earth'.[26]

However, all the crusaders saw within was treasure to loot. Some made a beeline for the ornate central altar, which was 'broken into bits and distributed among the soldiers, as was all the other sacred wealth of so great and infinite splendour'. Mules and saddled horses were brought into the Hagia Sophia, their hooves slipping on the marble beneath, so that the ill-gotten gains could be loaded up more easily. While all this was going on, 'a certain harlot, a sharer in their guilt, a minister of the furies, a servant of the demons, a worker of incantations and poisonings, insulting Christ, sat in the patriarch's seat, singing an obscene song and dancing frequently'. This crowning of a prostitute as leader of the eastern church scarred the consciousness of Greek rite Christians for centuries.[27]

It's normally assumed that the Knights Templar played little to no role in the sack of Constantinople. Their duties lay in the Holy Land and Iberian Peninsula, pushing back the boundaries of Islam and protecting Christian pilgrims. Many must have looked askance at events in the Byzantine capital, no matter how they hated its rulers. But other Franks were enthusiastic cheerleaders. Geoffrey of Villehardouin (c.1150-c.1213) was a knight and chronicler who both participated and advocated for the Fourth Crusade. He was withering about those crusaders who either never turned up in Venice to set sail or quitted during the crusade, unhappy with its direction.[28] Intriguingly, this implies that there were many, possibly among the military orders as well, who took a dim view of what the old Doge inflicted on the Byzantine empire.[29]

The second anti-Christian crusade was against the Cathars, a dualist and Gnostic variant of Christianity that had become wildly popular in the Languedoc region of southern France, much to the horror of the pope in Rome. They were also referred to as the Albigensians, as the city of Albi was a hotbed of Cathars.[30] If Constantinople left some crusaders, and Templars, feeling queasy, then this campaign on French soil against fellow Christians – no matter how much in error – got an initially lukewarm response. Pope Innocent responded by offering a plenary indulgence – that is the wiping away of one's sins – in return for just forty days of fighting against the Cathars. That was a better deal than the indulgences on offer for crusading in outremer.[31]

Innocent also deployed the arguments that Bernard of Clairvaux had developed to justify the existence of the Knights Templar but now applied it to attacking other Christians. Bernard himself had extended his idea of holy war by the sword to the Wendish pagans but never to a foe who believed in Christ. The Cathars refusal to believe in a bodily Christ, and therefore the virgin birth, placed them firmly outside the Catholic cosmos, the pope argued. They therefore had to be exterminated for false and heretical belief. Innocent was effectively criminalising 'thoughtcrime' centuries before the author George Orwell developed the concept in his dystopian novel, *1984*.

The result would be the burning of hundreds of Cathars at the stake and the massacre of 20,000 people in the French city of Béziers in July 1209. The atrocity at Béziers was the first major battle of the Albigensian crusade and was meant to set an example to the rest of Cathar-held France. Surrender or face the same fate. As the crusaders stood before the walls of the city, the military commanders turned to the papal legate, representing Innocent III, and asked how they would know who to kill at Béziers, as many of the inhabitants were believed to be loyal Roman Catholics.

What happened next was chronicled by Caesarius of Heisterbach (c.1180-c.1240), a Cistercian monk. The papal legate, Arnaud Amalric (died 1225), was the Cistercian abbot of Cîteaux, which Bernard had left to set up his own abbey at Clairvaux in 1115. So, the account from a Cistercian about a fellow Cistercian was not going to be hostile. Nevertheless, Caesarius captured the legate's chilling response to the commanders: 'Slay them all, God will recognise his own'. Or in the original Latin: Caedite eos. Novit enim Dominus qui sunt eius.

> 'When they discovered, from the admissions of some of them, that there were Catholics mingled with the heretics they said to the abbot "Sir, what shall we do, for we cannot distinguish between the faithful and the heretics." The abbot, like the others, was afraid that many, in fear of death, would pretend to be Catholics, and after their departure, would return to their heresy, and is said to have replied "Kill them all for the Lord knoweth them that are His" (2 Tim. ii. 19) and so a countless number in that town were slain.'[32]

Amalric later blamed ill-disciplined 'servants and other persons of low rank' for the slaughter but confirmed the number of dead at 20,000, 'irrespective of rank, sex or age'. There is a telling contrast between this vengeful killing and the bloodbath at the taking of Jerusalem in the First Crusade. The latter had seen a frenzy of murder, with the Muslims of the city fleeing to the Temple Mount as their last refuge and hope. Yet for those crusaders in 1099, Jerusalem was an emotionally and religious charged place in a strange land and peopled by pagans. By contrast, Béziers was on French soil and every Sunday, its church bells rang out to summon the faithful who spoke the same language as many of the attackers, if not most of them.

How did the Knights Templar react to this crusade? There were undoubtedly ties of blood across Cathar France, which has led some to wonder whether there were also ties of faith.[33] The bible of Templar esoteric theories, *The Holy Blood and the Holy Grail*, by Michael Baigent, Richard Leigh, and Henry Lincoln, states that the Templars 'maintained a certain warm rapport' with the Cathars of the Languedoc. The same lords in the region who backed the heretics also donated land to the Templars. The fourth grand master, Bertrand de Blanchefort, was said to have come from a Cathar family, which fought against the pope's Albigensian crusade.

The authors go further, claiming the Templars adopted a policy of studied neutrality during the anti-Cathar war because they believed that the only true crusade was against the Saracens. Sensing that the knights were sympathetic to their plight, Cathars fled to Templar preceptories seeking sanctuary where they were protected, sometimes by force of arms. The result of this was 'a major influx of Cathars into the Temple's ranks'. Having already absorbed Muslim and Jewish influences in outremer, the Templars were now exposed to Gnostic dualism by Cathars rising to senior positions within the order. These are the kind of claims about the Templars, fraternising with the enemies of Rome, that ultimately led to their downfall. The notion that they had become divorced from mainstream Roman Catholicism and secretly dabbled in heresy – even diabolism.[34]

The third anti-Christian crusade began as a war against Europe's remaining non-Christians – or pagans – in the Baltics. They consisted of different peoples living in northern Germany and modern Latvia, Estonia, and Lithuania who traded with Danes, Russians, and Finns. The area was prosperous, and cynics have long suggested that the invasion by Christian forces was economically motivated while dressed up in the language of the crusades.[35] The Livonian Crusade was initially spearheaded by a new order of holy warriors, the Livonian Brothers of the Sword, set up in 1202. However, after some setbacks and defeats, they merged into the Teutonic knights, who, like the Templars, were set up to aid pilgrims on the way to Jerusalem but expanded that remit considerably. Their full name was the Order of Brothers of the German House of Saint Mary in Jerusalem (Orden der Brüder vom Deutschen Haus der Heiligen Maria in Jerusalem).

Papal indulgences were extended to those fighting the pagans on similar terms to the crusades in the Holy Land and the Albigensian crusade. One pagan chief, Caupo of Turaida (died 1217), agreed to convert to Christianity and was taken by the bishop of Riga to Rome to meet Pope Innocent III, who presented him with a bible and a hundred gold pieces. His own people, however, took a dim view of his action and rebelled. Caupo was killed fighting alongside the Brothers of the Sword in the Battle of Saint Matthew's Day, in September 1217.[36]

Wherever the Teutonic knights conquered, they turned the local nobility into their vassals, monopolised trade, and were supported by the Cistercians, who spread their ever-growing Europe-wide network of monasteries into the region. Once pagan resistance had been broken, their lands devastated, and people wiped out, the Teutonic knights switched their attention to fellow Christians.

On 5 April 1242, the knights fought the Republic of Novgorod on the freezing ice of Lake Peipus, a battle that came to be known as The Battle on the Ice. This confrontation had nothing to do with combatting Islam or paganism but whether the Roman Catholic or Eastern Orthodox church would dominate what is now Russia. The knights were defeated but their crusade continued as they had now become wealthy exploiting the lands and subjects under their control. Later, they became embroiled in a war with the Christian city of Riga, which did eventually fall to the Teutonic knights.

After the death of Templar grand master Gilbert Horal in the year 1200, Philippe du Plessis, another Angevin, took over from 1201 to 1208. He had joined the

Third Crusade as a secular crusader but then became a Templar once in outremer. In his seven years leading the knights, there was little action in the Holy Land as the Fourth Crusade had diverted to Constantinople with disastrous results for the Byzantines. However, in 1202 he wrote a letter to Arnaud Amalric, the abbot of Cîteaux and papal legate who had told the crusaders at Béziers to slay all the city's inhabitants and let God work out who was a Cathar. Philippe had nothing but bad news to relate. Hundreds of thousands of people had died in the Levant due to the wrath of God in recent months.

'We wish to inform you of dreadful misfortunes, the unheard-of disasters, the unspeakable plagues, and the fitting punishment of God, which have come through our sinful actions.'

Despite a peace treaty being agreed between Saladin's brother, Al-Adil (1145–1218), who was the new Ayyubid ruler and often referred to as Saphadin by the crusaders, he had massed a large force of troops drawn from Egypt, Jerusalem and Damascus, which had taken to threatening Christians working on the land around Tripoli. Farmers had fled, abandoning their lands and villages. This and the arrival of a suffocating desert wind known as the 'simoon' had left three quarters of outremer's crops unharvested. But there was far worse.

In 1202, Philippe wrote that 'a frightening voice was heard in the sky, and a horrible lowing from the earth'. This was a massive earthquake caused by seismic activity on the Yammou^neh fault.[37] The main shock was felt from Sicily to Constantinople and modern Iran. The worst-affected cities were Tyre, Acre, Nablus, Damascus, and Tripoli. Philippe related that in Tyre, all the towers bar three came crashing down along with most of the city walls and nearly every house. The Templar castle of Chastel Blanc 'lost most of its walls, but the greater tower which we believed to be the most strongly and stoutly built in the world was so shaken and riven with cracks that we would have preferred it to fall down rather than stay standing in its weak condition'. Tortosa, by contrast, was preserved.

Estimates of the death toll vary but seismologists today reckon about 30,000 perished in the main shock, with up to a million dying during the subsequent famine and epidemics. Philippe referred in his letter to the 'corruption of the air' that brought disease. He believed a third of the people succumbed 'while there was hardly a living person who could find the energy to get out of bed'.

Under Philippe's successor, Guillaume de Chartres (c.1178–1218), the Templars were heavily involved in a spectacular victory on the Iberian Peninsula. This would prove to be the turning point in the centuries-long Reconquista. On 16 July 1212, Christian forces fought the Almohad caliphate at the Battle of Las Navas de Tolosa.[38] The Knights Templar, Knights Hospitaller, Order of Santiago, and crusaders from all over Europe confronted an Almohad army drawn not just from Al-Andalus but also the caliphate's north African provinces. This was a shocking reversal of fortune for the revived Islamic realm that had struck terror into the hearts of the kings of Castile, Léon, and Portugal. On the battlefield was the irrepressible papal legate and Cathar slayer, Arnaud Amalric. He wrote an account of what he saw to the Cistercian general chapter that summed up the success in all the different crusader theatres of combat, from the Baltics to Iberia and outremer.

> *'Blessed in all things is our Lord Jesus Christ, who through his mercy in our times, under the happy apostolate of the Lord Pope Innocent, has granted victories to the Catholic Christians over three plagues to humanity and enemies of his Holy Church, namely the eastern schismatics, the western heretics, and the southern Saracens.'*

Some historians argue that the church at the time did not see a direct linkage between the wars against the Cathars, Livonian pagans, and the eastern orthodox church in Russia and Constantinople. But there it is in black and white. The pope's right-hand man who was physically present on these crusades, or very close to them, had no doubt in his mind that the church was fighting a war on many fronts and the Knights Templar were in the frontline. At the Battle of Las Navas de Tolosa, the Almohads outnumbered the crusaders but yet again it was the disciplined formation of the Templars that helped assure victory and inflicted huge losses on the enemy.[39]

Queen Berengaria of León (c.1179–1246) wrote to her sister Blanche giving news of the battle and she put the death toll at 70,000 men and 15,000 women on the Muslim side. More conservative estimates give a figure of 20,000, which was the bulk of the Almohad army and ten times the Christian casualties. The treasure found in the Almohad tents in gold and silver was so vast that the crusaders had been unable to give it a value, Berengaria wrote. Twenty-thousand pack animals were required just to carry away the left-over javelins and arrows. So drastic was the loss that it dealt a fatal blow to the Almohad empire and led to the crusader conquest of the cities of Córdoba (1236), Jaén (1246) and Seville (1248). The Islamic caliphate in Iberia was reduced to the tip of the peninsula forming a rump state, the Emirate of Granada, eventually taken by King Ferdinand of Aragon and Queen Isabella of Castile in 1492.

Accusations of Templar perfidy continued throughout the thirteenth century, with the grand masters Gilbert Horal, Phillipe du Plessis, and Guillaume de Chartres criticised for seeking peace terms with the Saracens or renewing existing agreements. Guillaume received additional flak for reaching out to a new enemy on the horizon that was to sweep across the Middle East and into Europe: the Mongols.

Under Guillaume, the Fifth Crusade was launched by Pope Innocent III and then continued to be promoted after his death by Pope Honorius III (c.1150–1227). The Fourth Lateran Council met to plan the new Christian invasion, taking the unprecedented step of inviting the Knights Templar and Hospitaller to attend. There was a new spirit of inclusivity fostered by the papacy to ensure that everybody got a say in shaping the crusade. The underlying motive for this was to avoid a repetition of what had happened in the Fourth Crusade with Venice hijacking the whole venture for its own purposes.[40]

Honorius III was more than aware that knives were being stuck into the backs of the Templars and he was heartily sick of the vicious rumour mongering. In a letter to the prelates of Sicily dated 24 November 1218, he reminded them that both the Templars and Hospitallers 'had a special status among other Christians throughout the world' defending the faith by fighting the Lord's battles. But 'the devil has stirred up evil tongues against them: indeed, some people returning from outremer have so blackened their reputation, that if their innocence had not shone forth in the furnace like gold in time of need, we ourselves would have been forced by the rumours and the calumnies of their detractors to suspect that they had occasional committed crimes'. Honorius asked the papal legate in outremer, Pelagio Galvani (c.1165–1230), to investigate the accusations and he had found no wrongdoing, therefore 'these defenders of Jesus Christ should be granted large payments from the donations of the faithful'. So, as another crusade dawned, Rome gave the Templars a clean bill of health and told their critics to shut up.

Egypt was to be the primary focus of the Fifth Crusade and in 1219, the crusaders took the port city of Damietta from the Ayyubid ruler, Al-Kamil (c.1177–1238), known to the Franks as Meledin. The Templars played a key role in this victory and Al-Kamil reached out to Guillaume's successor as grand master, Peire de Montagut (died 1232), offering to exchange Jerusalem for Damietta. He also claimed to have the True Cross and promised to return it as well as agreeing to a meeting with Saint Francis of Assisi (c.1181–1226), who had come along on the crusade. This unlikely encounter occurred with Francis attempting unsuccessfully to convert Al-Kamil to Christianity.

These peace negotiations were continuously stymied by the Portuguese-born papal legate, Pelagio Galvani, who took a hardline position towards the Ayyubids. However, victory at Damietta was short-lived as Al-Kamil opened the sluice gates of the river Nile, forcing the bogged-down crusaders to flee Egypt.

Al-Kamil handed Jerusalem over to the Holy Roman Emperor, Frederick II (1194–1250), during the Sixth Crusade, as part of a ten-year peace treaty agreed in 1229. The Knights Templar did not welcome this restoring of the holy city to Christian control because under the terms of the deal, the Temple Mount remained under Muslim control. That meant that the Templars were unable to take back the Al-Aqsa Mosque as their headquarters. Plus, Frederick had been excommunicated by the pope during his ongoing rows with the papacy-leading to Pope Gregory IX (c.1145–1241) referring to him as 'preambulus Antichristi' – predecessor of the antichrist. The Templars were unwilling to support a king in such a sinful state. So, Frederick had to rely on the Teutonic knights while the Templars and Hospitallers were nowhere in sight.

Pope Gregory IX launched the Barons Crusade in 1239, restoring the Kingdom of Jerusalem's boundaries to almost where they had been before the Battle of Hattin. From the river Jordan to the Mediterranean Sea was almost wholly back in crusader hands. This, however, was to be a short-lived renaissance of Frankish control. In 1244, Jerusalem fell to the Khwarazmians. They were a Turkic people who had ruled an empire centred on Persia, which in the twelfth century dominated modern Iran and Afghanistan. However, in 1231, the Khwarazmians were conquered by the advancing Mongols, who were still to make their presence felt in the Levant. After that, the Khwarazmians were reduced to being mercenaries and the Ayyubids gladly hired their military muscle.

At the Battle of La Forbie in October 1244, the Templars, Hospitallers, and Teutonic knights encountered an Ayyubid army bolstered by Khwarazmian mercenaries. La Forbie was a small village, northeast of Gaza. It was about to witness a terrible blow against the very future of outremer. Some historians believe this calamity was more important than Hattin in terms of driving the final nails into the coffin of Pope Urban's dream of a Christian Holy Land.

The Khwarazmians proved to be devastatingly effective and by the close of battle, 5,000 crusaders lay dead, leaving only thirty-three Knights Templar, twenty-seven Hospitallers, and three Teutonic knights alive. Among those reportedly killed was the sixteenth grand master of the Knights Templar, Armand de Lavoie, also known as Armand de Périgord, although some accounts claim he was taken prisoner and perished around 1247.

The Barons Crusade had raised hopes that the glory days of outremer could be resurrected. Yet it all fell apart very quickly. The defeat at La Forbie threw into sharp relief the weakness of the crusader position in outremer.

This was reflected in deteriorating relations between the Knights Templar and Hospitaller, even resulting in incidents of violence between the two orders. Yet the Seventh Crusade raised hopes that fortunes could still be turned around. The leading figure was the charismatic and religiously zealous King Louis IX of France, who would go on to be made a saint by the church. In his capital, Paris, he constructed the still-standing Sainte-Chapelle, a riot of stained glass, to house the Crown of Thorns from the crucifixion of Jesus, for which he paid the stupendous sum of 135,000 livres, approximately half the national income of France.[41]

In August 1248, his fleet carrying 10,000 soldiers made its way to Cyprus where Louis stopped for eight months to gather supplies and more recruits from Europe, and what was left of outremer. While there, the king informed the Ayyubid ruler of Egypt, Al-Malik Al Salih (1205–1249), that he would be conquering his country and seizing back Jerusalem. Louis also received news of an enormous army advancing from the east. The Mongols were on the move. Excited at the thought of a pincer movement against the Muslim-controlled Levant, he sent emissaries to the Mongols offering gifts. Sadly, for Louis, this was construed as a grovelling offer of tribute from a mere vassal – and would he care to make the same payment ever year from now on? The French king declined.

The eighteenth grand master of the Knights Templar, Guillaume de Sonnac, sailed from Acre to Cyprus with news for Louis. He informed the king that Al-Salih had offered peace terms. This infuriated Louis, who blew up at Guillaume, ordering him to never conduct diplomatic talks with the enemy without his permission. This incident, like others, fuelled the perception that the Templars pursued their own geopolitical agenda quite separate from the secular rulers and prelates of the church. De Sonnac was chastened, and Louis made it abundantly clear that only war was on the table.

The French king landed in Egypt in 1249 with about 18,000 soldiers that included 2,500 knights and 5,000 crossbowmen. Damietta was taken with surprising ease. Reports filtered through that Al-Salih was dying either of tuberculosis or after having his leg amputated for a medical condition – an operation that was so often a death sentence in the Middle Ages. Against the advice of his generals, Louis decided to proceed from Damietta to Cairo. This was unfinished crusader business. If Amalric had taken Fatimid Egypt back in the 1160s, Jerusalem might still have been in Christian hands. The Ayyubid empire was now suffering a power vacuum at the top, so why not strike at this moment?

What Louis did not know was that the power vacuum was being filled by Al-Salih's wife and soon-to-be widow, Shajar al-Durr (died 1257). A resourceful woman who began her life as a slave; was bought by her future husband; and ended up sitting on his throne. Her reign lasted only eighty days, but she effectively ushered out the Ayyubid era begun by Saladin and brought in the Mamluks as the new rulers of the Muslim world. She had the distinction of being the first female ruler of Islamic Egypt and was referred to in Friday prayers at the mosques as 'the Queen of Muslims'.[42] Under her watch, Louis would falter badly.

His army, making their way towards Cairo, struck camp at a town called Mansourah, on a branch of the Nile delta. The Egyptians and crusaders bombarded each other for several weeks, reaching a stalemate. Local Bedouin then informed the French king that he could attack the town using a fordable crossing further downstream. The Nile was swollen but at that point, it was possible to get across. Louis made straight for the location where knights, and their horses, were able to traverse the Nile. De Sonnac and about 280 Templar knights forged ahead accompanied by Robert of Artois (1216–1250), brother of King Louis, and the commander of the English troops, Sir William Longespée (c.1212–1250).

Robert decided to attack before Louis had arrived with the main army. He led De Sonnac and Longespée with their men against some enemy soldiers who made for the town. Once inside, there was a bloody repetition of what had happened to the Templars under Bernard de Tremelay at the Siege of Ascalon in 1153. They were sucked into a warren of streets that became their mass grave. The English chronicler Matthew Paris (c.1200–1259) had Robert and William exchanging these touching words as they faced their doom:

Robert of Artois: *'Oh William! God fights against us–we can no longer hold out. I advise you save yourself alive, if you can, by flight, whilst your horse has strength to carry you, lest when you wish to you no longer can.'*

Sir William Longespée: *'Please God, the son of my father shall never fly from any Saracen I would rather die a good death than live a base life.*[43]

Robert then wheeled round and was promptly drowned trying to escape in the Nile. Seeing this, William opted to stand his ground and kill as many

Saracens as possible. According to Matthew Paris, his feet were cut off during the fighting and his horse collapsed under him yet 'still he continued to lop of the hands, heads, and feet, of such as attacked him'.

De Sonnac saw all but two of his 280 Templar knights slaughtered – and he lost an eye. A French chronicler, Jean de Joinville (1224–1317), who was with King Louis, attempted to pin the blame for what happened on De Sonnac – yet another example of Templar rashness. But Matthew Paris demurred, alleging that Robert had been insulting De Sonnac in the run-up to the tragic incident, accusing the Templars of having lost outremer, 'bellowing and swearing disgracefully as is the French custom'. More than likely, De Joinville was deflecting blame from the king's brother as Louis was his patron. While Matthew Paris was indulging in what would become a centuries-long English pastime of hating the French.

Louis became bogged down in months of fighting. The French king was cut off from Damietta by a Muslim blockade and very soon, famine and disease afflicted his camp. On 5 April 1250, Louis beat a retreat. The following day brought a renewed assault by the Ayyubids on the Franks with the now half-blind De Sonnac at the centre of the fray. The Templars built a barricade of sorts using bits of captured Saracen weaponry. As the enemy charged, they poured Greek Fire on top and set it alight. However, this did not deter the attackers who 'rushed upon the Templars among the scorching flames'. In a rather nasty touch, one of the Ayyubids blinded De Sonnac in his other eye after which, unable to defend himself, the grand master was hacked to pieces.

The French king was left in charge of a bedraggled army bereft of Templar strength and minus the cream of its noble knights. In addition, he was seriously incapacitated by dysentery. Louis may also have been a malaria sufferer and one recent theory, based on analysis of his jawbone, posits that he had scurvy as well. Researchers in 2019 looked at the jawbone interred at Notre Dame cathedral and concluded his diet was poor due to a refusal to eat the local food while on crusade.[44] Louis was captured and only released on 6 May after payment of a ransom totalling 400,000 livres tournois. He got the remains of his army released and had to surrender Damietta. Determined to make an impact in outremer, Louis stayed for another four years overseeing the refortification of Acre, Sidon, and Caesarea.

Meanwhile, a revolution was brewing in Cairo. Al-Salih's son, Turan Shah (died 1250), arrived from Damascus where he had been busy bribing troops and nobles to win their loyalty ahead of journeying to Cairo to claim the throne currently occupied by his father's widow, Shajar al-Durr. She was now referring to herself as the 'sultan' on dinar coins. Once in Egypt, he unwisely alienated the Bahri Mamluks, freed slaves who had served his father loyally. They were mostly of central Asian (Kipchak Turkic) origin. He also incurred the wrath of his stepmother by repeatedly asking her to hand over the wealth and jewels of his late father – and relinquish the throne. She complained bitterly to the Bahri Mamluks about his lack of respect for her position, as acting sultan, and they sympathised.

A group of Mamluk soldiers assassinated Turan Shah on 2 May 1250, bringing an end to the Ayyubid dynasty. At the same time, they declared that Shajar al-Durr should remain in charge of Egypt only now as the first of a new Mamluk dynasty. For the female sultan who had begun life as a slave, there must have been some quiet satisfaction in seeing people of low birth taking power. She married a Mamluk, Izz al-Din Aybak (died 1257), and appointed him as the Atabeg, or commander in chief. But unable to command the loyalty of the Syrian emirs, Shajar resigned as sultan and handed the throne to her husband. Yet as that failed to assuage opponents in Syria and Baghdad, Aybak went back to being the Atabeg, installing a 6-year-old Ayyubid princeling as his puppet sultan.

These tumultuous events in Egypt brought to prominence a Mamluk commander, Al-Zahir Baybars (c.1223–1277). A tall, slim man with fair skin and an eye that glinted due to cataracts. Fearless and ruthless, he would become the hammer of both the Franks and the approaching Mongols.

Chapter Seven

Retreat from the Holy Land

History is full of unexpected developments and the rise of the Mongol Empire must rank among one of the greatest shocks of all time. From out of the east burst a people who conquered everything in their path. Their achievement dwarfed the empire built by the Seljuks and others from the steppe who had moved westwards. In the opening years of the thirteenth century, the Mongol realm was centred on the Mongolian plateau and made up of warring tribal confederations: the Keraites, Khamag, Naiman, Mergid, and Tatar. They were united by a warlord, Temüjin, who in 1206 adopted the title Genghis (or Chinggis) Khan (c.1162–1227). In a very short time, he overwhelmed the neighbouring Xia and Jin kingdoms in modern China, which had imposed trade restrictions on the Mongols, severely damaging their economy.[1]

When Genghis Khan died in 1227, his grieving army was said to have carried his body back home to Mongolia, killing anyone they met on the way to conceal the route. His burial place was hidden from view by a thousand cavalry churning up the ground. In various accounts, it was claimed a river was diverted over the site or that he was placed under permafrost. Ever since, treasure hunters have wondered whether he was interred with priceless artefacts. According to one legend, if his tomb is ever found, the world will end.

The Khwarezmian Empire was the next domino to fall in 1231, which brought the Mongols to the frontiers of the Abbasid caliphate. This provoked widespread panic among Muslim and Christian rulers throughout the Middle East. For the Seljuks, there was alarm at this new threat from the east. Ironic given that they had emerged from the steppe sweeping aside all before them in the eleventh century. One might say they were about to receive a taste of their own medicine.

Christians were initially encouraged. Reports about the Mongols revealed that many had long ago converted to the Nestorian branch of Christianity. This was an old heresy condemned back in the fifth century CE at the Council of Ephesus (431 CE). It was based on a definition of Christ's human and divine natures developed by a Byzantine bishop, Nestorius (c.386–451 CE), whose views caused a storm in Europe but were better received among Christians in Persia and further east. Though he died in Egypt, his version of Christianity spread along the Silk Road to China where it took root in the seventh century CE.[2]

At the time of Genghis Khan, one of the strongest tribes in Mongolia – the Keraites – were Nestorians, as were other groups in the Mongol confederation. This gave rise to speculation that the legendary Christian king, Prester John, was a Christian Mongol tribal chief. One candidate being a Keraite leader, Toghrul (died 1203), and even Genghis Khan was cast as a possible Prester John.[3] But then a more troubling theory arose. Maybe the Mongols had defeated Prester John and even killed him.

In the 1240s, Pope Innocent IV (c.1195–1254) took an increasing interest in the Mongols. Not least because by the 1220s they were in modern Ukraine, sacking Kiev in 1240. The following year saw a battle at the Polish city of Legnica between the invaders and the Knights Templar, joined by the Hospitallers and Teutonic knights, which the Mongols won. Their tactics confused the western knights. For example, they used flags instead of yelling commands to direct their fighters. They feigned retreats then turned and attacked. And they used smoke to blind the enemy infantry, then fired ceaseless volleys of arrows. All these tactics combined decimated their enemies. The Mongols then set about destroying Templar fortresses and slaughtering knights.

On 11 April 1241, the Knights Templar were in battle again with the Mongols at the Battle of Mohi in the Kingdom of Hungary, which saw the Hungarian royal army destroyed. At the battle was the provincial Templar master, Rembald de Voczon, who may have been a veteran of Hattin. Up until the moment of engagement, the Hungarians were convinced they were facing a relatively small force and victory lay in their grasp. But on the day of battle, the Mongol numbers kept swelling until the Hungarian army panicked and attempted to flee through a gap deliberately left by the invaders. It was a death trap, and they were all cut down.[4]

The Mongols pursued King Béla IV of Hungary (1206–1270) down into modern Croatia and eventually besieged the terrified monarch at Klis castle. This had become a Templar fortress when King Andrew II of Hungary (c.1177–1235) entrusted the whole of Croatia and Dalmatia to the provincial Templar prior of Vrana, Pontius de Cruce, while he went off on the Fifth Crusade.[5] However, when it became clear that Béla was not present, the Mongols melted away. He had made his escape before they stormed the walls. As a footnote, Klis castle was used as the setting for the fictional city of Meereen in the hugely successful HBO history and fantasy series *Game of Thrones*.

In 1242, the European invasion petered out, with the Mongols refocusing on Russia, central Asia, and the Middle East. Why this happened remains a mystery. In 2016, scientists reported that analysis of wood samples from the period indicates unusually cold and wet weather between 1238 and 1241 that did not suit Mongolian battle tactics. It made the terrain boggy and unsuitable for horses and reduced the food supply as crops were spoiled.[6]

Alternatively, the death of Genghis Khan's successor – Ögedei Khan (c.1186–1241) – may have caused many Mongol leaders to head home as a succession crisis loomed. Some historians believe the Mongol invasion of Europe was never intended to be much more than a raid anyway.[7] However, the Mongols did return repeatedly to Europe, attacking Poland (1259, 1287), Byzantine-controlled Thrace (1265, 1324, 1337), Bulgaria (1271, 1274, 1280, 1285), Hungary (1285), Serbia (1291), and Germany (1340).

The papacy watched the Mongol incursions into Hungary, Poland, and the Holy Roman Empire with alarm. Pope Gregory IX pushed for a crusade against the Mongols in 1241, at the height of their activity in Europe. This was the pope who had excommunicated Emperor Frederick II, calling him the antichrist, and launched the Barons Crusade in the Holy Land. Four years later, in 1245, and a new pope, Innocent IV, decided to opt for dialogue. While the Mongol threat seemed to be receding, some outreach might convince them to stay away for good. The pope sent a papal nuncio, Giovanni da Pian del Carpini (c.1180–1252), to the third ruler of the Mongol empire, Güyük Khan (c.1206–1248), along with fellow Franciscan monks Benedict of Poland (c.1200–1280) and Stephen of Bohemia.[8]

The Mongols were a volatile and dangerous foe, in the papal view. They had bested the Knights Templar and seized their castles. These fearsome warriors had descended on Europe, reaching the city of Vienna. Gregory decided that to beat or contain the Mongols, they had to be understood. Or as he put it, it was necessary to find a 'solution against the Tatars' (remedium contra Tartaros). If only they could be convinced to stay away from Europe and ally with the crusaders in outremer to take on the Saracens together. Was it too much to hope for?

No papal ambassadors had journeyed so far east. Benedict of Poland was chosen as an envoy possibly because he had a smattering of the khan's language picked up from captured Mongolian soldiers in his native Poland. The trio set off not knowing what to expect. Their long trek was uneventful, and assisted by the Mongols, as the khan was clearly intrigued to know what this leader of the Christians wanted to say to him. On arrival at the khan's court, in the Mongol capital of Karakorum, they relayed the pope's wishes.

Güyük Khan gave his considered response – a demand for total submission. His letter is still retained in the Vatican archives. It revealed a total disregard for Rome's view that secular monarchs should bow the knee to Christ's vicar on earth. Instead, the khan insisted on slavish obedience to himself:

'You must say with a sincere heart: "We will be your subjects; we will give you our strength". You must in person come with your kings, all together, without exception, to render us service and pay us homage. Only then will we acknowledge your submission. And if you do not follow the order of God, and go against our orders, we will know you as our enemy.'

In 1258, Hülegü Khan (c.1217–1265), the grandson of Genghis Khan, took Baghdad. The Abbasid caliph, Al Musta'sim bi-llah (1213–1258), was reputedly murdered by being wrapped in a carpet and then trampled to death by the khan's cavalry. The idea being that royal blood should not be visibly shed. Another story has Hülegü locking the caliph into his treasure store without food or water, ordering him to feast on the riches he adored so much. The city was left a depopulated smoking ruin. Hülegü had demanded that the caliph accept him as an overlord in the same way his predecessors bowed to the Seljuks. But the over-confident caliph promised to unite the entire Islamic world to defy Hülegü. That proved to be the emptiest of threats.

The Mongols then moved on to Syria where they had formed an alliance with the Christians in Georgia and Armenia as well as Bohemond VI of Antioch (c.1237–1275).[9] Together, this Frankish-Mongolian force besieged and conquered Aleppo. From the Muslim perspective, the Mongols seemed to be working hand in glove with the crusaders. A view reinforced by the fact that Hülegü's mother, Sorghaghtani Beki (c.1190–1252), was a Nestorian Keraite and Hülegü's top general, Kitbuqa Noyan (died 1260), was also a Nestorian. When Kitbuqa, Bohemond, and the Armenian army entered Aleppo, they wasted no time slaughtering the Muslim and Jewish population of the city, then levelling the city's main mosque. In the aftermath of the Aleppo siege, the Knights Templar helped Bohemond seize back several towns including Lattakieh, Darkush, Kafr Debbin, and Jabala.

From the Templar standpoint, despite the alliances with the Mongols, they viewed the eastern foe with utmost suspicion. Unlike Bohemond, they were part of a Europe-wide organisation and brothers in Syria would have known that fellow brothers in Poland, Hungary, and Croatia had been killed by Mongol armies. The perspective of the Templars was far more global than the more narrowly focused secular princes.

In March 1260, Thomas Bérard (died 1273), the twentieth grand master of the Knights Templar, wrote to Amadeus of Morestello, treasurer of the Temple in England. The 'Tartars', as he called the Mongols, 'are now here in front of our walls, knocking at our gates, and now is not the time to hide their skirmishes under a bushel'. They had shaken Christendom to its foundations, bringing pain and fear. 'They rely on the power of their incredibly huge numbers and conquer provinces left and right with such great ease…'. Maybe, Thomas mused, they were a scourge sent from God to force repentance for sin.

Even Baghdad (which he calls Baldach) had been overrun and the caliph, 'the pope of the Saracens', had been murdered along with his children, household, and many citizens of the city. The Old Man of the Mountain and his Assassin cult had been destroyed. Aleppo had seen a 'huge number of Saracens' killed, and the walls razed in just a day. Bérard did not share Bohemond's faith in Mongol good intentions, realising that they were out to grab the whole region, regardless of who was in control. Templar castles were being strengthened 'to resist these Tartars'. He issued a chilling warning in his letter:

> *May you be in no doubt that unless help comes quickly to us from your countries, whatever our ability to resist the attack and onslaught of such a great horde, there is no doubt that the whole of Christendom this side of the sea will be subject to Tartar rule.*

As the Mongols menaced, Templar finances were in a mess. Bérard confided to the English treasurer that fortifying their castles and the city of Acre had resulted in significant 'runs on our money that it is recognised that we are in a dangerous financial situation'. Spending had gone up fourfold, yet there were no merchants from whom to borrow. Otherwise, Bérard noted, the order could have pawned its church ornaments 'such as crosses, chalices, incense-burners and all the other things in our houses'. He told the treasurer that if the European preceptories failed to generate sufficient wealth and channel it to outremer then the Templars would 'default completely in respect of the defence of the Holy Land'. To avoid that, assets might have to be liquidated. Possibly Bérard was mulling the sale of buildings and land across the Templar provinces to balance the books.

For the new Mamluk dynasty in Egypt, the Mongols posed an unexpected threat. Up until their arrival in the region, the Mamluk agenda had been to bring the remaining Ayyubid emirs in Syria under Egyptian control and to knock out the crusader states of outremer. That had all been proceeding satisfactorily until Hülegü appeared on the scene with an army numbering up to 300,000, though estimates vary widely. The western part of the Mongol realm under his control – the Ilkhanate – extended from the borders of what was left of the Byzantine empire through to modern Pakistan. His soldiers covered every ethnicity and faith from Chinese military engineers to Turkic bowmen.[10] They looked invincible.

A confrontation between Mamluks and Mongols was inevitable, and it took place at the Battle of Ain Jalut on 3 September 1260. It followed the usual strident demands from the Mongols – this time to surrender Egypt. Among many Muslims there was a growing fear that the invaders' ultimate intention was to reach and destroy Mecca, the holiest city in Islam. They had, after all, wrecked Baghdad and murdered the caliph. So, stopping the Mongols was both a political and religious imperative. The Mamluks won the battle under the leadership of their sultan, Saif ad-Din Qutuz (died 1260), but victory was secured by his ambitious general, Baybars. For reasons that are unclear, though unbridled ambition undoubtedly played a part, Baybars assassinated Qutuz shortly afterwards, becoming sultan himself.

The Knights Templar were already well acquainted with Baybars, who had played a key role in wiping out the knights in the Nile Delta when the grand master Guillaume de Sonnac had lost each of his eyes in consecutive battles. The collusion of the region's Christian princes with the Mongols enraged Baybars, who took an uncompromising stance towards the existence of outremer. The crusaders had to be driven into the sea. In 1263, he was besieging Acre and sacked nearby Nazareth. From March to April, he turned on the Hospitaller fortress at Arsuf. Having taken it, he promised the knights safe passage but the moment they emerged, he sold them all into slavery.

Then in 1266, he besieged the Templar castle of Safed. There are accounts that he convinced local Syrians fighting for the Templars, who were more than likely Turcopoles, to desert their posts. After defeating the knights, the same promise of safe passage was extended, only this time Baybars massacred the Templars as they exited the castle.

There is a curious story that on entering Safed, Baybars saw in the tower 'a big idol, under whose protection, according to the Franks, the fortress had been placed'. Given later accusations against the Templars that they worshipped a demon, Baphomet, it's tempting to imagine that what he viewed was a Satanic goat's head. But it's more likely that the idol in question was a revered saint's statue or even just a particularly gory crucifix.[11]

It's also worth noting that Safed, in modern Israel, has a long association with the magical rites of the Jewish Kabbalah. This mystical tradition within Judaism originated in Al-Andalus seeking hidden meanings believed to be in Jewish scripture. It's long been asserted that the Templars became associated with Kabbalistic beliefs while in the Holy Land seeking not just physical holy relics under the Temple Mount, but the truth about God suppressed by the Roman Catholic church.

With Hülegü's death in 1265, Baybars switched into hyperdrive. While the Mongols went through another succession crisis, there would be no Frankish-Mongol alliance to defend outremer. This was a window of opportunity that the Mamluk leader was not going to ignore. Safed fell in 1266. In 1268, Baybars subdued Beaufort Castle in southern Lebanon, which had been sold to the Knights Templar eight years earlier by a crusader prince, Julian Grenier, count of Sidon (died 1275), whose territory had been ravaged by the Mongols. The bankrupted Julian joined the Templars and lived long enough to see the castle seized by the Mamluks. With ruthless determination, Baybars extinguished one crusader castle and city after another. In 1268, he took Antioch with a great deal of bloodshed and in 1271, the last inland crusader castle, Montfort, was lost by the Teutonic knights to the Mamluks.

The Templar grand masters in charge before the order was crushed, grappled with an unpromising situation. In 1273, Guillaume de Beaujeu (c.1230–1291) became grand master, appointed at Tripoli, and he would be the last to reside in outremer. After him, the remaining grand masters were based off the coast of the Levant in Cyprus. In 1277, Baybars died – possibly by poison. Two years later, Qalawun as-Salihi (c.1222–1290) took over the Mamluk realm, establishing the Qalawunid dynasty. He set his sights on removing both the Franks and the Mongols from the region. In 1289, he reneged on a truce with the crusaders to take Tripoli, which was a huge blow to Christian outremer. The city reportedly ignored warnings from Guillaume of an imminent Mamluk assault and paid the price.[12]

The most significant Frankish holding left was the city of Acre, capital of the Kingdom of Jerusalem. Right up to the moment it was taken by the Mamluks, Acre was a wealthy trading hub in the eastern Mediterranean. Merchants from Genoa, Venice, and Pisa plied their trade and sometimes clashed over the sheer amount of money to be made in this lucrative entrepôt. The prosperity brought its attendant vices. Earlier in the thirteenth century, Acre's French-born bishop – Jacques de Vitry – described the city as being 'a monster or a beast, having nine heads, each fighting the other'.

De Vitry was scandalised by the low level of piety among local people. What was the point of the crusades if the Franks lost interest in their own faith? His writings reveal a man angered by what he saw. Christians had forgotten how to pray properly, and some were now circumcised 'in the manner of the Jews'. Many could only speak Arabic and the bishop had to deliver his sermons using an interpreter. Local priests were often married, and women went about veiled. Among those professing to be Christian were Nestorians, part of that long-condemned heresy. In short, the bishop had nothing good to say about Acre:

'Murders took place, both in public and private almost every day and night. Husbands strangled their wives by night when they displeased them. Women murdered their husbands with poisons and potions in accordance with ancient custom so that they might marry someone else… Who could be able to list all the crimes of this second Babylon, where Christians refused baptism to their Saracen servants, even though these Saracens earnestly and tearfully begged for it?'

On 5 April 1291, a Mamluk force of about 100,000 soldiers massed before the walls of Acre. On the Frankish side, the Templars – along with the Hospitallers and Teutonic knights – led the defence. There were no European monarchs or fresh recruits from the west to defend the city. From the battlements, the Templar grand master watched as the enemy set up a grim array of siege catapaults. Two of the machines were enormous, dubbed The Furious and The Victorious, capable of lobbing projectiles weighing over 300 pounds. At the head of this Mamluk army was a new leader. Qalawun had died the year before and his son, Al-Ashraf Khalil (died 1293), oversaw the onslaught. Above ground, the city was pounded remorselessly while below ground, the sappers set to work undermining the fortifications.

A contemporary chronicler wrote that 'nor was there an hour of the day without some hard fight being fought against the Saracens by the Templars' but on 18 May 1291, the Mamluks poured through the walls despite the best efforts of the knights. As defeat looked a certainty, Guillaume dropped his sword and staggered from the walls. His knights asked what the grand master was doing. Slowly, he raised his arm to reveal a bloody patch: 'I'm not running away. I am dead. Here is the blow'. Hours later, he succumbed to his wound and died.

The Mamluks ran amock through the streets of Acre. Most inhabitants made for the seashore to board boats for Cyprus. Hundreds of noble ladies carrying jewels and gold ornaments offered them to sailors for passage across the sea. As news of the city's fall spread, the same process was repeated in the remaining crusader-held towns. Outremer now emptied out of all its Franks, with Cyprus being the main destination.

Within Acre, some Templars rushed to the shore with their most valued possessions, while others made a last stand in their fortified compound. One dramatic account has the knights deliberately bringing down the mighty tower of their fortress onto both their own heads and those of the advancing Mamluks. Any knights who survived this suicidal act would have been slaughtered as they surrendered. Their white mantles emblazoned with red crosses marked them out for death.

One enduring legend about the Templars on that fateful day is that they spirited priceless treasure out of the city, down to the docks, and away in ships.

Included in that treasure was the Holy Grail, discovered in Jerusalem, and now being brought to Europe from the Holy Land. In the Netflix series *Knightfall*, we see the knights protecting this innocuous-looking cup as they flee down to the sea from the Mamluks. Sadly, they lose the Grail in the chaos and must go on a quest to recover it. There is no evidence that this incident occurred but it's certainly the case that as Acre succumbed, the crusading dream of Pope Urban vanished. Outremer was no more.[13]

Chapter Eight

The Last Templar Grand Master

In October 1291, the Knights Templar held a general chapter meeting in Cyprus and confirmed the election of Thibaud Gaudin as the new grand master. Another veteran Templar, Jacques de Molay (c.1240–1314), was appointed marshal, replacing Pierre de Severy, who had been killed at Acre. Gaudin lasted barely six months in the role before dying. The enormity of the tasks he faced must have compromised his health. He was succeeded by De Molay who could not have suspected that he would be the last grand master of the Knights Templar.

De Molay's date of birth is obscure but can be placed in the 1240s. It's been inferred he had Cathar connections on his mother's side of the family, even that he was born at Montségur castle, a nest of Catharism. De Molay was received into the order in 1265 at the Templar house in Beaune, France. He spent at least two decades in outremer when it was dominated by the Mamluks and Mongols. Scarcely can he have known a time when the Frankish kingdoms were not under severe threat. But it was also a period in which the Christian rulers had come to rely very heavily on the Knights Templar. Senior members of the order had the ear of the leaders of Christendom.

The conclusion that De Molay appears to have drawn from his time on active service in outremer was that the grand masters immediately before him lacked ambition. That included Gaudin. They had asked for too little, too late. Giving voice to the grumbles on the front line, De Molay echoed what must have been a widespread sentiment that the knights had been let down by the politicians back home. If only the Templars had been properly resourced, and Europe had mobilised as it had done for the First and Second Crusades, then Acre, Tripoli, and even Jerusalem might still be in Frankish hands.

After the fall of Acre in 1291, De Molay began a tour of Europe in the spring of 1293, banging the drum for another crusade. He reached out to Pope Boniface VIII (c.1230–1303), King Edward I of England (1239–1307), and James I of Aragon (1208–1276) among others. Edward had spearheaded the short-lived Ninth Crusade twenty years earlier, as a young prince, when Acre was still very much in Christian hands. He had dealt with the Mongols and crossed swords with the Mamluks but that all seemed a very long time ago.

There simply was not the appetite to board ships with thousands of troops and head for the Levant in the name of Christ.

The Templar grand master had some support in Rome from Pope Nicholas IV (1227–1292), who shared De Molay's belief that the fall of Acre deserved a strong response. He urged the French and English kings to consider funding another crusade and sent another Franciscan monk, John of Montecorvino (1247–1328), to the court of the Mongol emperor most often referred to as Kublai Khan (1215–1294). The Italian adventurer and merchant Marco Polo may have been there at the same time. Montecorvino stayed with the Mongols for many years and was made the first archbishop of Peking and patriarch of the Orient by the pope. However, he failed to forge any kind of alliance that would have reignited the crusades in the Levant.

The death of Pope Nicholas led to a reduction of fervour in Rome with regard to crusading. After the short reign of the nonagenarian Celestine V (1215–1296), ending in his resignation and confinement to his residence, Boniface VIII (c.1230–1303) was elected. Like previous popes, he desired a new crusade and was supportive of the Knights Templar, despite growing criticism. But England and France were spending their military budgets fighting each other over control of the southwestern French province of Gascony. This was bleeding the two countries dry, and France especially was burdened with war debt to the point where the king wanted to squeeze the church for cash.

This did not go unnoticed in Rome. In 1296, the pope issued a provocative bull, *Clericis laicos*, banning secular rulers from raking in church revenues without the express permission of the pope. No tax raids on monasteries and parishes unless Rome had been consulted first. The intention of the bull was to reinforce the independence of the church and the authority of the pope. Boniface also wanted to exert pressure on countries like England and France to consider funding a new crusade instead of scrapping over territory in Europe. Christian monarchs should be spending less time at each other's throats and instead, divert their energies to recovering the holy sites for Christendom. But times had changed, and Boniface was forced to back down faced with an outbreak of royal fury in both England and France.[1]

The French king – Philip IV 'the Fair' (1268–1314) – who would prove to be Boniface's nemesis, protested the loudest. He was the grandson of Louis IX, who had fought on two crusades and bankrupted France in the process.

So, money was a touchy subject for Philip, and he was in no mood to have faraway Rome lecturing him on how to tax his subjects. The pope, realising he had overstepped the mark, adopted a softer approach. To try to mollify Philip, Boniface canonised his grandfather, King Louis, in 1297. But that only served to bolster Philip's ego and belief in his own divine right to rule. He was now the descendant of a saint – yet one more reason not to be bossed around by a mere pontiff.[2]

Philip initiated a campaign of negative spin against Boniface. Stories began to circulate that the pope had murdered his elderly predecessor, Celestine V, by driving a nail into his head. Celestine had resigned due to old age and was very likely imprisoned by Boniface to keep him out of the way. He had died six months after his resignation at the papal castle in Fumone, southeast of Rome. Aged 81, he hardly posed a serious threat to Boniface.

But medieval popes had good reason to be nervous about having a second pope in the vicinity. Nearly every head of the Roman Catholic church during the Templar period was faced with an 'antipope' – and sometimes more than one. However, claiming that Boniface had driven a nail into his predecessor's head was a devastating accusation. A footnote to this story is that in 2013, an examination of Celestine's mortal remains found no evidence of trauma to his skull during life, evidencing foul play. So, Boniface and the nail was fake news.[3]

In 1301, Philip arrested the bishop of Pamiers, Bernard Saisset, who had been sent by Boniface to investigate the monarch's abuse of the church. The pope was incensed, arguing that his bishop had diplomatic immunity. Now it was Philip's turn to back down. However, Boniface was incandescent with rage. He fired off two papal bulls listing the church's grievances against Philip, to be read from every pulpit in France. Philip made very sure that did not happen. When the papal nuncio handed him the documents from Rome, the king burned them. Then he forged a replacement papal bull that did not contradict what Boniface had said – but changed the language to make the pontiff appear completely unhinged. Read from church pulpits, it would show that Boniface was a corrupt and dictatorial ogre.[4]

Now the two sides – French king and pope – were playing tit-for-tat. Boniface proposed an ecclesiastical council to deal with the errant king, so Philip convened France's Estates General – a parliament made up of all the country's social classes: nobility, church prelates, and the commons. Unsurprisingly it condemned the pope, with even France's bishops and clerics voting to support the king. The only exception being the abbot of Cîteaux, the birthplace of the Cistercian order, but for dissenting, he was arrested.

In reaction, Boniface scribbled another bull declaring again that monarchs are subordinate to the vicar of Christ. Then in April 1303, he excommunicated unnamed people who blocked the work of the church. In response, Philip's chief minister, Guillaume de Nogaret (1260–1313), publicly denounced the pope as a heretic and a thief, demanding his overthrow and arrest. For good measure, he made it known that the pope also endorsed sodomy. The temperature was certainly rising between Rome and Paris.[5]

Then the unthinkable happened. De Nogaret received reports that Boniface was about to excommunicate King Philip by name. He conspired with pro-French cardinals and a member of Rome's influential Colonna family – Sciarra Colonna (1270–1329) – who had backed the elderly Celestine, but despised Boniface. They were willing accomplices in De Nogaret's conspiracy to kidnap the pope, bring him back to Paris, and put him on trial.

De Nogaret and Colonna, with a group of armed men, stormed down to the pope's summer residence at Anagni, just outside Rome, and gave Boniface a severe beating. Colonna even slapping His Holiness across the face in what became dubbed the 'Outrage of Anagni'. Local soldiers managed to rescue the pope but weeks later, he died of a fever.

In this whole episode of king versus Pope, we see a foreshadowing of the tactics that Philip was about to deploy against the Knights Templar. The outlandish charges of heresy and sodomy followed by show trials and for the knights, imprisonment, and execution. The king had no qualms about using force against those who defied his will, no matter how sacred their person. His pursuit of the divine right to rule his own kingdom – and paying off his debts – led to both a reduction of papal power and influence as well as the destruction of the Knights Templar. An order of knights answerable only to the pope in Rome.

Acre had been lost but De Molay had not given up getting the order back onto the mainland. Being holed up in Cyprus was no substitute for running the Templar castles that had once dotted the landscape of the Levant. Safed, Gaza, Sidon, Beaufort, Chastel Blanc, and many others now lay in Mamluk hands. This was an unacceptable situation for a grand master who had been involved in all the final key battles on the mainland at places like Servantikar and Roche-Guillaume – now lost to the Mamluks. But one tiny piece of land offered some hope. The island of Ru'ad off the Syrian coast could be a bridgehead from which to retake the former stronghold of Tortosa and then on to Atlit and Acre.

Grounds for optimism emerged in 1299 and 1300 when the Mongols inflicted defeats on the Mamluks. They sent letters to the west inviting the crusaders to join in and smash the common enemy. This was heady stuff for the Templars, who resolved to hook up with the Mongols and get back into outremer. By July 1300, the Templars together with Henry II of Cyprus (1270–1324) – the last crowned King of Jerusalem – were conducting raids on Acre and Tortorsa – and even Alexandria and Rosetta in Egypt. The Mongols sent their ambassador to Cyprus, Italian-born Isol the Pisan, to accompany these expeditions.

By November 1300, De Molay had enough confidence to launch an attempted invasion of the former Templar fortress of Tortosa on the Syrian mainland. About 150 Templar knights were sent from Cyprus to Ru'ad with hundreds of soldiers for a seaborne assault. The plan was to attack by sea while the Mongols swooped in on land. Surrounded, the Mamluks would surely surrender. Tired of waiting for the Mongols, who had been delayed, De Molay charged ahead, entering Tortosa, and ransacking it. The Mongols did eventually turn up but by that stage, De Molay had pulled back his forces to Cyprus with a garrison left behind on Ru'ad island.

Having set foot once more in Tortosa, De Molay felt emboldened. He sent fevered dispatches to European monarchs and the pope demanding assistance – and preferably, another full-blown crusade. The pope gave permission for the Templars to continue holding Ru'ad, which they did under the command of the Templar Marshal, Barthélemy de Quincy (died 1302). But beyond that, there was little tangible assistance.

In 1302, the Mamluks decided to snuff out this offshore Templar outpost. They sent a fleet and besieged the Templar garrison, which was forced to surrender. Safe conduct was guaranteed but the Mamluks reneged on the terms as the gates opened, massacring the Turcopoles and taking many Templars as prisoners to Cairo. De Quincy had been killed already during the fighting. This was the final dismal chapter of the crusades.

All of which was noted in France where the king was determined to rein in papal power and bring the Templars, who he viewed as the pope's agents, to heel. His enforcer was a highly capable and intelligent operator, Guillaume de Nogaret. A man who possessed similar qualities to Henry VIII of England's adviser in the sixteenth century: Thomas Cromwell. Ruthless, focused, and lacking in any deference towards ecclesiastical power and privileges. Though unlike Cromwell, De Nogaret was not of low birth but came from a respectable noble family, with his father, Bertrand de Nogaret, having served on crusade with King Louis IX.

His hostile stance towards the Roman Catholic church may have been influenced by his grandfather being a Cathar – one of those heretics whose sect had been brutally suppressed during the Albigensian Crusade. Across France, there were thousands of families impacted by the papacy's decision to drown the Cathars in their own blood. Few in the Languedoc region would have lacked a grandparent or cousin who had not experienced the full wrath of the pope and the crusaders sent to commit horrific atrocities in the early thirteenth century. As Philip moved against the church, there would have been a wellspring of support in French society from those who recalled the massacres, burnings, and torture of their ancestors.[6]

De Nogaret viewed the Templars as creatures of the pope. Two-hundred years of papal bulls exempting them from royal authority certainly pointed in that direction – and Rome's favouring of the knights had not ceased. The knights in turn did their utmost to keep onside with whoever was pope. For example, under Boniface, in 1298, the Templars responded quickly to a request for funds from the pope when a wagonload of loot bound for Rome was stolen by the Colonna family. The Hospitallers were apparently less generous in their support, but the Templars gave His Holiness exactly the amount required. All of which flagged up something very important to De Nogaret and King Philip. That the Templars, despite all their setbacks in outremer, were still exceedingly rich. Wealthy, armed to the teeth, and unaccountable – little wonder the King of France resolved to do something about the knights.[7]

Even within the Roman Catholic church, there was a realisation that change was necessary. This was not the year 1095 or 1147. Several crusades later and the vision of Bernard of Clairvaux was yesterday's news. Nobody was queueing to take the cross or join a sacred military order in a messianic venture to retake Jerusalem. Rationalisation was the order of the day, with growing discussions behind closed doors about merging the Knights Templar and Knights Hospitaller, even allowing monarchs such as King Philip to have more control over this unified order. This reflected the changing balance of power between the pope and Europe's monarchs who were groping towards a sense of nationhood and baulking against the transnational papacy. That is a simplification but viewed from today, it's an easy-to-grasp explanation.

One man doing a lot of thinking about the orders was the Catalan church philosopher Ramon Llull (1232–1316). Born in Majorca in the same year that Christian forces entered the city of Medina Mayurqa, ending over 300 years of Muslim rule on the Spanish island. A self-taught church philosopher, he initially embraced the crusading ideal and, in the summer of 1301, went to Cyprus on news that the Templars and Mongols were about to hook up and retake cities on the mainland. When this failed to materialise, Llull increasingly emphasised the superiority of missionary work among Jews and Muslims – and eastern rite Christians such as Nestorians – to bring them into the Roman Catholic church. He was particularly insistent that all those involved in this godly activity learn Arabic – or whatever language the non-believers spoke.

Llull met De Molay on Cyprus and understood the need to couple peaceful missionary activity with the sword. He was no pacifist. But he came round strongly to the idea of merging the two orders under King Philip of France. After all, Philip's grandfather had been an exemplary, though unsuccessful, crusader leader with many saintly attributes. Why couldn't his grandson perform the same role? Philip liked what he heard, and the pope who succeeded Boniface – a Frenchman – swung round to the same view.

In June 1306, Pope Clement V (1264–1314) asked De Molay and the grand master of the Knights Hospitaller, Fulk of Villaret (died 1327), to submit separate reports addressing two key questions. One was the viability of another crusade against the Saracens while the other was their views on merging the two orders. De Molay had plenty to say about the first question but was clearly unhappy about the second.

Replying to Clement, he advised the church not to turn its back on the crusades – but to commit more than ever. It was true that Christian forces were in control of absolutely nothing in what had been outremer. There were no Frankish castles behind whose walls an army could retreat or cities that would throw open their gates. So, the next crusade had to be on the scale of the earliest crusades. Anything less would be annihilated by the Mamluks. As for those who had once been viewed as allies, such as the Armenians, De Molay warned that they would refuse to cooperate, suspecting that the Franks wanted to annex their kingdom.

'Hence, for these and many other reasons I could allege, in no way do I advise a small force, in fact I advise against it as strongly as I can and reject it totally so as to avoid bringing any shame and harm to Christendom.'

Instead, De Molay insisted on an 'all-embracing expedition to destroy the infidels and to restore the blood-spattered Holy Land of Christ'. The Templar grand master urged the pope to reach out as a matter of urgency to the kings of France, England, Germany, Sicily, and Aragon to demand they climb on board for yet another crusade. Genoa and Venice, as maritime powers, should provide large vessels to ship horses and provisions. And quoting Baybars, who he referred to as 'Bothendar', De Molay said that he had once been told that the Mamluk leader would retreat if faced by more than 30,000 Mongols or Franks.

The main crusading force should leave from Cyprus where De Molay would share top secret intelligence that would ensure success. Getting rather carried away with himself, the grand master then begged the pope to prepare ten galleys for the defence of Cyprus immediately. Control of the seas was essential to stop 'evil Christians' sending supplies to the Mamluks for money. This was a jibe at Genoese and Venetian merchants. If Clement would agree to all this, it would ensure the recovery 'in your lifetime the holy places in which our Lord Jesus Christ deigned to be born and die for the salvation of the human race'.

Regarding the proposed merger, it was impossible to argue against the economics of bringing the Templars and Hospitallers together, saving costs and achieving synergies. So, De Molay conceded that point. But then waffled on about the organisational difficulties it would pose with so many properties and pots of money to divide up. Clement saw through De Molay's special pleading. The challenge was not as insurmountable as the grand master was making out. The real issue was that the two orders had degenerated into rival fiefdoms. De Molay did concede that there certainly was competition between the Templars and Hospitallers, but he wrote it off as a healthy thing – kept everybody on their toes.

Louis IX had left France with a mountain of debt off the back of his crusading in Egypt. Even the cost of buying the Crown of Thorns paled next to the deficit incurred from military spending. But far from embarking on a policy of debt reduction, his grandson Philip was embroiled in a war with England over control of Gascony that only added to the problem.

To try to resolve his debt issues, he first refused to honour loans to the Lombards – Italian merchants operating in his realm. When they complained, he banished them and seized their goods and property. Similar treatment was then meted out to the Jewish money lenders, leading the king to expel all Jews from France in 1306. Just sixteen years before in 1290, King Edward I of England – also cash strapped – similarly banished the Jewish population of England and expropriated their property. He had already ordered out every Jewish family from Gascony in 1287. So, a precedent existed for Philip's drastic and highly discriminatory action.[8]

Philip was at loggerheads with Rome over taxing the clergy and as the situation deteriorated further, he debased the coinage repeatedly. What this meant was that the king ordered the mints to reduce the amount of silver in the currency. The French silver coin, known as the gros tournois, could be exchanged in 1285 for 3.95 grams of silver. But by 1303, after several of Philip's devaluations, it was only worth 1.35 grams of silver.

This resulted in inflation as the value of money declined. In turn, this led to growing social unrest as ordinary people found that their money was buying less and less. Starvation was blamed firmly on the king.[9] There is an unverifiable story that during a riot in Paris resulting from widespread discontent, the king took refuge in the Paris Temple. While there, he could not help noticing the chests of money and treasure deposited with the knights for safe keeping. If only – he thought – I could do to the Templars what I have done to the Lombards and Jews, then my problems might be solved.

In 1306, Pope Clement asked De Molay and the grand master of the Knights Hospitaller to join him in the French city of Poitiers on All Saints Day – 1 November. Both men were late by a matter of months arriving in the spring of 1307, for different reasons. De Molay was already aware that a trio of renegade Templars, expelled from the order, had been making serious allegations of impropriety to whoever in authority would listen. King James II of Aragon had sent them on their way, refusing to believe the stories, but Philip IV of France had proven to be far more receptive. So much so that he mentioned it to Clement at his papal coronation in 1305.

Clement assured De Molay that he would instigate an official enquiry and the grand master clearly felt this would exonerate the order and was reassured when the pope notified the king of his intention to investigate the matter. With the benefit of hindsight, it's hard to wonder how De Molay was unable to see the impending disaster. But at the time, he was clearly convinced that the king was not about to round on the Templars. He might have a beef with the pope, but the knights were beyond reproach.

On 12 October 1307, De Molay was a pallbearer at the funeral of the Latin Empress of Constantinople, Catherine I (1274–1307), who had died aged 32. Her husband was King Philip's brother, Charles, count of Valois (1270–1325). Honoured with performing such a role at a royal burial, the grand master had no reason to believe he was about to be the subject of an arrest warrant issued by the king. But the very next day – Friday, 13 October – De Molay was arrested by De Nogaret, in person, at the Paris Temple. Charles of Valois would later protest at his torture but proximity to the royal family offered no real protection in these circumstances. The king was bent on destroying the Knights Templar.

Chapter Nine

Arrest Warrants and Trials

On Friday the thirteenth, 1307, the warrants were enacted for the arrest of all Knights Templar. Their properties were seized, and knights flung into dungeons. Very soon, the sadistic torturers set to work extracting the desired confessions from men once regarded as holy warriors. The warrants had been issued some weeks before in total secrecy. The document pressed into the hands of bailiffs and seneschals all over France detailed crimes that were horrible to contemplate and terrible to hear. The Templars had committed acts behind closed doors that were 'an abominable work', 'a detestable disgrace', and 'set apart from humanity'.[1]

Through their deeds, they crucified Jesus all over again, the warrant read, only this time 'causing Him greater injuries than those he received on the Cross'. On becoming a Templar, it claimed, they denied Christ three times and spat on a crucifix. They then removed their clothes and were kissed by the visitor, a senior Templar official, 'on the lower part of the dorsal spine, secondly on the navel and finally on the mouth'. This, the warrant declared, was a disgrace to the dignity of humanity. Their initiation rite echoed the worshipping of the golden calf detailed in the biblical book of Exodus when the children of Israel turned their back on God, opting to venerate a useless metal idol.

Informers and denouncers had stepped forward to tell all. This included a former Templar, Esquin of Floryan, who had first approached King James II of Aragon to unburden himself of what he had seen going on within the order. But the Spanish king was unconvinced and sent the disgruntled knight on his way. However, he got a more willing audience in Philip. In a written statement, the ex-Templar confirmed the insults levelled against Christ, and the same-sex relations between knights, that were actively encouraged. In addition, 'they worship an idol which they call their god'. Esquin finished his statement by pointing out that he had been promised 3,000 Livres in cash payment from Templar assets if his allegations proved to be true.

In a single day, about 15,000 Templars – including knights, sergeants, chaplains, and servants – were rounded up for questioning. The entire assets of the order were also sequestered by the crown. Other monarchs in Europe looked with shock at what was going on in France. Attitudes varied between those who wondered if they now had an opportunity to balance their own budgets by seizing Templar wealth while others, in kingdoms like Portugal, felt a residual loyalty to the knights. They had, after all, been instrumental in driving the Moors southwards. And many of these kings had seen no evidence for what Philip and De Nogaret were alleging in their arrest warrant. They were also more than aware of Philip's track record with the papacy.

Philip had not explicitly informed the pope of the forthcoming arrests and with good reason. The news would have almost certainly leaked out, warning the Templars of their impending doom. The pope at this moment was Clement V, born Raymond Bertrand de Got, in the duchy of Aquitaine. His election to the papacy in 1305 had been amenable to both the English and French as Aquitaine was part of King Edward I of England's Angevin possessions, held on condition that Edward agreed to be a vassal to the French king. Therefore, this pope was viewed as a creature of both the English and French crowns. Crucially, he was not Italian, so unlike Boniface VIII, Clement was not embroiled in Roman family politics. Indeed, Clement was the first of seven successive popes who were all French and decided to base themselves at the papal palace in Avignon – in modern France – instead of sitting in Rome. It's been described as a period of 'Babylonian captivity' where the papacy was deemed a prisoner of the French king.

However, there were tensions in this relationship. Clement was initially unhappy that the knights under his control had been summarily arrested and imprisoned. Not only did the papacy feel that it should be consulted on taxation of church assets, but it believed that the state should hand over clerics for trial in church courts, not secular courts. Bad enough that Philip was squeezing monasteries and churches to pay for his wars, but launching a purge against the Templars, with no opportunity for them to prove their innocence, was a step too far. Clement begged Philip to let the church investigate the accusations against the knights in a balanced and reasonable manner.

The king treated the letter with utmost scorn. Not only were Templars arrested but De Nogaret had issued instructions to the bailiffs and seneschals to begin an immediate inventory of all Templar assets. He also specified that these officials could, in their duties, 'investigate the houses of other religious orders' if deemed relevant. The farms and vineyards of the Templars in France were to be entrusted straight away to the local nobility and their servants. So, even as the pope fumed, the order's property was being split up and handed away.

The cost of imprisoning so many Templars was enormous and deducted from seized Templar assets. In effect, they paid for their own torture. In addition, there was the cost of food, the salaries of guards, and the fees of priests coming to hear their confessions, or administer last rites in some cases. This was all meticulously recorded and deducted. Philip and De Nogaret detained the knights in spaces run by the secular authorities and not the church, which it was felt might go soft on the Templars. Initially, a large number were kept under lock and key at the Paris Temple, their own headquarters. But in the months that followed, they were dispersed to other sites around the city and wider France. This was essential to separate key people but also to follow the commissions that now held court, conducting public interrogations of the Templars.

From testimonies given at the commissions by jailed Templars, it was clear that from very soon after their arrests, torture began to be applied. The legacy of the Albigensian Crusade and other heretical movements had brought both the church and state round to the view that torture was an acceptable form of interrogation. In 1252, Pope Innocent IV issued a bull stating that the newly created papal inquisition could torture heretics provided their bones were not broken or lives endangered. This brought church-sanctioned torture in line with what the state was already doing in its prisons.

Yet Clement was distressed by intelligence he received in Avignon that the Templars were being tortured. In another letter to the king on 27 October 1307, he added a very carefully worded sentence that some might say was mealy-mouthed in light of what he was referring to in the prisons:

'To add to our grief, you have not yet released them (the Templars) but, according to our reports, have gone further and added a greater affliction to those who are already considerably afflicted by their imprisonment, an affliction which we consider it better not to mention for the moment for the sake of the church as much as yours, if you understand our meaning.'

The trials of the Templars would last years and in 1310, a group told the pope to his face that they had been tortured into confessing. From the day of their arrest, they had been subjected to degrading treatment intended to break their spirit. This included being fed just bread and water while confined to a cold, dank space with shackles on their hands and feet. One knight described having his feet burned by fire to such an extent that bones fell off in the days afterwards. In case this was greeted with incredulity, he produced the bones from his pocket. Some knights died during interrogation while others blurted out anything to end the horror.

De Molay and others confessed, then retracted their confessions, and then confessed again. This went on over a seven-year period of incarceration, judicial proceedings, and in 1310 – the mass burning of over fifty Templars. These unfortunates were taken to a field just outside Paris, near the convent of Saint-Antoine, and placed on an enormous pyre that was then set alight. Up until then, many Templars had assumed that the charges would, at the very least, lead to a long period of penance and, at the most, life in prison. As a result, they equivocated on their confessions, sometimes retracting what they had said. King Philip resolved to make an example that would speed up the whole process. One could say that this appalling scene, followed by further burnings, turned up the heat on the Templars.

What is abundantly clear from the arrest and subsequent trials of the Templars between 1307 and 1314 is that the high point of papal power had passed and a new age of monarchs flexing their political muscles had begun. One might even trace a direct line from the Templar trials, instigated by King Philip, through to the Protestant Reformation of England's King Henry VIII. Both events extending royal power over the church using very different pretexts. Philip portrayed his power grab as a move against heresy perpetrated by armed knights under papal control. Henry used the refusal of the pope to grant him a divorce from his first queen to end Rome's sway in his realm. Both had the same outcome – a dramatic reduction in papal power.

Most of Europe was not yet on board with the idea of annihilating the Knights Templar. Even those who would be most intimately involved in the interrogations, down to the torturer applying the thumbscrews, had to be convinced that these previously adored warriors for Christ were in fact agents of Satan. It was a big mental leap that required a barrage of propaganda to shift medieval public opinion. The same accusations would need to be hammered home repeatedly based on what had been outlined in the arrest warrants.

The deadliest of those accusations was heresy. This was defined by the church, being the experts on all matters spiritual. The primary motive for stamping out heresy was that the views of people like the Cathars and Waldensians posed a direct threat to the authority of the pope and his bishops. But with the Knights Templar, it was the king and his chief minister who led the onslaught against alleged Templar heresy, dragging the pope behind them. One historian has referred to this as the 'pontificalisation of the French monarchy' – the king assuming the role of pope in the national interest. He accused the knights of a form of heresy that sent chills down the spine.[2]

The Templars, it was declared, had been worshipping some kind of bestial demon behind closed doors. The demon was a creature named Baphomet. In occult and Satanist circles since the nineteenth century, Baphomet has typically been depicted as a goat-headed demon with a pentagram on its forehead giving a Christian-style mockery of a benediction. This image was the creation of Éliphas Lévi (1810–1875), who wrote many books on magic, alchemy, and the occult. His drawing of Baphomet was based on images going back centuries of horned creatures attending witches' sabbaths as well as the Tarot card – Le Diable.

The inquisitors who tortured imprisoned Templars may not have had the exact same image in their minds, but it would have been something similar. Medieval illuminated works and the gargoyles of Gothic cathedrals – so hated by Bernard of Clairvaux – often brought to life demonic creatures with horns, wings, and protruding tongues. Lévi was merely reinterpreting ancient goat-headed demons, not inventing them. These were beings from hell that interfered in human affairs, even trying to insinuate their way into churches. In some churches in the English county of Essex, 'devil doors' were built on the north side of churches to encourage the evil one to leave, lest he snatch the soul of an unbaptised child.

Cats also cropped up as alleged objects of Templar worship. They had long featured as agents of evil in Christian art and folklore. The twelfth-century Winchester Bible includes an image of a cat-shaped idol venerated on an altar. In a quite disturbing image from a thirteenth-century French religious work, we see the antichrist worshipped on one side by two Jews, and on the other by heretics, one of whom clutches a cat. During the witch-hunting craze of the fifteenth to seventeenth centuries, witches were believed to keep cats as companions on account of their sly and evil nature.[34]

Tribunals in Paris heard testimony from nine Templars who claimed to have seen a head worshipped in chapter meetings that took place across Europe from Paris to Limassol, Cyprus. Sometimes this head was painted on a beam, or it was fashioned from wood, silver, covered in gold leaf, or had four legs attached. One account claimed it was the mouldering head of the first grand master, Hugh de Payens. The idea of a talking head handing out instructions to the knights seems almost laughable, reminiscent of those coin-operated fortune-telling fairground machines from the early twentieth century or something akin to a ventriloquist's dummy. But these confessions from arrested or former Templars were treated with utmost seriousness and were regarded as a capital crime.[5]

Ralph of Gizy had seen the strange idol venerated at seven different chapter meetings, some chaired by Hugh de Pairaud, the visitor. In truth, nobody could quite agree on the identity of these magical heads. William of Arreblay, the preceptor of Soisy, thought that a silver head he had seen often at chapter meetings came from one of the 11,000 virgins massacred along with Saint Ursula in the third or fourth century CE because they refused to lose their virginity to an army of invading Huns.

John of la Casagne saw a large brazen idol in the shape of a man brought out of a box, wearing a dalmatic, the Byzantine-influenced robe worn by priests. The preceptor told La Casagne: 'Here is a friend of God, who speaks with God, when he wishes, to whom you must bring thanks, since he has led you to this state, which you desire greatly, and he fulfils that desire.' While venerating this curious idol, the brothers simultaneously spat at a crucifix. But what was this idol? Some Templars claimed it was a creature called Baphomet while others referred to it as Yalla, or just a nameless devil.

One recent theory asserts that the head being worshipped was that of Jesus Christ. The theory, expounded by author Keith Laidler, is that Jesus may have been linked to the cult of head worship common in the Middle East for millennia. The heads of heroes and holy men were taken after their death and venerated. A reference in the apocryphal (not accepted by the church) gospel of Nicodemus states that the author of this gospel, a pharisee drawn to the teachings of Jesus, carried a very lifelike head of Jesus around with him in the aftermath of the crucifixion.[6]

In the Gospel of John, Nicodemus visits the tomb of Christ at night. The inference being that he possessed the actual head of Christ in the spirit of those ancient head cults. Laidler also argues that the Templars began burying their own knights with their heads removed after learning about these belief systems while in Jerusalem. As for the head of Christ's whereabouts today, he believes it may be under the very ornately carved Apprentice Pillar at Rosslyn chapel in Scotland – famously featured in Dan Brown's novel *The Da Vinci Code*.

As the commissions and enquiries ground on through the years, the pressure on the ageing De Molay was enormous. Addressing the papal commission at Paris on 26 November 1309, two years after his arrest, a dishevelled grand master admitted that he was 'not as wise as he needed to be' when confronted by these allegations of heresy. He was not a great man of learning and lacked any money to mount a serious defence against such grave charges. The official account of this judicial hearing is very patronising in tone, with the bluff De Molay needing to have key documents read out in 'the vulgar tongue', and not church Latin. As De Molay conceded, he was not an intellectual or a lawyer, though these skill sets would certainly have been undeniably useful.

Under massive pressure from King Philip, the pope convened the Council of Vienne between 1311 and 1312 to withdraw all support from the Knights Templar. Just in case Clement lacked sufficient spine, Philip turned up in person towards the end of its deliberations to ensure the knights were condemned as heretics.

Along with the Templars, religious communities of women known as the Beguines were also labelled heretics at the council and threatened with being burned at the stake. The Beguines lived in semi-monastic conditions and, in their neighbourhoods, performed the role of priest and lay preacher. One of their greatest champions was Jacques de Vitry, who had so disapproved of the low morals he encountered in Acre when sent there as a bishop. He claimed that it was a Beguine, Marie of Oignies (1177–1213), who inspired him to become a priest. But unlike De Vitry, the church disliked these women who behaved as if they had been ordained, which was strictly forbidden by the Catholic church then as it is today. Women could be nuns, but not priests.

As so often happens at times of societal upheaval, women found themselves in the firing line. Philip was a king determined to have all aspects of his kingdom under his control. A band of armed men under direct papal control – the Templars – was unacceptable. So, it turned out, were groups of assertive and independently minded women living in communal houses with an undefined role in the church and society.[7]

By the time the council met, a prominent Beguine had already been tried and burned at the stake at the Place de Grève in Paris on 1 June 1310. A few years before, Louis IX had ordered the burning of hundreds of copies of the Jewish Talmud at the same spot during an antisemitic pogrom in the city. The woman condemned to die was Marguerite Porete, author of a mystical Christian work, *The Mirror of Simple Souls*, which to the church's horror had been written in French and not Latin. Marguerite was handed over for questioning to the Inquisitor of France, the leading Dominican William of Paris (died 1314), who also led the interrogations of the Knights Templar. After refusing to acknowledge the inquisitor's authority or confess under torture, she was led out and burned at the stake. Her bold refusal to recant, even as the flames rose, would be the hallmark of De Molay's death four years later.[8]

The Knights Templar were accused of two abhorrent crimes that were interwoven in the medieval mind: heresy and sodomy. Both undermined the natural world as created by the Almighty. Sodomy was not simply a sexual act but an attack on the universe – a sin that threatened to destabilise the whole edifice of Christianity. In short – it was lethal sex.

For such a dangerous activity, with earth-shattering consequences, sodomy was ill-defined. During the Middle Ages, sodomy extended to homosexuality, bestiality, masturbation, and oral sex. It was a catch-all term for what medieval society regarded as deviant. Saint Peter Damian (1007–1072), a leading cleric and religious thinker, was very specific about the different forms of sodomy and listed the appropriate punishments. For example, monks should be thrown out of the church for sex with men or women. While a man who 'fornicates between the thighs' must do a year of penance; 'in the rear' demanded three years; and with a sheep or mule required ten years of penance.

> *'For how may one be a cleric, or named as such, if according to his own judgement he does not fear to be soiled either by his own hands or those of another, fondling his own male parts or those of another, or fornicating with contemptible irrationality either between the thighs or in the rear?'*[9]

A man 'who engages with another man in feminine copulation', an act punishable in scripture by death, could be pardoned of his guilt but never admitted to the church. Peter Damian took fire at those who must have been stating that monk-on-monk sex was fine in comparison to a monk lying with a nun. He was not buying that argument. Monks lying together would be treated in the same way as one sharing a bed with a nun. It was unacceptable for them to remain inside the church.

Same-sex relations with men, or with animals, were bracketed together – but homosexuality seemed to pose a more pressing threat in the cloister or dormitory. A man who 'has been polluted with another man through the ardour of lust, he is ordered to pray not among Catholic Christians, but among the demonically possessed'. They have traded their flesh to demons by defying the laws of nature, Peter Damian continued. 'For when a man thrusts himself upon another man to commit impure acts, it is not from a natural carnal drive, but only the stimulus of diabolic impulse.'[10]

Sodomy was not just a physical act but the destruction of one's soul and the expulsion of the Holy Spirit. Those who engaged in acts of sodomy allowed the devil to enter. 'It makes the citizen of the heavenly Jerusalem into an heir of the Babylonian underworld.' These unnatural acts undermined the very 'walls of the heavenly homeland'. Sodomy 'gnaws the conscience like worms, burns the flesh like a fire, and pants with desire for pleasure'. In short, the sodomite was the worst form of heretic, threatening to bring down the entire edifice of Christianity if left unchallenged and unpunished.

The Third Lateran Council in 1179, presided over by Alexander III, and where William of Tyre had sought to curb Templar privileges, saw a toughening of Rome's stance on homosexuality within the church, described as the vice for which God had destroyed 'the five cities with fire'. Thomas Aquinas (1225–1274), a Dominican friar and church philosopher, later explained that when the sodomite violates the laws of nature, an injury is done to God – as the divine author of nature. Any sexual activity not directed towards making babies had to be prohibited if the universe was not to be thrown off balance: 'It is evident that, in accordance with the natural order, the union of the sexes among animals is ordered towards conception. From this it follows that every sexual intercourse that cannot lead to conception is opposed to man's animal nature.'[11]

As the popes of the early medieval period sought to enforce celibacy on priests – many of whom were secretly married or had concubines – they had to create an asexual masculine ideal. There is little doubt that in the twelfth and thirteenth centuries, the holy military orders, especially the Templars and Hospitallers, were very attractive to the church precisely because they exemplified the most masculine of traits while also observing the vow of total chastity. The Templars, with their use of violence to advance the cause of Christ, might not have sex lives but neither were they eunuchs. Indeed, the early medieval church was very explicit that a man had to be in full possession of his genitals to be a priest – or a Templar. Castration was not an alternative to complete abstinence.[12]

Not everybody was convinced that this asexual masculine ideal was achievable or desirable. One clerical writer, Serlo of Bayeux (c.1050–1113), even accused those in the church pushing hardest for celibacy of being 'sodomites' who wanted to punish married priests out of vindictiveness.[13] Among wider society, there was an incessant stream of gossip about priests failing to be chaste. Medieval poets and authors from Giovanni Boccacio (1313–1375) to Dante Alighieri (1265–1321) and Geoffrey Chaucer (c.1340s-1400) mocked church figures from priests to popes as being thoroughly licentious. Nobody could seriously curb their most natural urges.

With monks and friars accused of sodomy all the way down to the Protestant Reformation of the sixteenth century, it's perhaps not surprising that the Knights Templar would eventually face the same charge. An all-male organisation, sleeping in shared dormitories, recruiting young men who for decades were forced to deny their basic urges. For those who wanted to denigrate the knights, it took very little imagination to brand them as a nest of sodomites. De Nogaret's dungeon torturers simply got the knights to confess that this depravity was institutionalised, baked into the order's ethos and initiation rites.[14]

The evidence was made to look watertight. In statements made by Templars during the trials, there were over a hundred documented incidences of alleged homosexual acts being performed within the order – though only three involved sexual intercourse. William of Giac served in the household of De Molay in Cyprus and allegedly had sex with the last grand master three times in one night. Hugh of Narsac testified that De Molay had homosexual sex with a man called George, who died by drowning. Hugh was sure this was divine punishment for his terrible sin. A Spanish brother who worked close to De Molay had homosexual relations with another brother but only agreed to this because he was told it was the rules. But mostly it was kissing – on the mouth, torso, and backside.

De Pairaud, mentioned above, was also accused of taking Jean de Cugy 'behind an altar and kissing him on the base of the spine and the navel'. The added detail of this taking place behind an altar inferring that the act was not so much a part of the initiation ritual, conducted in the eyes of God, but for private pleasure. Ithier of Rochefort admitted to 'obscene' kisses; Nicholas of Sarra denied the holiness of Christ before stripping off and being kissed at the base of the spine, navel, and mouth: while Ralph of Grandeville had a same-sex encounter 'enjoined upon him' via the usual kisses.

At a hearing in the city of Cahors, famous for its money lenders, Peter Donaderi told how he had been received into the order thirty years before. Everything seemed routine enough as he shed his secular clothes and donned the mantle of the order. But then he returned to find the preceptor 'like a four-legged beast on knees and elbows', at which point he was told to kiss him on the spine and navel before spitting on a crucifix and denying Christ three times.

The overwhelming response from historians down the centuries to these accusations is that they were largely cooked up by Philip and De Nogaret. The king and his chief minister concocted a damning narrative backed up with confessions obtained under torture. However, from a modern perspective, this is problematic. How do we react in our own time to allegations of sexual abuse? Several respected organisations, in particular the Roman Catholic church, have been accused in recent decades of fostering an internal culture of institutionalised sexual abuse, so the idea of brushing these claims aside would be entirely unacceptable today. We should at least pause to consider the possibility that senior Templars abused their position to exploit young recruits. Is it right to automatically assume that an ex-Templar like Esquin of Floryan, not subjected to torture, fabricated his claims?

Or was it the case that in this all-male environment, consensual same-sex activity was very common? Any LGBT man in the Middle Ages, who never wished to be asked again by his family and neighbours when he was going to marry a woman and have children, had an escape route. Joining a monastery or a military order, like the Templars or Hospitallers, guaranteed plenty of all-male comradeship and close bonding. Only those who imagine that homosexuals needed the term invented by psychologists in the 1880s to realise their desires would flatly rule this out.

That said, those accusing the Templars of habitual sodomite practices knew that it was a sure-fire way to bring down an opponent in the Middle Ages. Adam Orleton (died 1345) was an English cleric and diplomat to the papal court at Avignon. He honed his skills as a clerical lawyer prosecuting Templars over the issue of sodomy. Years later in 1326, he would lead the charge in accusing King Edward II of England (1284–1327) of being a sodomite and therefore fit to be overthrown. The hapless monarch was heaved off his throne in a rebellion led by his wife, the queen, and allegedly murdered with a red-hot poker inserted up his backside. Orleton had learned in France that sodomy was a potent legal weapon to demolish the reputation of anybody – a king or an order of holy knights.

It is often stated that the Knights Templar had warning of the warrants and some managed to escape the clutches of the French king's agents. Furthermore, in the dead of night, the Templars emptied out their coffers – especially at the Paris Temple – and countless wagons trundled down to the port of La Rochelle, where the Templar fleet awaited. Once there, eighteen galleys were loaded up with men and treasure, then set sail, possibly for Switzerland, Scotland, or Portugal and then to lands beyond the seas yet to be discovered.

This story of the Templar fleet at La Rochelle was extracted from Jean de Châlons, a brother in the order, who claimed to have overheard Gerard de Villiers, master of France, hatching these plans. Like other Templars, many subjected to torture, De Châlons told a lurid tale about Templar initiation ceremonies. When being received into the order, he was shown an image of a crucifix in a missal (a book giving the order of service at mass) and was asked if he truly believed in the risen Christ. He replied: 'I truly believe.'

Then suddenly the senior Templar conducting the ceremony ordered him to deny Christ and spit on the image. De Châlons hesitated. He was then admonished and told to stop being disobedient or else he would be flung into a pit, something like an 'oubliette' – a tiny cell in which prisoners were starved to death. Shaking with terror, De Châlons obeyed denying Christ with his mouth, but not his heart. After that, 'he received a kiss which meant that he had been received'.

De Châlons rose to become a preceptor and learned many disturbing things about his own order. Apparently in that senior role he could punish any brother he hated by having them thrown into that pit. All De Châlons had to do was contact his superiors, pay some money, and it would be done. With his own eyes, he had seen poor unfortunates end their days in that dark and dank space with no food or water. This was symptomatic, he added, of the obsession with money and material goods within the Templars.

Along with heresy and sodomy, Philip was obsessed with the financial worth of the Templars. The kings of France had long depended on the order to help run the state finances and to borrow for wars and crusades, so they were in no doubt that the Templars were worth a great deal. It's often said that when Philip got to the Paris Temple, the cupboard was bare. That the dreamed-off riches he thought the brothers owned was an illusion. Or that the knights had spirited their wealth away having got notice of the arrest warrants.

Some Templar historians have speculated that graffiti on the walls of the fortress at Gisors, where many knights were held, includes the image of a large cart carrying treasure. Though why a Templar would scrawl pictures of a top-secret operation on the wall of his dungeon cell is anybody's guess. However, prisoners were wont to chisel or paint very intimate thoughts on walls in between torture sessions. An excellent example of this is the inquisition prison in Palermo, Sicily, where those accused of heresy painted images with a mixture of filth and water or urine. These were only uncovered fully in 2005 but give an incredible insight into the mindset of alleged heretics awaiting interrogation.

In 1946, the caretaker at Gisors, Roger Lhomoy, claimed to have found Templar treasure at the castle. Under the medieval battlements at Gisors, he had stumbled across an immense chapel with several large sarcophagi and thirty metal chests. He was convinced that this was wealth brought from the Paris Temple that never made it to La Rochelle.

The local council investigated and when neither the chests nor the chapel materialised, the caretaker was asked to find a job elsewhere. He went on to recount his story to Géraud-Marie de Sède, baron De Liéoux (1921–2004), who was an associate of Pierre Plantard, the man who invented the Priory of Sion in the 1950s. Another aristocratic friend of Plantard, Philippe Louis Henri Marie de Chérisey, ninth marquis De Chérisey (1923–1985), repeated the claim about Templar treasure at Gisors in 1967 but it has proven to be very elusive.

In 1312, five years after the Templars had been arrested, Clement V issued the bull of suppression: *Vox in excelso*. After centuries of privileges showered on the knights, the pope now disowned them. The name of the bull was very telling. Clement, quoting the biblical book of Jeremiah, declared that a voice had been heard from on high, full of lamentation and weeping. He went on to quote the verses that follow, applying them to the Templars:

'This house has aroused my anger and wrath, so that I will remove it from my sight because of the evil of its sons, for they have provoked me to anger, turning their backs to me, not their faces, and setting up their idols in the house in which my name is invoked, to defile it.'

Clement declared that the Knights Templar had given themselves up to demons. He had been warned at the time of his papal coronation that there was something wrong with the knights. There had been 'secret intimations' against De Molay, various preceptors, and brothers, but the church had not wanted to believe it. These warriors had been supported for so long in the vanguard of the crusades in outremer. It scarcely seemed possible, Clement continued, that they could fall into the 'sin of impious apostasy, the abominable vice of idolatry, the deadly crime of the sodomites, and various heresies'. Yet the church commissions had found this all to be true.

Thank goodness, King Philip had intervened in time. An illustrious monarch not at all motivated by greed, the pope noted. In fact, Philip had 'no intention of claiming or appropriating for himself anything from the Templars' property'. Instead, like his ancestors, he was fired by a holy zeal that forced his hand against the knights. Under oath, De Molay and the preceptors of Normandy, Outremer, Aquitaine, and Poitou had confirmed all the accusations made in Philip's arrest warrant – and more besides. There was nothing that could be done for the Knights Templar and what reputable young man would want to join them now anyway? It was time to shut the order down.

A subsequent bull, *Ad providam*, transferred Templar assets to the Knights Hospitaller, except for their holdings on the Iberian Peninsula. In effect, the situation regarding the rival order of Hospitallers had gone from proposed merger with the Templars to hostile takeover, enabled by the pope. One obvious question is why the Templars were subjected to a campaign of vilification and torture while the Hospitallers continued without harassment. Professor Malcolm Barber identified one economic motive being that Hospitaller wealth was overwhelmingly land based and they suffered as inflation rose under Philip, but rents remained fixed. Whereas the Templars had a more diversified portfolio with significant involvement in banking that protected their overall assets, also making them that much more attractive to a debt-ridden monarch.

Philip made sure that while the Hospitallers walked off with the Templars' assets, they would be forced to make several payments to the French crown including 200,000 livres tournois for royal goods the king claimed had been lodged at the Paris Temple, but which were now unaccounted for. Philip was making sure he got his cut of the action, which makes a mockery of Clement's earlier claim that the king was not in it for the money. Under Philip's successor and son, King Louis X (1289–1316), the Hospitallers would be forced to make further concessions including cancelling all the Templar debts of the French royal family.

Twenty years later, the Hospitallers were still paying out pensions to former Templars under terms agreed with the church. Knights who survived imprisonment and were freed after showing penance were pensioned off but reminded that their monastic vows still applied. However, some languished behind bars for many years and emerged in a pathetic state. One man who would never taste freedom was Jacques de Molay, last grand master of the order. He and the preceptor of Normandy, Geoffroi de Charney (died 1314), faced the grisliest form of execution, reserved for heretics.

But they had one last chance to save their skins. The two were led in front of a panel of church prelates and other senior figures who had decided, based on earlier confessions, to condemn the duo to life imprisonment. The same applied to the master of Aquitaine, Godefroi de Gonneville, and the master of Normandy, Hugues de Pairaud, who were standing alongside. But De Molay, now in his seventies, had reached the end of his tether. To the astonishment of everybody present, he retracted every confession made under torture. Seven years in a fetid medieval jail reduced the appeal of life imprisonment. De Charney chimed in and protested his innocence one last time.

This was a death sentence. But the church could not carry it out. The two men, De Molay and De Charney, were handed over on the same day to the secular authorities. At 4pm, on 18 March 1314 (the exact date is disputed), they were bound to the stake in front of a crowd. Small fires were lit under their feet and the piled-up wood began to crackle menacingly. In reports that may have been embellished since, De Molay is said to have borne the resulting agony without cries or groans. As the flames rose, and his body began to be consumed, the last grand master of the Knights Templar shouted:

'You who behold us perishing in the flames, shall decide our innocence. I summon Pope Clement V to appear in forty days and Philip the Fair in twelve months before the just and terrible throne of the ever-living God, to render an account of the blood which they have unjustly and wickedly shed!'

If this curse was uttered, then it worked. Clement V was dead by 20 April while Philip the Fair died later the same year on 29 November. Jacques de Molay was avenged.

Chapter Ten

Did the Templars Survive?

The burning at the stake of Jacques de Molay and the seizure of the order's assets should have brought the curtain down on the Knights Templar. It might have been just another bloodstained chapter in medieval history. However, the Templars have continued to capture the popular imagination ever since. Millions are convinced the knights discovered not only the Holy Grail but also the Ark of the Covenant and other sacred relics.

It's also stated that while in outremer, the knights imbibed ancient and mystical knowledge, as well as heretical forms of Christianity that had survived persecution in the Levant. Their wealth therefore was spiritual, not physical in the form of treasure. They were versed in the Jewish kabbalah, Muslim Sufism, and had learned the secrets of the Essenes and those Christians who believed that John the Baptist was the true Messiah and not a man from Nazareth called Jesus. The danger they posed to the church was the truth they had uncovered. This was why they had to be wiped out.

But did they disappear? To many, it is inconceivable that these brave knights with holy relics and ancient knowledge just fizzled out. The neo-Templars of the early nineteenth century were convinced they had not. On 4 November 1804, Bernard-Raymond Fabré-Palaprat (1773–1838) revealed the existence of a secret document: the Larmenius Charter. Otherwise known as the Charter of Transmission, it evidenced an unbroken line of Templar grand masters continuing from Jacques de Molay to the present day. A total of twenty-two grand masters were listed from 1324 to 1804. The present grand master was, of course, Fabré-Palaprat.[1]

The charter is named after John Mark Larmenius, who De Molay allegedly designated as his successor. His first act as the new clandestine grand master, operating under the radar, was to denounce the Knights Hospitaller and the Templars in Scotland who were banned from ever joining the genuine Templar order. Larmenius then handed on the position of grand master to a Templar in Alexandria, Egypt, called Franciscus Theobaldus, and the line continued. In 1705, Philippe Duke of Orléans (1674–1723) went public, declaring he was the current grand master.

The last Templar leader during the French monarchy was Louis Hercule Timoléon de Cossé, eighth duke of Brissac (1734–1792), who continued in the role despite the 1789 French revolution. However, he was hacked to death by a republican mob in 1792 who put his head on a spike. When the duke's property was auctioned off, the charter was rediscovered, as it supposedly fell from the drawer of a desk bought by an associate of Fabré-Palaprat. Once he was shown the document, Fabré-Palaprat wasted no time sticking his name down as the very latest grand master. To support his claim, he produced the sword, helmet, and breastplate of Jacques de Molay as well as some bones recovered from the execution site in 1314.

It's very easy to see parallels between Fabré-Palaprat and Pierre Plantard in the 1950s. Both men claimed to be leaders of a secret fraternity operating in the shadows – yet despite having only questionable evidence to back this up, and attracting considerable derision from critics, their stories had huge impact. Fabré-Palaprat went on to set up his own church, which attracted the cream of French society. On 18 January 1833, *The Morning Post* in England reported on the opening of a new 'Metropolitan Convent', which one assumes was a house of worship of some description, in the Cour Damiette, which was attended by 'an immense crowd'.

> *'The whole brotherhood performed in the costumes of the old knights of the Temple, mass was said, bread and wine consecrated, and M. Barginet, a well-known political writer, of Grenoble, delivered a sermon. I regret I was prevented being present at this extraordinary exhibition, which seems to have excited more ridicule than admiration.'*[2]

Whether a knight called John Mark Larmenius became the next grand master, one must wonder what happened to the thousands of decommissioned Templar knights, sergeants, and other retainers. Those who were still in the prime of life, unbroken by the inquisition, may have become swords-for-hire, if the military life still had appeal. While those with a more spiritual bent, or simply older, may have taken up a religious vocation as priests, monks, or lay preachers. Having been thoroughly institutionalised in a highly regimented and prayerful environment – one might even say brainwashed – it seems unlikely they went off to lead a normal existence.

Many, one must suspect, would have been suffering from some form of post-traumatic stress disorder (PTSD), unrecognised at the time. While in the order, fighting in outremer, they had experienced bloody defeats and terrifying escapes from the Mamluks. Then back at home, the shock of arrest, imprisonment, and torture. All of this would have left even the toughest of knights in poor mental shape. One can picture an old Templar in a tavern clutching a tankard of ale with a shaking hand, chewing over the bitterest of memories.[3]

The hotheads among the Templars, enraged at their treatment and the execution of their grand master, would have sought to continue their previous life in some way. Perhaps finding a kingdom in Europe where the Templars were still held in high esteem. The Iberian Peninsula was the obvious destination. In Portugal, the news from France came as an unpleasant surprise. The kingdom was still consolidating its gains from the Moors and had no wish to see the Templars suddenly vanish.

Five years after De Molay was executed, King Diniz of Portugal (1261–1325) petitioned Pope John XXII (1249–1334), who had previously been bishop of Porto, Portugal's second city, to set up a new order that would absorb all the Templar assets – including personnel. This was agreed in a papal bull of 1319. The Order of Christ (Ordem do Cristo) took over Tomar and other Templar sites. The order was basically the continuation of the Templars under new branding. Over the next 250 years, they would spearhead the Portuguese 'age of discovery', being the first Europeans to explore the coastline of Africa and reach Brazil – the sails of their ships emblazoned with the distinctive red cross of the order. Not surprisingly, many have seen this as the continuation of the Templar mission, spreading Christianity at the tip of a sword, under new management.

In neo-Templar and Freemason lore, some Templar knights fled to Scotland after the arrest warrants were issued in France. Those ships that set sail from La Rochelle, groaning with Templar treasure from outremer, are believed to have headed north in search of a hiding place. One item that needed concealing was the Holy Grail, the theory runs. For many modern Grail hunters, the eventual home of the Grail, the mummified head of Jesus Christ, and an eye-watering amount of silver and gold was a secret crypt at Rosslyn Chapel, near the Scottish capital Edinburgh, built by the Sinclair family, who are local gentry of Viking and Norman heritage. It's claimed that the Grail lies under the nave, held in place by sand brought from Jerusalem. However, the chapel staff are at pains to point out that Rosslyn was built in 1446, over 130 years after De Molay was executed, so either the Holy Grail had a previous hiding place, or it simply is not there.

In 1314, the year the Templars were banned by Pope Clement, the Scottish achieved a stunning victory against their biggest enemy, England, at the Battle of Bannockburn. An army led by Robert the Bruce (1274–1329) vanquished the forces of King Edward II. This has given rise to a theory that the balance was tipped in Scotland's favour by Templar knights fighting in their signature formation. It's not a theory that endears itself to Scottish nationalists, who would rather believe they won through their own efforts.[4]

The locating of fleeing Knights Templar in Scotland was partly the work of the Scottish Freemason Andrew Michael Ramsay (1696–1743). He had been raised a Calvinist but converted to Roman Catholicism and then embraced Freemasonry. Ramsay was a Jacobite supporter of the Stuart claim to the English throne and, like other Jacobites, lived in exile in France. In a speech delivered on 27 December 1736, he claimed that medieval stone masons, the ancestors of the Freemasons, had enjoyed a close relationship with the Hospitallers. Did he believe this? One view is that Ramsay wanted to give Freemasonry a more romantic history that would encourage bourgeois and aristocratic people to join. He certainly let the crusader cat out of the bag.

After his death, other writers switched to the Knights Templar as the partners of medieval stone masons. An elaborate mythology developed in which the Templars learned the secrets of the ancients, and passed that knowledge down the line of grand masters. The Freemasons today are the inheritors of this wisdom. Though masonic spokespeople routinely insist that the link to the Templars is not literally believed, but an origin myth.[5]

Ironically, many of the alleged connections between the Templars and Freemasons were first articulated by anti-masonic writers. In 1806, the French Jesuit priest and writer Augustin Barruel (1741–1820) received a letter from a man calling himself Jean-Baptiste Simonini, which spun a wild, antisemitic theory that the French revolution had been planned by a conspiracy of Jews, Freemasons, and the Illuminati. Barruel was already peddling anti-masonic theories and simply decided to fold the Jews and the Illuminati into this poisonous mix. He also claimed that the conspiracy to overthrow Christian civilisation was of long standing and had included the Knights Templar. Regrettably, Baruel's writings went on to inform *The Protocols of the Elders of Zion*, a forgery by the Tsarist secret police used to legitimise pogroms against Russian Jews at the turn of the twentieth century.[6]

Since the Knights Templar were crushed, they have been depicted as both the good and the bad guys. During the Renaissance, they were cast as malign magicians. In 1531, a German scholar, Henry Cornelius Agrippa (1486–1535), wrote about the Templars in his book, *De Oculta philosophia*, condemning them as something akin to witches. At the time Agrippa was writing, Europe was in the grip of a witch-hunting mania, accompanied by an increasing intellectual interest in the occult. Agrippa believed that the power of demons could be transferred into seemingly inanimate objects, or idols. He is infuriatingly vague, but it seems he is referring to the worship of Baphomet, accompanied by orgiastic rites – one of his pet obsessions – that summoned up the evil one.[7]

His emphasis on Templar sorcery is pertinent. The evidence is strong that both the French kings and popes of the fourteenth century believed in the power of malicious magic, what is referred to as the left-hand path. Pope John XXII, for example, thought he had been the subject of an assassination plot by an Italian noble who had crafted a silver bronze of the pontiff that included an unlucky Zodiac sign plus the inscription: 'demon of the west'. In 1320, he officially integrated black magic into the crime of heresy. Though Agrippa cast the Templars as evil magicians, to his credit he did oppose the persecution and burning of witches in his own lifetime.

In the same century as Agrippa, the French clerical writer Guillaume Paradin (1510–1590) embellished the charges made against the Templars. He wrote that young novices were taken to a dark cave where they were forced to worship an idol covered in human skin with glowing carbuncles for eyes. They drank a revolting potion made from the ashes of a dead knight. If an illegitimate child was born from a forbidden union between a Templar knight and a woman, it would be killed, then roasted, and the remains used to anoint the idol. All of which, Paradin observed, echoed the disgusting rites of the Bacchanalian cult in ancient Rome.

But others gave the Templars a more positive press. They came to see the knights as freethinking mystics persecuted by an overbearing church. In this regard, they were associated with all forms of Gnosticism, especially the Cathars. During the Protestant Reformation, the Templars became proto-Protestants, courageous Christians broken by the despotic pontiff in Rome. As Catholic monarchs, like Mary Tudor in England, burned Protestants at the stake, an identification with Jacques de Molay was obvious, elevating him to the status of conscientious martyr. Even if this was not true, and they had remained loyal to Rome throughout their existence, it spoke volumes about the perfidious nature of the papacy that it could turn so viciously on its own creation.[8]

Fast forward to the twentieth century, and we have the little-known novel *Alamut*, by Vladimir Bartol (1903–1967), an author born in Trieste, now in Italy but then part of the Austro-Hungarian empire, and died in Yugoslavia, then under Communist rule. His novel was set in the Assassin fortress at Alamut and is told from the perspective of a 'houri', a woman called Halima who works in the paradisical garden where trainee assassins are sent to experience heaven, but then drugged again and returned to the Old Man of the Mountain to become slavish killers.[9]

This book inspired one of the best-selling video games of all time: *Assassins Creed*. In the game (and movie spin-off), the Knights Templar are the bad guys seeking to impose order through mind control, whereas the Assassins fight to protect free will. The Templars have set up an evil corporate giant, Abstergo Industries, developing the Animus, a device that enables users to relive the memories of their ancestors. The Templars then kidnap descendants of Assassins to gather information that will destroy them. Fantastical though it undoubtedly is, the game echoes the propaganda of Philip and De Nogaret, presenting us with Templars steeped in ungodly intentions and horrific rituals.

The historian Peter Partner (1924–2015) finished his insightful work on the Templars, *The Murdered Magicians*, by stating that the knights did nothing to 'build the Temple of Wisdom', nor were they destroyed because of 'the operation of demonic forces but as a result of their own mediocrity and lack of nerve'. At their trials they had little to say in their defence, and while they may have been great soldiers, they were 'short-sighted politicians'. Indeed, Partner concludes, the Templars were very ordinary people.

In an otherwise brilliant book, this seems an unfair conclusion. Hugh de Payens, and his small band of friends, conceived of something that the times demanded. It required a spark of true inspiration to create the Knights Templar. They tapped into a new spirit, a desire to fight for one's faith. The concept is, of course, very problematic – as it was then. But nobody can doubt they succeeded beyond their wildest expectations. In a few short years, the Knights Templar had papal protection, hundreds of busy preceptories across Europe, and an army organised almost on modern lines, on which the rulers of outremer came to depend. Every ambitious young noble, without an estate to inherit, wanted to become a Templar knight.

Their story arc is like the proverbial rollercoaster ride, taking us first on a vertiginous ascent followed by a precipitous decline. If they had little to say at their trials, it was because these knights who had devoted so much to the crusades were stupefied. Locked in dungeons, broken by torturers, and dragged through the streets to be burned at the stake. Little wonder that countless generations have continued to empathise with their sudden disgrace and, for some, painful death.

We all want to be Templars. Discovering some hidden truth or object with immense sacral power. Brave, fearless, the first into battle and the last out. Yet so few of us make the grade in our very ordinary lives. So, we project what we would like to be on an incredible group of knights who shone so brightly for two centuries, before being betrayed and destroyed.

Notes

Chapter One: The Crusades: 'Deus Le Vult!'
1. Robert the Monk, *Historia Hierosolimitana*, Fordham University, Internet Medieval Source Book, Halsall, Paul, 1997
2. Boas, Adrian, (editor), *The Crusader World*, Routledge, first edition, 2015, ISBN: 9780415824941
3. Di Branco, Marco, Wolf, Kordula, *Hindered Passages. The Failed Muslim Conquest of Southern Italy*, Journal of Transcultural Medieval Studies, Vol. 1, Issue 1, 2014
4. Janosik, Daniel J., *John of Damascus, First Apologist to the Muslims: The Trinity and Christian Apologetics in the Early Islamic Period*, Pickwick Publications, 2016, ISBN: 9781498289825
5. Abu-Munshar, Maher Y., *The Attitude of Christians towards the first Muslim Fath (Conquest) or Islamic Jerusalem*, Journal of Islamic Jerusalem Studies, Summer 2008
6. Irenaeus of Lyons, *Against Heresies*, Aeterna Press, 2016, ISBN: 9781785169267
7. Haberl, Charles G, *The Neo-Mandaic Dialect of Khorramshahr*, Harrassowitz, 2009, ISBN: 9783447058742
8. Barber, Malcolm, *The Trial of the Templars*, Cambridge University Press, 1978, ISBN: 9781107645769
9. McGlynn, Sean, *Kill Them All, Cathars and Carnage in the Albigensian Crusade*, The History Press, 2018, ISBN: 9780750984317
10. Picknett Lynn, Prince, Clive, *The Templar Revelation*, Corgi edition, 2007, ISBN: 9780552155403
11. Sypiański, Jakub, *Arabo-Byzantine relations in the 9th and 10th centuries as an area of cultural rivalry*, HAL Open Science, December 2011
12. Clot, Andre, *Harun Al-Rashid: and the World of the Thousand and One Nights*, Saqi Books, 2005, ISBN: 9780863565502
13. Ellenblum, Ronnie, *The Collapse of the Eastern Mediterranean: Climate Change and the Decline of the East, 950–1072*, Cambridge University Press, 2013, ISBN: 9781107688735
14. Çetin, Altan, *Oghuz Turks in the Account of a Mamluk Historian*, Journal of Islamic Studies, Vol. 20, Issue 3, September 2009, pp. 376–382
15. Streater, Jasper, *The Battle of Manzikert*, History Today, Vol 17, Issue 4, April 1967
16. West, Charles, *And how, if you are a Christian, can you hate the emperor?*, Bonn University Press (Vandenhoeck & Ruprecht, Germany, pp. 411–430, ISBN: 9783847110880
17. Mayne, Richard, "East and West in 1054", *The Cambridge Historical Journal*, Vol. 11, No. 2, 1954, pp. 133–148
18. Isidore of Seville, *The Etymologies*, Cambridge University Press, 2010, ISBN: 9780521145916
19. Joranson, Einar, *The Problem of the Spurious Letter of Emperor Alexius to the Court of Flanders*, The American Historical Review, Oxford University Press, Vol. 55, No. 4, pp. 811–832
20. Cushing, Kathleen, *Reform and the Papacy in the Eleventh Century*, Manchester University Press, 2005, ISBN: 9780719058349
21. Langan, John, *The Elements of St Augustine's Just War Theory*, The Journal of Religious Ethics Vol. 12, No. 1, Spring 1984, pp. 19–38
22. *The Church of the Holy Sepulchre in Jerusalem*, The Roman Anglican, December 5, 2017, blog
23. Nkrumah, Gamal, *The Crazed Caliph*, Al-Ahram weekly online, Issue No. 976, December 2009
24. Albert of Aachen, *History of the Journey to Jerusalem*, Translation: Susan B. Edgington, Routledge, 2013, ISBN: 9781409466543

25. Eidelberg, Shlomo, (edited and translated), *The Jews and the Crusaders, The Hebrew Chronicles of the First and Second Crusades,* University of Wisconsin Press, 1977, ISBN: 0881255416

26. Ibid: Eidelberg, Shlomo, *The Jews and the Crusaders, The Hebrew Chronicles of the First and Second Crusades*

27. Stow, Kenneth, *Conversion, Apostasy, and Apprehensiveness: Emicho of Flonheim and the Fear of Jews in the Twelfth Century,* Speculum, The University of Chicago Press, Vol. 76, No. 4, 2001, pp. 911–933

28. Ocker, Christopher, *Ritual Murder and the Subjectivity of Christ: A Choice in Medieval Christianity,* Harvard Theological Review, Vol. 91, Issue 2, April 1998, pp. 153–192

29. Kedar, Benjamin Z., *Crusade Historians and the Massacres of 1096,* Jewish History, Vol. 12, No. 2, 1998, pp. 11–31

30. Garstad, Benjamin, (translator), *Apocalypse of Pseudo-Methodius,* Dumbarton Oaks Medieval Library, 2008, ISBN: 9780674053076

31. Pynes, Sam, *Explaining the 1096 Massacres in the Context of the First Crusade,* University of Central Florida, 2019, History of Christianity Commons

32. Ibid: Shlomo, Eidelberg, *The Jews and the Crusaders, The Hebrew Chronicles of the First and Second Crusades*

33. Komnene, Anna, *The Alexiad,* Masterworks Classics, Stonewall Press, 2015, ISBN: 9781627301121

34. Ralph of Caen, *The Gesta Tancredi of Ralph of Caen,* Routledge, first edition, 2010, ISBN: 9781409400325

35. Robert the Monk, *Historia Iherosolimitana,* Sweetenham, Carol (translator), Ashgate Publishing, 2005, ISBN: 9780754658627

36. D'Aguilers, Raymond, *Historia Francorum Qui Ceperunt Iherusalem,* The American Philosophical Society Press, 1968, ISBN: 9781422380116

Chapter Two: Mysterious Origins of the Knights Templar

1. Riley-Smith, J.S.C., *Peace Never Established: The Case of the Kingdom of Jerusalem,* Transactions of the Royal Historical Society, Cambridge University Press, Vol. 28, 1978, pp. 87–102

2. Ciggaar, Krijna Nelly, Davids, Adelbert, Teule, Herman G. B., *East and West in the Crusader States, Context, Contacts, Confrontations,* Acta of the Congress held at Hernen Castle, May 1993, Vol. 1, 1996, ISBN: 9789068317923

3. Ibid: Ellenblum, Ronnie, *The Collapse of the Eastern Mediterranean: Climate Change and the Decline of the East*

4. William of Tyre, *A History of Deeds Done Beyond the Sea,* Babcock, Emily A., Krey, A.C. (translated), Columbia University Press, 1943

5. Ibid: William of Tyre, *A History of Deeds Done Beyond the Sea*

6. Brockhaus, Hannah, *The relics St. Helena brought to Rome from the Holy Land,* Catholic News Agency, August 18, 2022

7. Cavendish, Richard, *The Discovery of the Holy Lance,* History Today, Vol. 48, Issue 6, June 1998

8. Gibson, Shimon, *Archival notes on Robinson's Arch and the Temple Mount/Haram al-Sharif in Jerusalem,* Palestine Exploration Quarterly, August 14, 2020, Vol. 153, Issue 3, pp. 222–243

9. Lawler, Andrew, *No Way Out: How the Opening of a Tunnel Blocked the Path to Peace in Jerusalem,* Politico, February 10, 2021

10. Colby, Frederick, S., *Narrating Muhammad's Night Journey: Tracing the Development of the Ibn Abbas Ascension Discourse,* State University of New York Press, 2008, ISBN: 9780791475171

11. Kedar, Benjamin Z., "On the Origins of the Earliest Laws of Frankish Jerusalem: The Canons of the Council of Nablus, 1120", *Speculum,* Vol. 74, No. 2, April 1999

12. Karras, Ruth Mazo, "The Regulation of Sodomy in the Latin East and West", *Speculum,* Vol. 94, Issue 4, pp. 969–986

13. Rubenstein, Jay, *Nebuchadnezzar's Dream: The Crusades, Apocalyptic Prophecy, and the End of History*, OUP USA, 2019, ISBN: 9780190274207
14. Ritchie, R.L. Graeme, "The Normans in Scotland", *The English Historical Review*, Vol. 70, No. 275, April 1955, pp. 276–278
15. Banks, Grace, Blackhall, Sheena, *Aberdeenshire Folk Tales*, The History Press, 2013, ISBN: 9780752497588
16. Brown, Dan, *The Da Vinci Code*, Corgi (first edition), 2009, ISBN: 9780552159715
17. Barber, Malcolm, Bate, Keith, *The Templars*, Manchester University Press, 2002, ISBN: 9780719051104
18. Wood, Herbert, "The Templars in Ireland", *Proceedings of the Royal Irish Academy: Archaeology, Culture, History, Literature*, Vol. 26, 1906/1907, pp. 327–377
19. Bulst-Thiele, Marie Luise, *Sacrae Domus Militiae Templi Hierosolymitani magistri : Untersuchungen z. Geschichte d. Templerordens 1118/19–1314*, Vandenhoeck und Ruprecht, 1974, ISBN: 3525823533
20. Bartlett, W. B., *Assassins: The Story of Medieval Islam's Secret Sect*, The History Press, 2009, ISBN: 9780752452050
21. Lewis, Bernard, *Assassins: A Radical Sect in Islam*, Basic Books (reissue edition), 2002, ISBN: 9780465004980
22. Maalouf, Amin, *The Crusades through Arab eyes*, Saqi Books, 2006 edition, ISBN: 9780863560231
23. Gibb, H.A.R. (translator), *The Damascus Chronicle of the Crusades – extracted and translated from the chronicle of Ibn Al-Qalanisi*, Dover Publications, New York, 2002, ISBN: 9780486425191
24. Duby, Georges, *The Three Orders: Feudal Society Imagined*, University of Chicago Press, 1982, ISBN: 9780226167725
25. Riley-Smith, J., *The Knights Hospitaller in the Levant, c.1070–1309*, Palgrave Macmillan, 2012, ISBN: 9781349331628
26. Nicholson, Helen J., *The Knights Hospitaller*, Boydell Press, 2006, ISBN: 9781843830382
27. Barber, Malcolm, "The Order of Saint Lazarus and the Crusades", *The Catholic Historical Review*, Catholic University of America Press, Vol. 80, No. 3, 1994, pp. 439–456
28. Baigent, Michael, Leigh, Richard, Lincoln, Henry, *The Holy Blood and the Holy Grail*, Jonathan Cape, 1982, ISBN: 9780224017350
29. Schorn, Daniel, "The Priory of Sion", CBS News, April 27, 2006
30. Wallace-Murphy, Tim, Hopkins, Marilyn, *Custodians of Truth: The Continuance of Rex Deus*, Red Wheel/Weiser, 2005, ISBN: 9781578633234

Chapter Three: Templar Heroes and Villains

1. Bernard of Clairvaux, *In Praise of the New Knighthood: A Treatise on the Knights Templar and the Holy Places of Jerusalem*, Cistercian Publications, 2001, ISBN: 9780879071202
2. Jessee, Scott, "Crusaders and Templars: Robert the Burgundian Lord of Craon and Sable and his Descendants, 1095–1192", *Medieval Prosopography*, Board of Trustees of Western Michigan University, Vol. 30, 2015, pp. 31–58
3. MacEvitt, Christopher, *The Crusades and the Christian World of the East: Rough Tolerance*, University of Pennsylvania Press, 2007, ISBN: 9780812240504
4. Runciman, Steven, *A History of the Crusades, Vol. 3*, Penguin, 1990, ISBN: 9780140137057
5. Bar Hebraeus, Budge, Ernest Alfred Wallis, *The chronography of Gregory Abu'l Faraj, the son of Aaron, the Hebrew physician, commonly known as Bar Hebraeus*, Oxford University Press, 1932
6. Constable, Giles, "The Second Crusade as seen by contemporaries", *Traditio*, Cambridge University Press, 1953, Vol. 9, pp. 213–279
7. Brundage, James A., *The Crusades*, The Marquette University Press, 1962
8. Lamb, Alastair, "The Search for Prester John", *History Today*, February 20, 2018 (originally appeared May 1957)

9. Fryde, Natalie, "Abelard and the Church's Policy Towards the Jews", *Anglo-Norman Studies XXIV Proceedings of the Battle Conference 2001*, Boydell & Brewer, pp. 99–108
10. Enelow, H.G., "Anacletus II (Pietro Pierleoni)", *Jewish Encyclopedia*
11. MISSING
12. David, Charles Wendell (translation), *The Conquest of Lisbon – De Expugnatione Lyxbonensi*, Columbia University Press, 2001, ISBN: 9780231121231
13. Fierro, Maribel, "The Legal Policies of the Almohad Caliphs and Ibn Rushd's Bidayat al-Mujtahid", *Journal of Islamic Studies*, September 1999, Vol. 10, Issue 3, pp. 226–248
14. Safran, Janina M., "Identity and Differentiation in Ninth-Century al-Andalus", *Speculum*, 2001, Vol. 76, No. 3, pp. 573–598
15. Murray, Alan V., *The Crusades: An Encyclopedia (4 volumes)*, ABC-CLIO, 2006, ISBN: 9781576078624
16. Branco, Maria JoãoViolante, *D. Sancho I: O Filho do Fundador*, Circulo de Leitores, 2006
17. Lay, Stephen, "Miracles, Martyrs and the Cult of Henry the Crusader in Lisbon", *Portuguese Studies*, 2001, Vol. 24, No. 1, pp. 7–31
18. Drake, Matt, "Knights Templar secret tunnels 'leading to Treasure Tower' discovered in Israel", *The Independent*, October 28, 2019
19. Lockley, Mike, "Relics including the Holy Grail and lost Ark of the Covenant 'under Midlands Manor House'", *Birmingham Mail*, July 25, 2021
20. Read, Piers Paul, *The Templars*, Weidenfeld & Nicholson, 2003, ISBN: 9780753810873
21. Parker, John, "The Attempted Byzantine Alliance with the Sicilian Norman Kingdom (1166–7) /Papers of the British School in Rome", *Studies in Italian Medieval History*, 1956, Vol. 24, pp. 86–93
22. Odo of Deuil, *De Profectione Ludovici VII in Orientem*, W.W. Norton & Co., 1965, ISBN: 9780393096620
23. Howlett, Richard, *Chronicles of the Reigns of Stephen, Henry II, and Richard I*, Cambridge University Press, 2012, ISBN: 9781108052269
24. Chambers, Frank McMinn, "Some Legends concerning Eleanor of Aquitaine", *Speculum/ The University of Chicago Press*, 1941, Vol. 16, No. 4, pp. 459–468
25. Richards, D.S., (editor), *The Chronicle of Ibn al-Athir for the Crusading Period from al-Kamil fi'l-Ta'rikh. Part 2*, Routledge, 2010, ISBN: 9780754669517
26. Henry of Huntingdon, *Historia Anglorum. The History of the English from AC 55 to AD 1154*, Cambridge University Press, 2012, ISBN: 9781108051415
27. Robinson, James Harvey, *Readings in European History. Vol. 1*, Ginn & Company, 1904
28. Kingsford, Charles Lethbridge, Archer, Thomas Andrew, *The Crusades: the story of the Latin Kingdom of Jerusalem*, Palala Press, 2015, ISBN: 9781355847601
29. Lewis, Kevin James, *The Counts of Tripoli and Lebanon in the Twelfth Century: Sons of Saint-Gilles (Rulers of the Latin East)*, Routledge, 2017, ISBN: 9781472458902
30. Estrin, Daniel, "Israeli strike leaves Gaza's oldest mosque in ruins", NPR, December 9, 2023
31. Ibn Munqidh, Usamah, *The Book of Contemplation: Islam and the Crusades*, Penguin Classics, 2008, ISBN: 9780140455137
32. Ali, Adam, "A Game of Thrones…Fatimid Style", *Medievalists.net*
33. William of Tyre, *Historia rerum in partibus transmarinis gestarum, XXIII, 1, Patrologia Latina 201*, Brundage, James (translated), *The Crusades: A Documentary History*, Marquette University Press, 1962
34. Zajac, Bill, Nicholson, Helen (translated), *Monumenta Germaniae Historica Scriptores*
35. Attiya, Hussein M., "Knowledge of Arabic in the Crusader States in the twelfth and thirteenth centuries", *Journal of Medieval History*, 1999, Vol. 25, Issue 3, pp. 203–213
36. Halm, Heinz, *Kalifen und Assassinen: Ägypten und der Vordere Orient zur Zeit der ersten Kreuzzüge 1074–1171*, C.H. Beck, 2021, ISBN: 9783406661631
37. Brett, Michael, *The Fatimid Empire*, Edinburgh University Press, 2017, ISBN: 9780748640768

38. Walter Map, *De Nugis Curialum: Courtiers' Trifles (Oxford Medieval Texts)*, OUP Oxford, 1983, ISBN: 9780198222361
39. "Third Lateran Council – 1179 AD", *Papal Encyclicals Online*
40. Schonfield, Hugh J., *The Passover Plot*, Disinformation Co; Anniversary Edition, 2005, ISBN: 9781932857092
41. Joyce, Donovan, *The Jesus Scroll*, Sphere, 1975, ISBN: 9780722151037
42. Baigent, Michael, Leigh, Richard, Lincoln, Henry, *The Holy Blood and the Holy Grail*, Arrow (second edition), 1996, ISBN: 9780099682417
43. Eco, Umberto, *Foucault's Pendulum*, Vintage, 2001, ISBN: 9780099287155
44. Fulton, Michael S., *Contest for Egypt: The Collapse of the Fatimid Caliphate, the Ebb of Crusader Influence, and the Rise of Saladin*, Brill, 2022, ISBN: 9789004512276
45. Clay, R.M., *Medieval Hospitals of England*, Routledge, 1966, ISBN: 9780714612928
46. Hosler, John D., "The Prayer of Usama ibn Mundiqh", Yale University Press, 2022
47. Stubbs, William (Editor), *The Historical Works of Master Ralph de Diceto, Dean of London*, Cambridge University Press, 2012, ISBN: 9781108049346
48. Barber, Malcolm, *The New Knighthood: A History of the Order of the Temple*, Cambridge University Press, 2012, ISBN: 9781107604735

Chapter Four: Getting Rich Quick

1. Perkins, Clarence, 'The Wealth of the Knights Templar in England and the Disposition of it after their Dissolution', *The American Historical Review*, 1910, Vol. 15, No. 2
2. Lourie, Elena, "The Will of Alfonso I, El Batallador, King of Aragon and Navarre: A Reassessment", *Speculum*, The University of Chicago Press, Vol. 50, No. 4, October 1975, pp. 635–651
3. Harari, Yuval, "The military role of the Frankish Turcopoles: A reassessment", *Mediterranean Historical Review*, Vol. 12, Issue 1, 1997
4. Lord, Dr Evelyn, *The Knights Templar in Britain*, Longman (first edition), 2001, ISBN: 9780582472877
5. Dalton, Paul, White, Graeme, J., *King Stephen's Reign*, Boydell Press, 2008, ISBN: 9781843833611
6. Slavin, Philip, "Landed estates of the Knights Templar in England and Wales and their management in the early fourteenth century", *Journal of Historical Geography*, Vol. 42, October 2013, pp. 36–49
7. Lees, Beatrice A., "Records of the Templars in England in the Twelfth Century", *Economic History*, Royal Economic Society, Vol. 3, No. 11, February 1936, pp. 293–295
8. Carraz, Damien, "Templars and Hospitallers in the Cities of the West and the Latin East (Twelfth to Thirteenth Centuries)", *Crusades*, Vol. 12, Issue 1, 17 February 2023, pp. 103–120
9. Ferris, Eleanor, "The Financial Relations of the Knights Templar to the English Crown", *The American Historical Review*, Vol. 8, No. 1, October 1902, pp. 1–17
10. Barber, Malcolm, *The Trial of the Templars*, Cambridge University Press, 1978, ISBN: 9781107645769
11. De La Torre, Ignacio, *The London and Paris Temples: A Comparative Analysis of their Financial Services for the Kings during the Thirteenth Century*, Routledge (first edition), 2008, ISBN: 9781315555553
12. Carpenter, David, *Henry III: The Rise to Power and Personal Rule, 1207–1258 (The English Monarchs Series)*, Yale University Press, 2021, ISBN: 9780300259193
13. Dorin, Rowan, *No Return: Jews, Christian Usurers, and the Spread of Mass Expulsion in Medieval Europe (Histories of Economic Life Book 34)*, Princeton University Press, 2023, ISBN: 9780691240923
14. Jacobs, Joseph, "The Jews of Angevin England: Documents and Records from Latin and Hebrew Sources, Printed and Manuscript, for the first time collected and translated", *The Economic Journal*, Vol. 4, Issue 14, June 1, 1894, pp. 275–279

15. Jacobs, Joseph, "Aaron of Lincoln", *The Jewish Quarterly Review*, Vol. 10, No. 4, July 1898, pp. 629–648
16. Howlett, Richard (editor), *Vol. 1: The First Four Books of Historia rerum Anglicarum of William of Newburgh*, Cambridge University Press, 2012 (first published 1884), ISBN: 9781139380669
17. Hill, J.W.F., *Medieval Lincoln*, Cambridge University Press, 1948
18. Bartlett, Suzanne, *Licoricia of Winchester: Marriage, Motherhood and Murder in the Medieval Anglo-Jewish Community*, Vallentine Mitchell & Co Ltd, 2015, ISBN: 9780853038320
19. Al Bustani, Hareth, "Templar Banking: How to go from donated rags to vast riches", *Medievalists.net*

Chapter Five: The Holy Grail, Knights Templar, and King Arthur

1. 'Down the centuries at Priddy', Weston Mercury, 5 February 2007
2. 'And Did those Feet...? The 'Legend' of Christ's visit to Britain', Smith, A.W., Folklore, Vol. 100, Issue 1, 1989, pp. 63–68
3. 'De Antiquitate Glastonie Ecclesie', William of Malmesbury, 1247
4. Gerould, Gordon Hall, 'King Arthur and Politics', *Speculum*, 1927, Vol. 2, No. 1, pp. 33–51
5. Weinraub, Eugene J., 'Chretien's Jewish Grail: A New Investigation of the Imagery and Significance of Chretien de Troyes's Grail Episode based on Medieval Hebraic sources', *North Carolina Studies in the Romance Languages and Literatures*, 1976, p. 136
6. De Troyes, Chrétien, *Perceval: The Story of the Grail*, Yale University Press, 1999, ISBN: 9780300075861
7. Hosler, John, *Henry II: A Medieval Soldier at War, 1147–1189*, Brill, 2007, ISBN: 9789004157248
8. Barber, Malcolm, *The Crusader States*, Yale University Press, 2012, ISBN: 9780300113129

Chapter Six: Accusations of Treachery

1. Giebfried, John, "The Crusader Rebranding of Jerusalem's Temple Mount", *Comitatus: A Journal of Medieval and Renaissance Studies*, 2013, Vol. 44, pp. 77–94
2. Schein, Sylvia, "The changing traditions of the Temple Mount in the central Middle Ages", *Traditio*, 1984, Vol. 40, pp. 175–195
3. Theoderich of Würzburg, *Guide to the Holy Land*, Italica Press, 2008, ISBN: 9780934977036
4. Brewer, Keagan, Kane, James, *The Conquest of the Holy Land by Salah al-Din*, Routledge, 2020, ISBN: 9780367729752
5. Delaville Le Roulx, Joseph, *Les Hospitaliers en Terre Sainte et a Chypre (1100–1310)*, E. Leroux, 1904
6. Humphreys, Stephen R., "The Emergence of the Mamluk Army", *Studia Islamica*, 1977, No. 45, pp. 67–99
7. Schuster, Ruth, "Crusader Princess' Escape Tunnel from Muslim Armies found in Tiberias", *Haaretz*, June 15, 2017
8. Morgan, Margaret Ruth, *The Chronicle of Ernoul and the Continuations of William of Tyre*, Oxford University Press, 1974, ISBN: 9780198218517
9. Lee, Jeffrey, "Crusader, deserter and traitor: the life and legacy of Raymond III of Tripoli", *History Extra*, February 15, 2017
10. Brand Charles M., "The Byzantines and Saladin, 1185–1192: Opponents of the Third Crusade", *Speculum*, 1962, Vol. 37, No. 2, pp. 167–181
11. Bird, Jessalynn, Peters, Edward, Powell, James M., "Crusade and Christendom: Annotated Documents in Translation from Innocent III to the Fall of Acre", *The Middle Ages Series/ University of Pennsylvania Press*, 2013, p. 536
12. Dolan, John P., "A Note on Emperor Frederick II and Jewish Tolerance", *Jewish Social Studies*, 1960, Vol. 22, No. 3, pp. 165–174
13. Loud, G.A., *The Crusade of Frederick Barbarossa. The History of the Expedition of the Emperor Frederick and Related Texts*, Routledge, 2013, ISBN: 9781472413963

14. Freed, John, *Frederick Barbarossa: the Prince and the Myth*, Yale University Press, 2016, ISBN: 9780300122763
15. Cobham, Claude Delaval, *Excerpta Cypria: Materials for a History of Cyprus*, Cambridge University Press, 1908
16. Stubbs, William, *Itinerarium Peregrinorum et Gesta Regis Ricardi*, Rolls Series, 1864
17. Maalouf, Amin, *The Crusades through Arab Eyes*, Saqi Books, 2006, ISBN: 9780863560231
18. Richard of Devizes, Geoffrey de Vinsauf, *Chronicles of Crusades: Contemporary Narratives of the Crusade of Richard Coeur de Lion*, George Bell and Sons, 1908
19. Tyerman, Christopher, *God's War: A New History of the Crusades*, Penguin, 2007, ISBN: 9780140269802
20. MISSING
21. Reston, James, *Warriors of God: Richard the Lionheart and Saladin in the Third Crusade*, Anchor Books, 2002, ISBN: 9780385495622
22. Ailes, Marianne (translator), Barber, Malcolm (translator), *The History of the Holy War: Ambroise's Estoire de la Guerre Sainte*, Boydell Press, 2011, ISBN: 9781843836629
23. Williams, Patrick A., "The Assassination of Conrad of Montferrat: another suspect?", *Traditio*, Cambridge University Press, 1970, Vol. 26, pp. 381–389
24. Round, J. H., "The Saladin Tithe", *The English Historical Review*, 1916, Vol. 31, No. 123, pp. 447–450
25. McLynn, Frank, *Lionheart and Lackland: King Richard, King John and the Wars of Conquest*, Vintage, 2007, ISBN: 9780712694179
26. Choniates, Nicetas, *O City of Byzantium, Annals of Niketas Choniates*, Wayne State University Press, 1984, ISBN: 9780814317648
27. Roudometof, Victor, *Globalization and Orthodox Christianity: The Transformations of a Religious Tradition*, Routledge, 2013, ISBN: 978135014698
28. Geoffrey de Villehardouin, Marzials, Frank T. (translated), *Memoirs or Chronicle of the Fourth Crusade and the Conquest of Constantinople*, J. M. Dent, 1908
29. Queller, Donald E., Compton, Thomas K., Campbell, Donald A., "The Fourth Crusade: The Neglected Majority", *Speculum*, 1974, Vol. 49, No. 3, pp. 441–465
30. Sibly, W.A., Sibly, M.D., *The History of the Albigensian Crusade: Peter of Les Vaux-de-Cernay's Historia Albigensis*, Boydell Press, 1998, ISBN: 9780851158075
31. Sumption, Jonathan, *The Albigensian Crusade*, Faber & Faber, 1999, ISBN: 9780571200023
32. Caesarius of Heisterbach, *The Dialogue on Miracles*, George Routledge & Sons, 1929
33. McGlynn, Sean, *Kill Them All: Cathars and Carnage in the Albigensian Crusade*, Spellmount, 2015, ISBN: 9780752486321
34. Baigent, Michael, Leigh, Richard, Lincoln, Henry, *The Holy Blood and the Holy Grail*, Jonathan Cape, 1982, ISBN: 9780224017350
35. Tamm, Marek, "How to justify a crusade? The conquest of Livonia and new crusade rhetoric in the early thirteenth century", *Journal of Medieval History*, 2013, Vol. 39, Issue 4, pp. 431–455
36. Venning, Timothy, Frankopan, Peter, *A Chronology of the Crusades*, Routledge, 2019, ISBN: 9780367870775
37. Daeron, M., Klinger Y., Tapponier, P., Elias, A., Jacques E., Sursock, A., "Sources of the large A.D. 1202 and 1759 Near East earthquakes", *Geology*, July 2005
38. Cantor-Echols, David, "Kingship, Crusade, and the Battle of Las Navas de Tolosa in the Chronica latina regum Castellae", *Romance Quarterly*, 2013, Vol. 60, Issue 2, pp. 102–113
39. Gomez, Miguel Dolan, "Templar dispatches from the battlefield: a new source for the battle of Las Navas de Tolosa", *Journal of Medieval Iberian Studies*, 2021, Vol. 13, Issue 3
40. "Fourth Lateran Council: 1215", *Papal Encyclicals Online*
41. Gaposchkin, M. Cecilia, Field, Sean L., *The Sanctity of Louis IX: Early Lives of Saint Louis by Geoffrey of Beaulieu and William of Chartres*, Cornell University Press, 2013, ISBN: 9780801478185

42. Arafa E., "The Legitimacy of Shajar al-Durr reign as represented in light of a rare dinar", *Egyptian Journal of Archaeological and Restoration Studies*, 2016, Vol. 6, Issue 1, pp. 65–70
43. Wedgwood, Ethel, *The Memoirs of the Lord of Joinville*, John Murray, 1906
44. Daley, Jason, "Fear of Foreign Food may have led to the death of this crusader king", *Smithsonian Magazine*, June 25, 2019

Chapter Seven: Retreat from the Holy Land

1. Jackson, Peter, *From Genghis Khan to Tamerlane: The Reawakening of Mongol Asia*, Yale University Press, 2023, ISBN: 9780300251128
2. Ho, T.N., "Ancient Stone marks China's First Encounter with Christianity", *Christianity Today*, November 11, 2022
3. Atwood, Christopher P. (translated), *The Secret History of the Mongols*, Penguin Classics, 2023, ISBN: 9780241197912
4. Rady, Martyn (editor), Bak, M. Janos (editor), Veszpremy, Laszlo (editor), *Anonymous and Master Roger*, Central European University Press, 2010, ISBN: 9789639776951
5. Laszlovszky, Jozsef (editor), Hunyadi, Zsolt, *The Crusades and the Military Orders*, CEU Medievalia, 2001, ISBN: 9639241423
6. Kramer, Sarah, "Scientists finally know what stopped Mongol Hordes from conquering Europe", *Science Alert*, May 28, 2016
7. Maiorov, Alexander V., "The First Mongol Invasion of Europe: Goals and Results", *Journal of the Royal Asiatic Society*, Cambridge University Press, June 28, 2021
8. Czarnowus, Anna, "The Mongols, Eastern Europe, and Western Europe: The Mirabilia Tradition in Benedict of Poland's Historia Tartarorum and John of Plano Carpini's Historia Mongalorum", *Literature Compass*, 2014, Vol. 11, Issue 7, pp. 484–495
9. Amitai, Reuven, "Mongol Raids into Palestine (AD 1260 and 1300)", *The Journal of the Royal Asiatic Society of Great Britain and Ireland*, Cambridge University Press, 1987, No. 2, pp. 236–255
10. Ali, Adam, "Mamluks vs. Mongols", *Medievalists.net*
11. "The Templar Idol at Safed", *Archives de l'Orient Latin*, 1884, Tome II, Chapter IV
12. Barber, Malcolm, *The New Knighthood: A History of the Order of the Temple*, Cambridge University Press, 2012, ISBN: 9781107604735
13. Ali B, "Knightfall recap: The ultimate guide to season 1", *Sky History*

Chapter Eight: The Last Templar Grand Master

1. Curley, M. Mildred, "An episode in the conflict between Boniface VIII and Philip the Fair", *The Catholic Historical Review*, 1927, Vol. 13, No. 2, pp. 194–226
2. Gaposchkin, M. Cecilia, *The Making of Saint Louis: Kingship, Sanctity, and Crusade in the Later Middle Ages*, Cornell University Press, 2010, ISBN: 9780801476259
3. Bennett-Smith, Meredith, "Celestine V, 13th Century Pope, examined; skeleton rules out murder by head trauma", *Huffpost*, May 11, 2013
4. Menache, Sophia, "A Propaganda Campaign in the Reign of Philip the Fair, 1302–1303", *French History*, 1990, Vol. 4, Issue 4, pp. 427–454
5. Cavendish, Richard, "Boniface VIII's Bull Unam Sanctam", *History Today*, November 11, 2002, Vol. 52, Issue II
6. Frale, Barbara, "The Chinon chart. Papal absolution to the last Templar, Master Jacques de Molay", *Journal of Medieval History*, 2004, Vol. 30, Issue 2, pp. 109–134
7. Frale, Barbara, *The Templars: The Secret History Revealed*, Maverick House, 2009, ISBN: 9781905379606
8. Schwarzfuchs, Simon R., "The Expulsion of the Jews from France (1306)", *The Jewish Quarterly Review*, 1967, Vol. 57, pp. 482–489

9. De La Torre, Ignacio, *The Debate on the Trial of the Templars (1307–1314)*, Routledge, 2010, ISBN: 9781315615349

Chapter Nine: Arrest Warrants and Trials
1. Barber, Malcolm, Bate, Keith, *The Templars: Selected Sources (Manchester Medieval Sources)*, Manchester University Press, 2002, ISBN: 9780719051104
2. Julien, Thery, "A Heresy of State: Philip the Fair, the Trial of the 'Perfidious Templars', and the Pontificalization of the French Monarchy", *The Journal of Medieval Religious Cultures*, 2013, Vol. 39, Issue 2, pp. 117–148
3. Jones, Malcolm, *The Secret Middle Ages*, The History Press Ltd., 2004, ISBN: 9780750938747
4. Strickland, Debra Higgs, *Saracens, Demons & Jews – making monsters in medieval art*, Princeton University Press, 2003, ISBN: 9780691057194
5. Barber, Malcolm, *The Trial of the Templars*, Cambridge University Press, 1978, ISBN: 9781107645769
6. Laidler, Keith, *The Head of God: The Lost Treasure of the Templars*, Phoenix, 2005, ISBN: 9780752826899
7. Miller, Tanya Stabler, *The Beguines of Medieval Paris: Gender, Patronage, and Spiritual Authority (The Middle Ages Series)*, University of Pennsylvania Press, 2014, ISBN: 9780812246070
8. Babinsky, Ellen, *Marguerite Porete: The Mirror of Simple Souls*, Paulist Press, 1993, ISBN: 9780809134274
9. St. Peter Damian, *The Book of Gomorrah and St Peter Damian's struggle against ecclesiastical corruption*, Matthew Cullinan Hoffman, 2015, ISBN: 9780996704205
10. Karlen, Arno, "The Homosexual Heresy", *The Chaucer Review*, 1971, Vol. 6, No. 1, pp. 44–63
11. Thomas Aquinas, *Summa Theologica*, Ave Maria Press, 2000, ISBN: 9780870610639
12. Thibodeaux, Jennifer D., *The Manly Priest: Clerical Celibacy, Masculinity, and Reform in England and Normandy, 1066–1300*, University of Pennsylvania Press, 2015, ISBN: 9780812247527
13. Boswell, John, *Christianity, Social Tolerance, and Homosexuality: Gay People in Western Europe from the Beginning of the Christian Era to the Fourteenth Century*, University of Chicago Press, 2005, ISBN: 9780226067117
14. Gilmour-Gryson, Anne, "Sodomy and the Knights Templar", *Journal of the History of Sexuality*, 1996, Vol. 7, No.2, pp. 151–183

Chapter Ten: Did the Templars Survive?
1. 'The Story of Modern Templary', *The Courier Journal, Louisville*, 27 August 1901
2. 'Private Correspondence', *The Morning Post*, 18 January 1833
3. Sohn, Emily, 'Medieval knights may have suffered post-traumatic stress', *NBC News*, 20 December 2011
4. Newsroom, 'How crusading Templars gave Bruce the edge at Bannockburn', *The Scotsman*, 5 December 2009
5. Iribarren, Isabel, 'From Black Magic to Heresy: A Doctrinal Leap in the Pontificate of John XXII', *Church History*, 2007, Vol. 76, No. 1, pp. 32–60
6. Barruel, Augustin, *Memoirs illustrating the history of Jacobinism, Vol. 1 – the antichristian conspiracy*, Real View Books, 1995 (first published 1798), ISBN: 9780964115057
7. Partner, Peter, *The Murdered Magicians: Templars and their myth*, Aquarian Press, 1987, ISBN: 9780850305340
8. Addison, Charles, *The History of the Knights Templar*, Skyhorse Publishing, 2012, ISBN: 9781616088460
9. Bartol, Vladimir, *Alamut*, North Atlantic Books, 2008, ISBN: 9781556436819

Bibliography

Chapter One: The Crusades: 'Deus Le Vult!'
Barber, Malcolm, *The Trial of the Templars*, Cambridge University Press, 1978, ISBN: 9781107645769
Boas, Adrian, (editor), *The Crusader World*, Routledge, first edition, 2015, ISBN: 9780415824941
Clot, Andre, *Harun Al-Rashid: and the World of the Thousand and One Nights*, Saqi Books, 2005, ISBN: 9780863565502
Cushing, Kathleen, *Reform and the Papacy in the Eleventh Century*, Manchester University Press, 2005, ISBN: 9780719058349
Eidelberg, Shlomo, (edited and translated), *The Jews and the Crusaders, The Hebrew Chronicles of the First and Second Crusades*, University of Wisconsin Press, 1977, ISBN: 0881255416
Ellenblum, Ronnie, *The Collapse of the Eastern Mediterranean: Climate Change and the Decline of the East, 950–1072*, Cambridge University Press, 2013, ISBN: 9781107688735
Haberl, Charles G, *The Neo-Mandaic Dialect of Khorramshahr*, Harrassowitz, 2009, ISBN: 9783447058742
Irenaeus of Lyons, *Against Heresies*, Aeterna Press, 2016, ISBN: 9781785169267
Janosik, Daniel J., *John of Damascus, First Apologist to the Muslims: The Trinity and Christian Apologetics in the Early Islamic Period*, Pickwick Publications, 2016, ISBN: 9781498289825
Komnene, Anna, *The Alexiad*, Masterworks Classics, Stonewall Press, 2015, ISBN: 9781627301121
McGlynn, Sean, *Kill Them All, Cathars and Carnage in the Albigensian Crusade*, The History Press, 2018, ISBN: 9780750984317
Picknett Lynn, Prince, Clive, *The Templar Revelation*, Corgi edition, 2007, ISBN: 9780552155403
Ralph of Caen, *The Gesta Tancredi of Ralph of Caen*, Routledge, first edition, 2010, ISBN: 9781409400325
Robert the Monk, *Historia Iherosolimitana*, Sweetenham, Carol (translator), Ashgate Publishing, 2005, ISBN: 9780754658627
Tyerman, Christopher, (editor), *Chronicles of the First Crusade*, Penguin Classics, 2012, ISBN: 9780241955222

Chapter Two: Mysterious Origins of the Knights Templar
Baigent, Michael, Leigh, Richard, Lincoln, Henry, *The Holy Blood and the Holy Grail*, Jonathan Cape, 1982, ISBN: 9780224017350
Banks, Grace, Blackhall, Sheena, *Aberdeenshire Folk Tales*, The History Press, 2013, ISBN: 9780752497588
Barber, Malcolm, Bate, Keith, *The Templars*, Manchester University Press, 2002, ISBN: 9780719051104
Bartlett, W. B., *Assassins: The Story of Medieval Islam's Secret Sect*, The History Press, 2009, ISBN: 9780752452050
Brown, Dan, *The Da Vinci Code*, Corgi (first edition), 2009, ISBN: 9780552159715
Banks, Grace, Blackhall, Sheena, *Aberdeenshire Folk Tales*, The History Press, 2013, ISBN: 9780752497588
Ciggaar, Krijna Nelly, Davids, Adelbert, Teule, Herman G. B., *East and West in the Crusader States, Context, Contacts, Confrontations*, Acta of the Congress held at Hernen Castle, May 1993, Vol. 1, 1996, ISBN: 9789068317923

Colby, Frederick, S., *Narrating Muhammad's Night Journey: Tracing the Development of the Ibn Abbas Ascension Discourse,* State University of New York Press, 2008, ISBN: 9780791475171

Duby, Georges, *The Three Orders: Feudal Society Imagined,* University of Chicago Press, 1982, ISBN: 9780226167725

Gibb, H.A.R. (translator), *The Damascus Chronicle of the Crusades – extracted and translated from the chronicle of Ibn Al-Qalanisi,* Dover Publications, New York, 2002, ISBN: 9780486425191

Lewis, Bernard, *Assassins: A Radical Sect in Islam,* Basic Books (reissue edition), 2002, ISBN: 9780465004980

Nicholson, Helen J., *The Knights Hospitaller,* Boydell Press, 2006, ISBN: 9781843830382

Nicholson, Helen J., *The Knights Templar,* Sutton Publishing Ltd., 2001, ISBN: 9780750925174

Maalouf, Amin, *The Crusades through Arab eyes,* Saqi Books, 2006 edition, ISBN: 9780863560231

Riley-Smith, J., *The Knights Hospitaller in the Levant, c.1070–1309,* Palgrave Macmillan, 2012, ISBN: 9781349331628

Wallace-Murphy, Tim, Hopkins, Marilyn, *Custodians of Truth: The Continuance of Rex Deus,* Red Wheel/Weiser, 2005, ISBN: 9781578633234

William of Tyre, *A History of Deeds Done Beyond the Sea,* Babcock, Emily A., Krey, A.C. (translated), Columbia University Press, 1943

Chapter Three: Templar Heroes and Villains

Baigent, Michael, Leigh, Richard, Lincoln, Henry, *The Holy Blood and the Holy Grail,* Arrow (second edition), 1996, ISBN: 9780099682417

Barber, Malcolm, *The New Knighthood: A History of the Order of the Temple,* Cambridge University Press, 2012, ISBN: 9781107604735

Bar Hebraeus, Budge, Ernest Alfred Wallis, *The chronography of Gregory Abu'l Faraj, the son of Aaron, the Hebrew physician, commonly known as Bar Hebraeus,* Oxford University Press, 1932

Bernard of Clairvaux, *In Praise of the New Knighthood: A Treatise on the Knights Templar and the Holy Places of Jerusalem,* Cistercian Publications, 2001, ISBN: 9780879071202

Branco, Maria JoãoViolante, *D. Sancho I: O Filho do Fundador,* Circulo de Leitores, 2006

Brett, Michael, *The Fatimid Empire,* Edinburgh University Press, 2017, ISBN: 9780748640768

Brundage, James A., *The Crusades,* The Marquette University Press, 1962

David, Charles Wendell (translation), *The Conquest of Lisbon – De Expugnatione Lyxbonensi,* Columbia University Press, 2001, ISBN: 9780231121231

Eco, Umberto, *Foucault's Pendulum,* Vintage, 2001, ISBN: 9780099287155

Fulton, Michael S., *Contest for Egypt: The Collapse of the Fatimid Caliphate, the Ebb of Crusader Influence, and the Rise of Saladin,* Brill, 2022, ISBN: 9789004512276

Joyce, Donovan, *The Jesus Scroll,* Sphere, 1975, ISBN: 9780722151037

Henry of Huntingdon, *Historia Anglorum. The History of the English from AC 55 to AD 1154,* Cambridge University Press, 2012, ISBN: 9781108051415

Hosler, John D., 'The Prayer of Usama ibn Mundiqh', Yale University Press, 2022

Howlett, Richard, *Chronicles of the Reigns of Stephen, Henry II, and Richard I,* Cambridge University Press, 2012, ISBN: 9781108052269

Ibn Munqidh, Usamah, *The Book of Contemplation: Islam and the Crusades,* Penguin Classics, 2008, ISBN: 9780140455137

Kennedy, Hugh, *Muslim Spain and Portugal,* Routledge, 1996, ISBN: 9780582495159

Kingsford, Charles Lethbridge, Archer, Thomas Andrew, *The Crusades: the story of the Latin Kingdom of Jerusalem,* Palala Press, 2015, ISBN: 9781355847601

Lewis, Kevin James, *The Counts of Tripoli and Lebanon in the Twelfth Century: Sons of Saint-Gilles (Rulers of the Latin East),* Routledge, 2017, ISBN: 9781472458902

MacEvitt, Christopher, *The Crusades and the Christian World of the East: Rough Tolerance,* University of Pennsylvania Press, 2007, ISBN: 9780812240504

Murray, Alan V., *The Crusades: An Encycopedia (4 volumes)*, ABC-CLIO, 2006, ISBN: 9781576078624

Odo of Deuil, *De Profectione Ludovici VII in Orientem*, W.W. Norton & Co., 1965, ISBN: 9780393096620

Read, Piers Paul, *The Templars*, Weidenfeld & Nicholson, 2003, ISBN: 9780753810873

Richards, D.S., (editor), *The Chronicle of Ibn al-Athir for the Crusading Period from al-Kamil fi'l-Ta'rikh. Part 2*, Routledge, 2010, ISBN: 9780754669517

Runciman, Steven, *A History of the Crusades, Vol. 3*, Penguin, 1990, ISBN: 9780140137057

Schonfield, Hugh J., *The Passover Plot*, Disinformation Co; Anniversary Edition, 2005, ISBN: 9781932857092

Stubbs, William (Editor), *The Historical Works of Master Ralph de Diceto, Dean of London*, Cambridge University Press, 2012, ISBN: 9781108049346

Walter Map, *De Nugis Curialum: Courtiers' Trifles (Oxford Medieval Texts)*, OUP Oxford, 1983, ISBN: 9780198222361

William of Tyre, *Historia rerum in partibus transmarinis gestarum, XXIII, 1, Patrologia Latina 201*, Brundage, James (translated), *The Crusades: A Documentary History*, Marquette University Press, 1962

Zajac, Bill, Nicholson, Helen (translated), *Monumenta Germaniae Historica Scriptores*

Chapter Four: Getting Rich Quick

Barber, Malcolm, *The Trial of the Templars*, Cambridge University Press, 1978, ISBN: 9781107645769

Bartlett, Suzanne, *Licoricia of Winchester: Marriage, Motherhood and Murder in the Medieval Anglo-Jewish Community*, Vallentine Mitchell & Co Ltd, 2015, ISBN: 9780853038320

Carpenter, David, *Henry III: The Rise to Power and Personal Rule, 1207–1258 (The English Monarchs Series)*, Yale University Press, 2021, ISBN: 9780300259193

Dalton, Paul, White, Graeme, J., *King Stephen's Reign*, Boydell Press, 2008, ISBN: 9781843833611

De La Torre, Ignacio, *The London and Paris Temples: A Comparative Analysis of their Financial Services for the Kings during the Thirteenth Century*, Routledge (first edition), 2008, ISBN: 9781315555553

Dorin, Rowan, *No Return: Jews, Christian Usurers, and the Spread of Mass Expulsion in Medieval Europe (Histories of Economic Life Book 34)*, Princeton University Press, 2023, ISBN: 9780691240923

Hill, J.W.F., *Medieval Lincoln*, Cambridge University Press, 1948

Howlett, Richard (editor), *Vol. 1: The First Four Books of Historia rerum Anglicarum of William of Newburgh*, Cambridge University Press, 2012 (first published 1884), ISBN: 9781139380669

Lord, Dr Evelyn, *The Knights Templar in Britain*, Longman (first edition), 2001, ISBN: 9780582472877

Slavin, Philip, 'Landed estates of the Knights Templar in England and Wales and their management in the early fourteenth century', *Journal of Historical Geography*, Vol. 42, October 2013, pp. 36–49

Chapter Five: The Holy Grail, Knights Templar, and King Arthur

Barber, Malcolm, *The Crusader States*, Yale University Press, 2012, ISBN: 9780300113129

De Troyes, Chrétien, *Perceval: The Story of the Grail*, Yale University Press, 1999, ISBN: 9780300075861

Hosler, John, *Henry II: A Medieval Soldier at War, 1147–1189*, Brill, 2007, ISBN: 9789004157248

Chapter Six: Accusations of Treachery

Ailes, Marianne (translator), Barber, Malcolm (translator), *The History of the Holy War: Ambroise's Estoire de la Guerre Sainte*, Boydell Press, 2011, ISBN: 9781843836629

Brewer, Keagan, Kane, James, *The Conquest of the Holy Land by Salah al-Din*, Routledge, 2020, ISBN: 9780367729752

Caesarius of Heisterbach, *The Dialogue on Miracles*, George Routledge & Sons, 1929

Choniates, Nicetas, *O City of Byzantium, Annals of Niketas Choniates,* Wayne State University Press, 1984, ISBN: 9780814317648

Cobham, Claude Delaval, *Excerpta Cypria: Materials for a History of Cyprus,* Cambridge University Press, 1908

Delaville Le Roulx, Joseph, *Les Hospitaliers en Terre Sainte et a Chypre (1100–1310),* E. Leroux, 1904

Freed, John, *Frederick Barbarossa: the Prince and the Myth,* Yale University Press, 2016, ISBN: 9780300122763

Gaposchkin, M. Cecilia, Field, Sean L., *The Sanctity of Louis IX: Early Lives of Saint Louis by Geoffrey of Beaulieu and William of Chartres,* Cornell University Press, 2013, ISBN: 9780801478185

Geoffrey de Villehardouin, Marzials, Frank T. (translated), *Memoirs or Chronicle of the Fourth Crusade and the Conquest of Constantinople,* J. M. Dent, 1908

Loud, G.A., *The Crusade of Frederick Barbarossa. The History of the Expedition of the Emperor Frederick and Related Texts,* Routledge, 2013, ISBN: 9781472413963

Maalouf, Amin, *The Crusades through Arab Eyes,* Saqi Books, 2006, ISBN: 9780863560231

McGlynn, Sean, *Kill Them All: Cathars and Carnage in the Albigensian Crusade,* Spellmount, 2015, ISBN: 9780752486321

McLynn, Frank, *Lionheart and Lackland: King Richard, King John and the Wars of Conquest,* Vintage, 2007, ISBN: 9780712694179

Morgan, Margaret Ruth, *The Chronicle of Ernoul and the Continuations of William of Tyre,* Oxford University Press, 1974, ISBN: 9780198218517

Reston, James, *Warriors of God: Richard the Lionheart and Saladin in the Third Crusade,* Anchor Books, 2002, ISBN: 9780385495622

Richard of Devizes, Geoffrey de Vinsauf, *Chronicles of Crusades: Contemporary Narratives of the Crusade of Richard Coeur de Lion,* George Bell and Sons, 1908

Roudometof, Victor, *Globalization and Orthodox Christianity: The Transformations of a Religious Tradition,* Routledge, 2013, ISBN: 978135014698

Sibly, W.A., Sibly, M.D., *The History of the Albigensian Crusade: Peter of Les Vaux-de-Cernay's Historia Albigensis,* Boydell Press, 1998, ISBN: 9780851158075

Stubbs, William, *Itinerarium Peregrinorum et Gesta Regis Ricardi,* Rolls Series, 1864

Sumption, Jonathan, *The Albigensian Crusade,* Faber & Faber, 1999, ISBN: 9780571200023

Theoderich of Würzburg, *Guide to the Holy Land,* Italica Press, 2008, ISBN: 9780934977036

Tyerman, Christopher, *God's War: A New History of the Crusades,* Penguin, 2007, ISBN: 9780140269802

Venning, Timothy, Frankopan, Peter, *A Chronology of the Crusades,* Routledge, 2019, ISBN: 9780367870775

Wedgwood, Ethel, *The Memoirs of the Lord of Joinville,* John Murray, 1906

Chapter Seven: Retreat from the Holy Land

Atwood, Christopher P. (translated), *The Secret History of the Mongols,* Penguin Classics, 2023, ISBN: 9780241197912

Barber, Malcolm, *The New Knighthood: A History of the Order of the Temple,* Cambridge University Press, 2012, ISBN: 9781107604735

Jackson, Peter, *From Genghis Khan to Tamerlane: The Reawakening of Mongol Asia,* Yale University Press, 2023, ISBN: 9780300251128

Laszlovszky, Jozsef (editor), Hunyadi, Zsolt, *The Crusades and the Military Orders,* CEU Medievalia, 2001, ISBN: 9639241423

Rady, Martyn (editor), Bak, M. Janos (editor), Veszpremy, Laszlo (editor), *Anonymous and Master Roger,* Central European University Press, 2010, ISBN: 9789639776951

Southern, R. W., *The Penguin History of the Church: Western Society and the Church in the Middle Ages,* Penguin, 1990, ISBN: 9780140137552

Chapter Eight: The Last Templar Grand Master

Frale, Barbara, *The Templars: The Secret History Revealed*, Maverick House, 2009, ISBN: 9781905379606

De La Torre, Ignacio, *The Debate on the Trial of the Templars (1307–1314)*, Routledge, 2010, ISBN: 9781315615349

Gaposchkin, M. Cecilia, *The Making of Saint Louis: Kingship, Sanctity, and Crusade in the Later Middle Ages*, Cornell University Press, 2010, ISBN: 9780801476259

Chapter Nine: Arrest Warrants and Trials

Babinsky, Ellen, *Marguerite Porete: The Mirror of Simple Souls*, Paulist Press, 1993, ISBN: 9780809134274

Barber, Malcolm, *The Trial of the Templars*, Cambridge University Press, 1978, ISBN: 9781107645769

Boswell, John, *Christianity, Social Tolerance, and Homosexuality: Gay People in Western Europe from the Beginning of the Christian Era to the Fourteenth Century*, University of Chicago Press, 2005, ISBN: 9780226067117

Demurger, Alain, *The Persecution of the Templars*, Profile Books, 2018, ISBN: 9781782833291

Dodd, Gwilym (Editor), *The Reign of Edward II: New Perspectives*, York Medieval Press, 2006, ISBN: 9781903153192

Jones, Malcolm, *The Secret Middle Ages*, The History Press Ltd., 2004, ISBN: 9780750938747

Laidler, Keith, *The Head of God: The Lost Treasure of the Templars*, Phoenix, 2005, ISBN: 9780752826899

Miller, Tanya Stabler, *The Beguines of Medieval Paris: Gender, Patronage, and Spiritual Authority (The Middle Ages Series)*, University of Pennsylvania Press, 2014, ISBN: 9780812246070

Morgan, Glyn, *Secret Essex*, Ian Henry Publications, 1982, ISBN: 0860258599

St. Peter Damian, *The Book of Gomorrah and St Peter Damian's struggle against ecclesiastical corruption*, Matthew Cullinan Hoffman, 2015, ISBN: 9780996704205

Strickland, Debra Higgs, *Saracens, Demons & Jews – making monsters in medieval art*, Princeton University Press, 2003, ISBN: 9780691057194

Thibodeaux, Jennifer D., *The Manly Priest: Clerical Celibacy, Masculinity, and Reform in England and Normandy, 1066–1300*, University of Pennsylvania Press, 2015, ISBN: 9780812247527

Thomas Aquinas, *Summa Theologica*, Ave Maria Press, 2000, ISBN: 9780870610639

Chapter Ten: Did the Templars Survive?

Addison, Charles, *The History of the Knights Templar*, Skyhorse Publishing, 2012, ISBN: 9781616088460

Barruel, Augustin, *Memoirs illustrating the history of Jacobinism, Vol. 1 – the antichristian conspiracy*, Real View Books, 1995 (first published 1798), ISBN: 9780964115057

Partner, Peter, *The Murdered Magicians: Templars and their myth*, Aquarian Press, 1987, ISBN: 9780850305340

Index

Dear Reader,

We hope you have enjoyed this book, but why not share your views on social media? You can also follow our pages to see more about our other products: facebook.com/penandswordbooks or follow us on X @penswordbooks

You can also view our products at www.pen-and-sword.co.uk (UK and ROW) or www.penandswordbooks.com (North America).

To keep up to date with our latest releases and online catalogues, please sign up to our newsletter at: www.pen-and-sword.co.uk/newsletter

If you would like a printed catalogue with our latest books, then please email: enquiries@pen-and-sword.co.uk or telephone: 01226 734555 (UK and ROW) or email: uspen-and-sword@casematepublishers.com or telephone: (610) 853-9131 (North America).

We respect your privacy and we will only use personal information to send you information about our products.

Thank you!